CRITICAL INSIGHTS

Midwestern Literature

CRITICAL INSIGHTS

Midwestern Literature

Editor
Ronald Primeau
Central Michigan University

SALEM PRESS
A Division of EBSCO Information Services, Inc.
Ipswich, Massachusetts

GREY HOUSE PUBLISHING

∞ The paper used in these volumes conforms to the American National Standard
for Permanence of Paper for Printed Library Materials, Z39.48-1992 (R1997).

Library of Congress Cataloging-in-Publication Data

Midwestern literature / editor, Ronald Primeau. -- [1st ed.].
   p. : ill. ; cm. -- (Critical insights)
Includes bibliographical references and index.
ISBN: 978-1-61925-216-5
1. American literature--Middle West--History and criticism.   2. Middle West--
Intellectual life.   3. Middle West--In literature.   4. Authors, American--Homes
and haunts--Middle West. I. Primeau, Ronald. II. Series: Critical insights.

PS273 .M54 2013
810.9/977

PRINTED IN THE UNITED STATES OF AMERICA

Contents

Critical Contexts

Critical Readings

Resources

Dedication

Arvid "Gus" Sponberg died August 7, 2013 while working on an essay for this volume. Gus' scholarship, amazing teaching, and generosity with younger colleagues are a cherished legacy. He was a driving force at Indiana's Valparaiso University for 42 years and will be deeply missed.

About This Volume

Ronald Primeau

This volume brings together fifteen original essays with thorough coverage and innovative exploration as the main goals. Three overview essays survey the historical and cultural context of Midwestern literature, present how critical commentary on the literature took shape over time, and explore Midwestern plays and playwrights over three centuries. A comparative essay examines similarities in certain techniques of Toni Morrison and Richard Powers, and Sarah Warren-Riley turns the critical lens of Freud's views of melancholy and mourning on Godfrey St. Peter in Willa Cather's *The Professor's House.*

Major writers studied closely include Cather, Morrison, and Carl Sandburg. Cather is looked at in a new way: as an outsider who discovers the Midwest after being reared elsewhere. Morrison "invokes Africa" from Ohio and—in Maureen Eke's terms— "Africa is constantly transforming, being transformed, negotiated, interrogated or recast or reconstructed" in Morrison's "performance of Africa in *Beloved* and *Song of Solomon.*" Carl Sandburg, for Phillip A. Greasley, developed *Chicago Poems* from his power as a journalist, biographer, children's author, and figure of considerable political importance, both nationally and internationally.

The essays that follow take a new look at what it means to be a Midwestern writer as well as what revisiting regionalist studies brings to the study of literature. Marcia Noe introduces new questions in her historical and cultural overview of Midwestern writers. Sara Kosiba explores the critical contexts in which these questions have been nurtured and have evolved. David Radavich reviews the history of Midwestern plays and playwrights, showing how the Midwestern treatments of drama differ from other regions.

Alternative views on what it means to be Midwestern are abundant. For Patricia Oman, the Midwest as Nowhere allows Toni Morrison and Richard Powers to project their stories on empty space in the way of classical *topos*, or the location of topics for material. Oman sees these two authors as Midwestern in a way not often discussed. Marilyn Atlas explains a similar conflict in Patricia Hampl's ambivalence about whether her writing would have fared better if she had written memoirs about a place considered to be *somewhere* rather than *nowhere*. Hampl struggled with the internalized oppression when one is considered to be "less because one is in the wrong place"—until she banishes that oppression and accepts and celebrates her Minnesota home. John Rohrkemper suggests that native Virginian Cather came to see the Midwest like one of her own pioneers "as a place of difference rather than familiarity," bringing to her work "the exuberance of the novelist as discoverer."

In yet another take on what it means to be Midwestern, Jurrit Daalder locates David Foster Wallace's generally overlooked Midwestern roots in his first novel *The Broom of the System.* In the face of Foster's fictionalizing of the places he had called home, Daalder traces Wallace's ambivalent attitudes toward his childhood memories in the region. In *Broom,* Wallace both fears and loves the region of his origin, a paradox Daalder suggests makes the Midwest at once peripheral and central to Foster's work. This conflict accounts for much of the "geographical and spiritual loneliness" in Wallace's work on the whole.

From another point of view, the self-effacing humor noted by Christian Knoeller in Mike Perry's "trope of poking fun at ourselves" creates a distancing effect about the links between identity and the sense of place of one's region. Providing many examples of typically Midwestern, self-deprecating humor as a device for negotiating the ambivalence of identification with place, Knoeller allows us to see clearly that the double-edged weapon of poking fun at oneself is a particularly effective—if at times overlooked—Midwestern trope.

Guy Szuberla provides yet another perspective, this one on how immigrants to the Midwest negotiate their new identities through complex uses of humor. Szuberla probes "immigrant inferiority" in Peter DeVries' comic treatment of regional differences in a "map of desire characters use to escape their origins." DeVries' "parodic treatments of the myth of origins" are central to his characters' "comic efforts to escape" their feelings of inferiority as the characters use humor to both "flee from" and eventually accept the importance of their origins. Eventually, they find peace and understanding in "an indelible imprint and forged pattern of the Midwest." Throughout its long history and up to what being Midwestern means now in a postmodernist context, the essays in this volume raise questions about a regional identity that we are only beginning to explore.

Several essays also take note of groups whose identities as Midwesterners have been ignored or distorted. William Barillas shows how Tomás Rivera expands on who is included as "Midwestern" by subverting the more romantic conceptions of conventional Midwestern pastoral literature. ...And the Earth Did Not Devour Him moves significantly away from pastoral conventions of Willa Cather or Jim Harrison in its emphasis on social class, race, and ethnicity. Rivera's Mexican-American migrant workers are not accepted as Midwesterners by folks in the upper Midwest. The migrant workers do not own land and are exploited by employers with their labor receiving no recognition toward earning an identity. Rivera thus undermines the conventional take on the Midwestern pastoral and moves toward a realism that embraces politics, like the Chicano rights movement of the 1960s and 1970s. Similarly, Matthew Low emphasizes major differences between Native America's and white America's accounts of the bison hunt. Low compares the Euro-American texts to the technique of *mise en abyme* in works by Zitkala-Ša, Standing Bear, James Welch, and others in the context of Gerald Vizenor's concept of "survivance" in Native American narratives. The Anglo-American accounts distorted the story of the bison hunt into elaborate colonized narratives that promoted "settlement, enterprise, and commerce" at the expense of people and the land. Low notes that, at the end of Cormac McCarthy's *Blood Meridian*, images of slaughtered bison are "superimposed upon the preceding images of massacred human beings to reinforce the theme that the Euro-American settlement of the trans-Mississippi West was a supremely violent and senseless enterprise for both human kind and the natural world."

Many of these essays reexamine how we define Midwestern literature, consider whether the region is somewhere or nowhere (and why that matters), and how authors might use absence itself as a location for settings not possible elsewhere. Some authors born in the Midwest are not considered to be writing Midwestern literature. Others, born and reared elsewhere, become Midwestern in special ways as they grow into the roles. The essays also expand the bounds of what we usually think to be literature in a more narrow sense by including humor and sports as essential ingredients in an author's repertoire. Scott D. Emmert rereads the Iowa pastoral through the idyllic lens of baseball books, finding both nostalgia and self-mockery in the Midwestern literature of sports books and films. Emmert's commentaries on a number of books, films, and a musical demonstrate how "Iowans use sports, most emphatically baseball, to project and protect the conception that their optimism, cooperation, and unity are sustained by a pastoral heritage."

From widely varied perspectives, the scholars' work collected here offers corrective readings of several authors and more expansive ways to see others. The contributors ask new questions, reinforce the way in which traditions are both sustained and undermined, and provide much evidence that Midwestern literature remains a subject of endless fascination and importance.

On Midwestern Literature _____

Ronald Primeau

We look for a sense of place when reading literature, in order to understand one important source of the feelings, values, experiences, and meaning we find. Poems, novels, plays, or memoirs emerge from the landscape, architecture, way of life, and beliefs of people living in specific places. Midwestern literature arises from small towns, large cities, and rural settings and is as diverse as the people who live in the region.

A "regionalist" approach to American literature assumes distinct patterns in the content, the styles of writing, and the culture and values nurtured in different geographical locations. For some time, Midwestern writing was considered less important or interesting than stories of other regions. However, starting out as the Old Northwest Territory and continuing today as the Midwest, the country's heartland contains perhaps the richest and most varied literature anywhere in the country. Midwestern literature is uniquely diverse because people have come to the region from everywhere—from all other areas of the country and most parts of the world. Located in the middle of the nation, the region is not only home to millions, but a crucial geographical space that people pass through on their way to someplace else. The Midwest becomes, therefore, an important part of many literary quests. The region has long provided the pathways of national growth, adventure, and exploration. The enormous number of people who have settled in the Midwest have recorded their experiences in a wide variety of literary genres. The sense of place we have come to know in this literature is created through descriptions of actual places as well as imaginative constructions of the region. Midwestern literature is often also a social, cultural, or rhetorical construction of the geographical locale, values, and way of life of the region.

Where is the Midwest? Today the region includes 12 states and extends from Ohio and Michigan to the east; Indiana, Illinois,

Missouri, and Kansas to the south; westward to Nebraska, North Dakota, and South Dakota; north-central to Minnesota and Wisconsin; and Iowa in the middle. This is the area of America's first westward migration—into Ohio and then the Great Lakes and plains, with farmlands, villages, and cities built by the railroads and industrialization. Much early Midwestern literature was, therefore, travel narratives and stories of relocation and settlement.

Why study Midwestern literature? For some time, it was the least known writing in the country, and its concerns, questions, and contributions to our national identity reward our increased attention. Moreover, at a time when the country is becoming more homogenous, we need to preserve customs and traditions, ways of speaking and writing, and values that might otherwise be lost to standardization. Midwestern writers also champion individualism tested every day by pressures from marketplace competition. Progressive and populist political views have been espoused by many Midwestern poets, novelists, and journalists. Many find optimism and a sense of hope in Midwestern stories as opposed to the increasing cynicism expressed elsewhere. Reading Midwestern writers also teaches us much about American language dialects. For example, a Midwestern dialect is what we have come to see as standard in national media news coverage.

It is significant to note that four of the eight literary Nobel Prize-winning Americans have been Midwesterners: Sinclair Lewis (1930), Ernest Hemingway (1954), Saul Bellow (1976), and Toni Morrison (1993). In addition, the Nobel Peace Prize was awarded to Midwestern writer Jane Addams in 1931.

How diverse is Midwestern life and culture? Among Midwestern phenomena are the architecture of Frank Lloyd Wright, Meredith Wilson's *The Music Man* (1957), many Native American songs and dances, Chicago blues, McGuffey readers, philanthropist Fannie Hurst, "British" poet T.S. Eliot, Harlem Renaissance poet Langston Hughes, Jane Addams, astronaut John Glenn, TV journalist Eric Sevareid, former US poet laureate Rita Dove, Orville and Wilbur Wright, Second City "Improv" Comedy, *The Wizard of Oz*, The Motown Sound, and Abraham Lincoln.

The long and rich history of Midwestern literature stretches back into the early days of the nation. Midwestern authors are indebted to Native American oral traditions, the journals and diaries of pioneers and settlers, and the wide variety of writing by immigrants and those who migrated from the South to Midwestern cities. In "The Origins and Development of the Literature of the Midwest", David D. Anderson has identified three facts that are "fundamental to a discussion of the Midwest as an authentic American region with a history, a myth, a psyche, and a culture that produces and, in turn, is shaped by its literature" (11). First, the Midwest is distinctively American "rather than a European or aboriginal creation." The region is also a product of eighteenth-century rationalism and its belief in progress and the possibility of change. The land occupies, Anderson notes, "a unique geographical position as the American Heartland, astride the main path of American destiny, the land route to the Pacific and beyond." A developing American identity, forged on a commitment to progress and occupying its own geographical place, created for the Midwest what Anderson calls "an identity, a reality, and a psyche which combine to produce the substance of a literature that is at once regional, national, and universal" (11). Anderson also identifies events and values in the early Midwest that would shape its people and literature. Among these are a commitment to Jacksonian democracy, free public education, the prohibition of slavery, commitment to a free and open society, and a problematic application of Darwin's "survival of the fittest" to economics in ways that would threaten these values. By the end of the nineteenth century, authors throughout the region were creating complex literary works sharing a distinctly Midwestern identity.

The heart of Midwestern literature is found in the stories, characters, and themes of its most well-known works. Mark Twain's *The Adventures of Huckleberry Finn* (1884) captures the quest motif, the joy of escape, the search for freedom, the celebration of the rebel, the bold rejection of what is narrow and stifling, the capturing of local customs, and the vibrant language of everyday life in Twain's Missouri. Read alongside Twain's *Life on the Mississippi* (1883), the book exudes a Midwestern reveling in motion itself, as the hero struggles against forces threatening his individuality. The book celebrates that Midwestern optimism even as it is constantly challenged by potential detours.

For most readers, fiction is the best-known genre of Midwestern literature, exploring a very broad range of topics, from scathing satire to celebration of everyday life and ventures to other worlds. In *Sister Carrie* (1900) and *An American Tragedy* (1925), Theodore Dreiser used his journalistic background to explore the challenges of industrialization and the development and survival of individuality. Upton Sinclair captured the brutality and inhuman conditions of meat packing plants in *The Jungle* (1906). Novels such as *The Sun Also Rises* (1926) and *A Farewell to Arms* (1929) are built of Ernest Hemingway's sparse Midwestern style and perspective; he also set his Nick Adams stories ("Big Two-Hearted River") in Michigan where the rivers, woods, and streams might heal the scars of war. F. Scott Fitzgerald's *The Great Gatsby* (1925) presents a critique of economic "success" alongside the visionary hope of the westward quest. Many Midwestern fiction writers have also sprung whole new worlds from their Midwestern sense of place: among them, the considerable body of science fiction by Ray Bradbury and L. Frank Baum's *The Wonderful Wizard of Oz* (1900), wherein Dorothy reminds Toto that they are no longer in Kansas.

Midwestern literature also includes distinguished books for children and young adult literature. Consider one writer who exemplifies the great range of works for children. Born in Michigan in 1944, Patricia Polacco descended from grandparents who were Russian immigrants. From 1987 to the present, she has created dozens of books introducing children to the cultural heritage of the Old World and her experiences in the Midwest. In *The Keeping Quilt* (1988), her immigrant family uses the cloth from outgrown clothes to make quilts for babies, weddings, and to cover the dying. A sequel, *The Blessing Cup,* appeared in 2013. In *Thunder Cake (*1990), a grandmother helps her granddaughter (and readers) deal with storms. An Amish girl tries to understand why she is plain in *Just Plain Fancy* (1990). In *The Bee Tree* (1993), a grandfather places honey on a book during a search for bees to show symbolically that reading is sweet. *Mrs. Mack (1998)* and *Thank You, Mr. Faulkner* (1998) are among her many tributes to teachers. In *Lemonade Club* (2007), a girl shaves her head to support a friend who has cancer. Polacco recreates, in so many ways, the lives of her ancestors and her own experiences growing up in the Midwest. She writes about adjusting to siblings, overcoming bullies, and the joys and pains of growing up. She is devoted to passing on stories across generations; celebrating Russian, Jewish, and Amish life; and expanding the world children experience through books.

Midwestern literature is shaped by and creates experiences on the prairies, plains, and farms as well as in large cities and small towns. These very different landscapes gave rise to increasingly complex Midwestern traits as the country expanded, the population diversified, and the cultural, political, and artistic beliefs took shape. Literary conventions, styles, and innovations followed the expansion of the nation's Heartland.

For many, the term "Midwestern" immediately conjures the picture of a rural setting: farmlands, prairies, the plains, and early exploration of wilderness areas. In fact, many of our experiences of what we think to be "the West" in films, TV, and other popular culture may more accurately be scenes of the open spaces of the Midwest. Much of the literature of the region attempts to capture rural life in a complexity that ranges from solid values, hard work, and simple routine to the challenges posed by the wild and untamed. Midwestern rural experiences and values are depicted in so many different ways by writers across the region. From Jane Smiley's powerful stories set on Iowa farms to Vachel Lindsay's praise for the Illinois prairies and William Stafford's poems on the Kansas landscape, we find a predominant harmony with nature that serves as a precursor to more recent ecocritical studies on preserving the environment.

Paul Gruchow's depiction of nature in Minnesota stands alongside Jim Harrison's healing powers of the land, rivers, and streams of Northern Michigan. Gene Stratton Porter's portrayal of hard working people on Indiana farms supports active environmental concerns. The Wisconsin woods, villages, and river banks in works by August Derleth complement Larry Woiwode's recurring discovery of the deepest sources of humanity in rural North Dakota. Similarly, the sacred words of Black Elk grow out of his Native American heritage, which seeks harmony with the land in South Dakota. Many authors forge key elements of their political world views from values nurtured in these rural scenes and pastoral life. In Ohio, Louis Bromfield created fiction, in which strength born of country life is leveled against threats of industrialization and attacks on individuality. Willa Cather's American Dream of the fulfilled individual takes shape in the rural Nebraska landscape. Mark Twain's ear for accurately capturing the language of rural life stoked both the irony of Huck Finn and the quest motif of journeying down the Mississippi.

While these widely varied experiences are found in other regions as well, Midwestern literature is relentless in its commitment to individualism, work ethic, optimism, progress, care for the environment, and savvy about the difficulties, drudgery, and threats from mechanization, easy money, and other shortcuts to what can actually be won only through persistence and reliance on the vitality of the human spirit. Midwestern rural life is not a stereotype to be dismissed. Neither is it so unique that many of its elements cannot be found elsewhere. But several elements of the Midwestern agrarian way of life make it distinctive. Because the region took shape as a result of pioneer exploration and westward expansion, the joys and pains of new settlement made the Midwestern countryside fresh, hopeful, and challenging. At the same time, threats of industrialization, standardization, and two World Wars underscored constant disruptions to the wholesomeness and serenity of the landscape. The values of the rural Midwest also played a large role in populism and the advance of democratic decision-making, which together led to land grant institutions and educational opportunity. None of these scenes remains pristine or naïve, as the integrity and promise of hard work are regularly challenged by the harshness of society, economics, weather, and the problems of daily life. Once again, Midwestern rural life depicts the variety of regional experiences and serves as an antidote to the standardization and homogenization threatening uniqueness and individuality in the country as a whole.

While the Midwestern pastoral tradition has long expressed ties to the land, over time, the literature of the region has reached even deeper into its own traditions to provide insights into and action on today's environmental problems. In *The Midwestern Pastoral,* William Barillas has noted how, in Midwestern literature, "pastoral, which can be conservative or progressive, has changed over time with response to new social and ecological imperatives" (3). Rather than the oversimplified or even stereotyped country values, which some readers might come to expect in Midwestern literature, Barillas emphasizes "ethical development" in pastoral works, particularly those by Willa Cather, Aldo Leopold, Theodore Roethke, James Wright, and Jim Harrison. For Barillas, contemporary writers "continue the study of place and culture begun by earlier Midwesterners" (206). He quotes Larry Woiwode's "The Spirit of Place" on the spirituality of the Midwestern pastoral: "Those of us at the center of America can retain what we presently possess or, even better, turn further inward toward what we're inherently clearing away from the falseness and superficiality that is constantly and electronically beamed into us from either coast, as if by its repetitiveness, it could become the truth" (207). Barillas underscores the importance of Midwestern literature's attachment to the land for the possibilities it affords us in light of environmental challenges we now face : "We have in the region's literature a vision of a land full of natural resources—fields, forests, rivers, and lakes—which can bring people cultural as well as economic rewards if they learn, as have many writers and artists, to love Midwestern places for their intrinsic beauty and spiritual worth" (225).

Urban Midwestern literature has also portrayed a powerful collision between the optimism identified with the region and the challenges of survival in a sometimes brutal environment. Consider two examples in the sense of place that prides itself on Carl Sandburg's "broad-shouldered" Chicago as well as the publishing centers created by Dudley Randall and Naomi Long Madgett in Detroit.

Chicago grew up on Lake Michigan and became an industrial complex, railroad hub, and center of commerce and financial markets. The city's World Columbia Exposition in 1893 was a showcase of emerging Midwestern pride and progress. Chicago architecture, Jane Addams' Hull House, the Chicago literary Renaissance, and the founding of *Poetry* magazine made the city a center of literary production. Its location drew immigrants and the ethnic diversity of Northern migration. Carl Sandburg's *Chicago Poems* (1916) praised toughness and political conviction. In the 1930s Chicago, writers created WPA projects, and there followed a series of storytellers who communicated the deep roots of the city's neighborhoods in works by Nelson Algren, James Farrell, Saul Bellow, and Lorraine Hansberry. Midwestern humor emerged in works by Ben Hecht, George Ade, and many others. In our time, Chicago has become a vibrant center for live theatre, with an astonishing number and range of repertory companies flourishing. For over 100 years, the city has been a center of Midwestern poetry from Carl Sandburg to Pulitzer Prize-winner Gwendolyn Brooks as well as the debut of the Poetry Slam in the city's oldest bar, The Green Mill Cocktail Lounge. And there is so much more: Chicago's blues poetry, journalistic writing, and an array of distinguished memoirs by—among others—Ronne Hartsfield, Douglas Bukowski, Robert B. Stepto, and Sara Paretsky (famous for her stories featuring detective V. I. Warshawski).

One of the greatest plays of the twentieth century features the Younger family, who migrated to the Midwest and settled on Chicago's South Side. Lorraine Hansberry's *A Raisin in the Sun* debuted in 1959 and has been revived repeatedly over time. The Youngers' quest for Midwestern opportunity is a search for the American Dream. Hansberry takes her title from St. Louis-born Langston Hughes' poem "Montage of a Dream Deferred," which asks what happens to a dream that is stifled so many times and for so long. Does it "sag" or "explode" or "dry up like a raisin in the sun"? The most immediate threat the Youngers face is from "The Neighborhood Improvement Association," which is dedicated to keeping "colored" people out of "white neighborhoods." But the Youngers will not let their dreams dry up, and as the play ends, they are ready to move into the previously segregated neighborhood of Clybourne Park. Though we do not know what will happen when they move, Hansberry explores the Midwestern belief that hard work and perseverance can overcome the obstacles the Youngers face. While the ambivalent ending remains a source of the play's power, Midwestern playwright Bruce Norris has returned to the question of what happened as the Youngers moved on. In *Clybourne Park* (2010), he takes us back to the neighborhood they moved into, where we also meet the people who sold them the house and learn much that happened in the interim.

Among other Midwestern cities, Detroit is notable for the publishing opportunities created for African American poets by two distinguished presses. Dudley Randall founded Broadside Press in 1963 and published numerous African American poets in the next two decades. In 1972, Naomi Long Madgett founded Lotus Press, which has given rise to many poetic debuts ever since. Madgett is currently poet laureate of Detroit. Of course, many other Midwestern cities have given us significant writers from St. Louis to Cleveland, Omaha, Indianapolis, Kansas City, Minneapolis, and other cities. Distinguishing Midwestern ingredients in these writers' voices and in the characters they create are toughness, grit, and a dogged though conflicted faith in progress as it is challenged by the difficulties of urban geography and competitiveness.

Particularly in its urban centers, Midwestern journalists have long had a pervasive influence on the region's burgeoning literature. Reportorial accuracy, investigative research, detailed character study, informed perspective on political issues, and a searing search for truth united the journalists and fiction writers throughout the region. Journalist and critic William Dean Howells was an important editor and leading figure in advancing the careers of so many younger authors. One notable example was his review of Paul Laurence Dunbar in 1896. The review launched the career of Dayton's poet laureate. As editor of the influential *Mirror,* William Marion Reedy provided an important venue for Midwestern writers, greatly expanding their readership and placing many in the canons of world literature. Poet and editor Harriet Monroe continued the work of establishing credibility and respect for Midwestern writers when she founded *Poetry: A Magazine of Verse* in 1912. The three decades spanning 1890-1920 saw a prolific outpouring of activity that came to be known as "the Chicago Literary Renaissance" led by journalists, poets, and storytellers shaping many new forms of Midwestern writing.

One of the most powerful novels of American Naturalism, where once benevolent nature has seemed to turn indifferent to human needs, is Frank Norris' *The Pit*. The novel portrays a Midwestern financial center that grinds up people like cattle at the stockyards. In 1900, Chicago is filled with the riches of the Gilded Age, where people live in mansions, attend opera balls, and make their fortunes trading commodities in the Board of Trade Building, "the monstrous sphinx with blind eyes" (26). Railways rise up on the plains, waterways receive shipments from Sheboygan and Duluth, and terminals fill up with people all "reeking with fatigue" (39). The city is so dominating that it takes on the role of a character in the plot: "It was Empire, the resistless subjugation of all this central world of the lakes and the prairies" (39). This heart of the nation offered opportunity for immigrants and for those migrating from the South, but it was also "brutal in its ambitions, arrogant in the new found knowledge of its strength, prodigal of its wealth, infinite in its desires" (39).

These oppositions unfold in *The Pit* through the clashes between the sensitivity of the arts and the hardboiled and calculating manner of commercial enterprise, in which profit seems to depend on the failure of others. These tensions extend beyond the financial markets and into the city, which is a mass of contradictions between the beauty of the architecture, museums, educational institutions, and the magnificent lakefront and the brutality of the weather, competitiveness, conflict, and an impersonal system. Norris presents a world that is "terrible at the center but gentle and perfidious around the edges with a reach going way beyond the city" (39). Opportunities beckon, but a great pit awaits to devour all.

With equal rigor and productivity, Midwestern writers created rich portrayals of life in small towns and villages in the region.

Many of these stories sketched the small town as an innocent and almost idyllic way of life. Others, however, such as Carl Van Doren, attacked the narrowness and hypocrisy in what they called a "revolt from the village." In *Winesburg, Ohio* (1919) Sherwood Anderson created a prototype of the richness and complexity of Midwestern small town literature. Anderson's characters experienced what he called "grotesques"—loneliness, conflict, and confusion—but somehow endured and stood for the hope that such frustration can lead to growth and strength. Others have not been so optimistic. In *Main Street* (1920), Sinclair Lewis took on the mean-spiritedness and sterility of small towns, and Edgar Lee Masters' *Spoon River Anthology* (1915) captured the voices of a town's people baring their souls in monologues from their tombstones. The picture is not flattering.

Spoon River Anthology (1915) introduced representative small town people from Western Illinois whose experiences have been hailed as universal. As frequent users of social media, today's readers are especially intrigued by Masters' graveside soliloquies, in which the dead come back from the grave to have one more say about what happened to them in their town. In many ways similar to Facebook, the characters of Masters' work project roles, present their perspectives, and debate with others about events and beliefs. Bankers, lawyers, preachers, reporters, housewives, and judges debate politics, discuss law enforcement, express the joys and regrets of their lives, plead their cases when they feel wronged, and reveal sexual affairs as well as acts of unrequited kindness. We meet many good people as well as those who expose, perhaps for the first time, their own or the town's treachery, deceit, and revenge. Especially intriguing are the disagreements readers must sort through for themselves. Masters was a lawyer and presents many of the speeches as a kind of testimony for his readers/ jurors to interpret and, ultimately, reach their own conclusions.

Contrasts in tone and attitudes are common in Midwestern literature. In fact, one way to understand the variety in the works is to look for deliberate patterns of contrast, opposites that coexist at the center of the values of the region. The quietness of rural scenes and the steadiness of agrarian values stand alongside the noise, harshness, and conflicts of urban life. Midwestern literary characters are both constantly in motion and content to sit still. Road literature travels on the highways of the heartland on a perpetual quest, and yet villages and towns emphasize a quiet permanence of tradition not so eager to flee or chase anything too far from home.

In his introduction to *The Dictionary of Midwestern Literature*: *Volume One*, Phillip A. Greasley summarizes the dazzling balancing act that Midwestern literature not only manages, but actually seeks: "A future orientation coexists with reverence for the past; aspiration to the ideal is complemented by pragmatism born of experience. Recognition of limits coexists with commitment to dreams and determination to mold a positive, value-based future" (2). This delicate balancing act Greasley describes may be the clearest and most accurate way to define the literature and culture of the region. A passionate striving is activated more fully by restraint. Commitment to the past and to tradition sparks innovation and exploration. Restlessness drives the quest to the realization that valuing home matters as much as the journey. The authors' dreams are limitless, but they seek egalitarian and democratic goals founded on limits. Optimistic attitudes burst forth alongside sometimes bitter and scathing satire. Rather than falling into any pattern that is overly predictable or stereotyped, the literature of the often unpredictable Midwest strives to immerse itself in, and work through, these and other conflicts of everyday life.

A sense of place provides for readers not only setting in literature, but also many clues about the tone, symbols, voice, meaning, and values expressed. Whether on farms or in cities, floating down a river, or trudging through a driving snow storm, the source of experiences comes in significant measure from contact with the land. Again, contrasts are the substance of the literature: in wheat fields and on urban pavements; in small-town meeting halls; skyscrapers or convention centers; on two-lane roads or super highways; on the prairies and open plains or in factories, stockyards, or office buildings, Midwestern literary characters are at once stoical, skeptical, optimistic, open, hard-working, dedicated to democratic ideals, and endowed with hope for the future. They welcome and work their way through conflicts between commitment to the environment and dehumanizing industrialization, the struggle to achieve individualism in the face of crushing corporate interests, and preserving tradition while moving forward toward innovation. These conflicts are inevitable and to be embraced, the literature tells us, because only by accepting and living through these struggles, do we survive and thrive.

Midwestern literature expresses its longstanding traditional values, which are evolving as well as the region takes an even more active role in a complex and changing world. Over time, Midwestern rural, urban, and small town settings have changed in response current issues and the region's expanded presence in global affairs. In "Re-Centering the Center," Edward Watts has noted significant changes in the literature and our responses to it. Watts suggests that our attention to Midwestern literature has, at times, considered mostly the concerns of literature that is often at least 100 years old: "Writers are described as 'regionalist' if they represent with an emphasis on realistic technique conditions in American small towns and farms at the moment of industrialization and urbanization—representations characterized by a tendency to romanticize the past and protect local identity" (860). While the study of the origins and longstanding traditions of Midwestern literature remain important, Watts commends many scholars for recognizing that later Midwestern authors moved their works into "the post-industrial moment" (860). Watts challenges us to continue the process of reconfiguring "the place of Midwestern regionalism and to read their narratives into the current moment reviving them for contemporary readers and creating new strategies for teaching and reading these texts"(860). He cautions that Midwestern literature is "still too often written out of 'American' literature courses by the enduring geographical provincialism and the self-referentiality of the coastal cultural, academic, and publishing centers of the nation" (860). Our responsibilities are to read and study the literature in its long tradition and current manifestations, to preserve knowledge of past conventions and acknowledge and discover the enormous benefits of what is developing in the current literature of the region.

Perhaps in the end, an art form as complex and varied as Midwestern literature will defy definition. Various genres are classified together because of the conventions and styles they use and the experiences they depict. Characters and themes that are repeated—attitudes of determination, hope, and the ability to endure ambivalence and conflict—all arise from a landscape situated in the middle of the nation. Midwestern literature boasts some of the first significant American expression, experimentation with literary forms, a persistent commitment to the importance of finding meaning in the land and everyday experience, tenacious support for democratic values, and a diverse cultural and stylistic tapestry with a common geography strong enough to hold together what continues to evolve.

So what can be said with certainty about Midwestern literature? First, it is a huge collection of works that cannot be defined fully in an essay of any length. Second, there is a continuous debate among critics and readers about Midwestern literature's origins, meaning, impact, and importance. Third, the writing of the region encompasses every literary genre and seems to cluster into groupings of rural, small-town, and city settings. Finally, there is an agreed upon list of major concerns and values found in the literature, but these values are expressed most often alongside challenges and threats that make any resolution conflicted. In a typical work of Midwestern literature, opportunity is met with challenge and struggle. Living through the ambivalence is at the core of the Midwestern experience. Conflicts can be destructive or restorative: presenting a fall or the healing and growth after a fall. Above all, the literature invites its readers to feel deeply its sense of place—in all its complexity—and grow wiser and more human in the process.

Works Cited

Anderson, David D. "The Origins and Development of the Literature of the Midwest" in *Dictionary of Midwestern Literature, Volume One, The Authors*. Ed. Phillip A Greasley. Bloomington: U of Indiana P, 2001. 10-24.

Barillas, William. *The Midwestern Pastoral.* Athens: Ohio UP, 2006.

Greasley, Phillip A. Introduction. *Dictionary of Midwestern Literature: Volume One, The Authors.* Ed. Greasley. Bloomington: U of Indiana P, 2001. 1-8.

Watts, Edward. "Re-Centering the Center," *American Literary History*, Volume 21, Number 4 Winter 2009. 859-868.

CRITICAL
CONTEXTS

Midwestern Literature in Historical and Cultural Context

Marcia Noe

What makes the Midwest the Midwest? For many of us, it's a grain elevator rising against a blazing blue sky, the rattle of the 'L' rambling through Chicago's Loop, the scent of new-mown hay in an Indiana meadow, the luscious sweetness of a custard at a Wisconsin dairy stand, the thrill of a red-winged blackbird perched on a cattail near an Iowa creek.

That the word "Midwest" can evoke such varying images suggests that it is surely more than the sum total of the twelve states that historian Frederick Jackson Turner named in *The Frontier in American History* (1948): the five states of the Old Northwest (Michigan, Wisconsin, Illinois, Ohio, and Indiana), as well as Iowa, Minnesota, North Dakota, South Dakota, Nebraska, Kansas, and Missouri. Some would argue, along with cultural geographer James Shortridge, that the Midwest exists not so much as a definite geographical location than as an idea that people have developed about a region where people are honest and kind and everybody lives in peace and harmony. That such a place may not, in fact, exist is less important than the idea that it does exist as the Great Good Place in the minds of many.

Where did this construction of the Midwest come from? To a large degree, it is a product of the literary imaginations of people who lived there, people who visited, and the people who need to see the region in this way. Moreover, it is a product of historical and cultural forces. The earliest novel that we can call Midwestern was written by an Englishman, Gilbert Imlay. In *The Emigrants* (1793), the Illinois Great Lakes region is the eventual destination of a family that has been financially ruined by poor judgment and bad luck. The family views this Middle Western locale, rich in land and resources, as an ideal place to start over.

Other travelers and sojourners came to the Midwest when our nation was young and wrote about its natural beauty and charm; among them are Washington Irving, Walt Whitman, Henry David Thoreau, and Margaret Fuller. Many nineteenth- and early twentieth-century Midwestern authors continued to portray the Midwest as a heartland where virtuous folk live in harmony with Nature and each other on its farms and in its towns. William Dean Howells's *A Boy's Town* (1890), James Whitcomb Riley's *Home-Folks* (1900), Clarence Darrow's *Farmington* (1904), Zona Gale's *Friendship Village* (1908), Francis Grierson's *The Valley of Shadows* (1909), many of the poems in Carl Sandburg's *Cornhuskers* (1918), and Sherwood Anderson's *Tar: A Midwestern Childhood* (1926) are just of few of the Midwestern works that fondly recall a pre-industrial, rural, small-town Midwest.

The early works of Midwestern literature that celebrate farm and small town Midwestern life are grounded in agrarian values, a philosophy that can trace its roots to the eighteenth-century French Physiocrats, who believed that land was the only true source of wealth. Nature is good, they held, therefore, and the farmer, who works the land, becomes virtuous because of his contact with the land. He derives his livelihood from it and is, therefore, fully entitled to the fruits of his labor. Early in our nation's history, agrarian statesmen such as Benjamin Franklin and Thomas Jefferson espoused these principles in their writings and advocated public policy and legislation that favored the farmer. Agrarianism was the basis for Jefferson's dream of a democratic civilization in the virgin land of the West, where every man had a chance to prosper as an independent landowner, if he worked hard and became competent. Jefferson's hope for America was based on this vision of a natural aristocracy of landowning farmers, free and equal, happy and virtuous because they earned their living from the land. Agrarian beliefs formed the foundation of much of the signature legislation of the mid-nineteenth century, such as the Homestead Act of 1862, which encouraged agrarian settlement through the ten-dollar sale of 160 acres to small farmers if they lived on their acreage for at least five years. Another example is the Morrill Act of 1862, which funded the land grant colleges, institutions of higher education that focused on the study of agriculture and practical trades.

Agrarian values are reflected in much of nineteenth- and early twentieth-century Midwestern literature. Willa Cather's *O Pioneers!* (1913) is the story of a female farmer, Alexandra Bergson, who inherits the family farm in Nebraska and becomes independent, successful, and wealthy because of her hard work, intelligence, and vision for the land. Similarly, Cather's 1932 short story, "Neighbour Rosicky," relates the story of Anton Rosicky, who trades an unsatisfying life in the city for the freedom and independence he derives from owning and working his own land in Nebraska. Times are sometimes hard, but Rosicky perseveres; enjoys a happy family life and, at the end of his life, becomes one with the land he loves .

The counter-narrative to these books, seen by many scholars as stemming from a Midwestern literary movement known as the 'Revolt from the Village', tells a different story, a story of social change as Thomas Jefferson's agrarian dream for small farmers was eclipsed by those who promoted growth, development, commercialism, and acquisitiveness in the villages, farms, and towns of the Middle West, as well as in the nation as a whole. During the nineteenth century, the most significant cultural change in the United States was the shift from a rural society to an urban one. In 1850, sixty-four percent of American workers lived on farms; by the turn of the century, nearly that many were city dwellers. This dramatic change from an agricultural to an industrial economy transformed American rural life, and its effect on Midwestern farms and small towns was immense. The Big Three village rebels (although each denied that he was part of a Revolt from the Village movement) were the poet Edgar Lee Masters and novelists Sherwood Anderson and Sinclair Lewis. They recorded these cultural changes in Midwestern rural life and the subsequent sense of loss and longing for an earlier, better day in *Spoon River Anthology* (1915), *Winesburg, Ohio* (1919), and *Main Street* (1920), respectively.

While an earlier generation of writers– the prairie realists— had offered Americans an unflinching look at the harsh realities of settling the frontier and farming in the Midwest (Edward Eggleston's

The Mystery of Metropolisville [1873], Joseph Kirkland' s *Zury: The Meanest Man in Spring County* [1887], E.W. Howe's *The Story of a Country Town* [1883], and Hamlin Garland's *Main-Travelled Roads* [1891] are four good examples), their literary successors in the early twentieth century brought their themes of dispossession and disillusionment to the town, undermining the myth of the Midwestern village as the locus of virtue, harmony, and community. Instead, they wrote of narrow-minded and conformist characters, who ostracized outsiders and dissenters while worshipping the Gospel of Prosperity and adhering to the code of keeping up appearances. Both of these values were reinforced by the advance of industry and its accompanying commercial mentality on their once-idyllic Midwestern havens.

A writer who focused heavily on the changes that industrialization brought to the Midwest was Booth Tarkington, whose *Growth* trilogy chronicled, over the course of three novels, the development of Midland City—based on Tarkington's native Indianapolis—from a town of gracious old homes and an established social hierarchy to a gritty, noisy, factory-filled metropolis: *The Turmoil* (1915), *The Magnificent Ambersons* (1918), and *The Midlander* (1923). *The Magnificent Ambersons*, which won the Pulitzer Prize for Fiction in 1919, relates these social and economic changes from the perspective of one of the town's reigning families, the Ambersons, who lose their money and social standing because they fail to adjust successfully to the new ways. Others who wrote about how the death of the agrarian dream in an industrializing America affected the Midwestern town were Louis Bromfield (*The Green Bay Tree*, 1924), Sherwood Anderson (*Poor White*, 1920), and Ruth Suckow (*New Hope*, 1942)

The shift from an agricultural to an industrial economy also involved a migration pattern in which country people moved into urban areas to take advantage of better paying jobs and cultural and educational opportunities. One of these migration patterns was that of African Americas and working class whites, who left the South in the early decades of the twentieth century for cities like Chicago and Detroit, where they imagined there would be better opportunities.

Richard Wright's *Black Boy* (1945), Harriette Arnow's *The Dollmaker* (1954), and several of the poems in Gwendolyn Brooks's *A Street in Bronzeville* (1945) reflect such migration experiences. A slightly different black migration story is seen in Langston Hughes's *Not Without Laughter* (1930); the protagonist's sister, Harriet, abandons her small-town Kansas beginnings to find success on the Chicago vaudeville blues scene.

Earlier migration patterns had brought the Scandinavians, the Irish, the Germans, the Dutch and others from the Old World to the Midwest. These new Midwesterners recorded the experience of coming to the region to homestead and build communities in rural areas or work in its urban factories in novels such as Upton Sinclair's 1906 *The Jungle*, which features a Lithuanian protagonist; Edna Ferber's 1924 Pulitzer Prize-winning *So Big*, which focuses on a Dutch community; Ole Rølvaag's 1927 *Giants in the Earth*, which depicts on a Norwegian pioneer family; James T. Farrell's 1935 *Studs Lonigan*, with its examination of Irish-American life in Chicago Irish; and Herbert Krause's 1939 *Wind Without Rain*, which portrays German immigrants on the prairie..

Carl Sandburg's *Chicago Poems* (1916) reflects the diversity of Chicago's immigrant population in poems such as "Fish Crier" (Russian Jewish), "The Shovel Man," "Onion Days," and "Child of the Romans" (Italian), "Happiness" (Hungarian), and "The Right to Grief" (Bohemian). Throughout these poems, Sandburg emphasizes the wide income gap between rich and poor, as well as the challenges immigrants faced: disease, infant and early childhood mortality, long hours of low-paying work in unsafe conditions, and corporate opposition to labor unions and its indifference to the sufferings of working people.

Those emigrating from the Old World brought with them cultural experiences that often clashed with those whose ancestors came over in earlier times. This clash of cultures in the Midwest pitted the Yankee descendants of the Puritans, who valued individualism, freedom, and civil liberties, against the newcomers: mainly Catholics and Lutherans from Germany and Scandinavia, whose cultural orientation was more authoritarian and hierarchical, as historian Jon Gjerde argues.

The twentieth century—dubbed the Machine Age—brought huge changes in the way Americans saw themselves and the world that they lived in. Four major thinkers—Darwin, Marx, Einstein, and Freud—bridged the nineteenth and twentieth centuries and laid the groundwork for Modernism. Their theories shared the common effect of displacing Man from his traditional place at the center of the universe and marginalizing and diminishing him: Freud showed him to be at the mercy of needs and that his drives centered in his unconscious; Darwin portrayed him as having evolved from a higher form of animal life, rather than having been specially created by a Divine Being; Marx's theory of dialectical materialism argued that economic changes, rather than human agency, drives human history; and Einstein changed the shape of the Universe and the flow of time, dwarfing Man with theories of relative rates of time passing in a curved universe.

In addition to these theoretical developments that diminished Man, three main cultural shifts in the United States, discussed by historian Henry F. May, put an end to Victorianism and ushered in modern times: a loss of belief in the old values and sources of authority, a loss of faith in progress, and a revolt against tradition in the arts. All of these new theories and cultural changes, seen in the United States as a whole, were also evident in the literature produced by Midwesterners in the early years of the twentieth century. These writers rejected the notion that progress was inevitable. Theodore Dreiser, for example, revealed in *Sister Carrie* (1900), *Jennie Gerhardt* (1911), and *An American Tragedy* (1925) that his characters were at the mercy of the vagaries of fate, circumstance, their environment, and their own drives. These writers also rejected the genteel tradition of literature, which held that what we read should make us better people and that only certain subjects, such as love, religion, patriotism, and heroic deeds done by noble people, were appropriate literary material. They similarly dismissed the belief that only certain forms of literature, such as poetry that rhymed and novels with plots, could be considered real literature.

The Poetry Revolution of the early twentieth century was led by Midwestern poets who violated all of these rules. Masters's *Spoon River* poems aren't about kings and warriors; many of the speakers of these dramatic monologues are working-class people, among them a prostitute, a cooper, a blacksmith, and a laundress. Among the subjects broached are venereal disease, adultery, political corruption, alcoholism, rape, and abortion, clearly not subjects fit for the poetry of the genteel tradition.

Two Chicago magazines, *Poetry*, founded in 1912 by Harriet Monroe, and *The Little Review*, founded in 1914 by Margaret Anderson, published poetry written in free verse that featured everyday subjects and the oral speech patterns of ordinary people. While *Poetry* became famous for publishing T.S. Eliot's *The Lovesong of J. Alfred Prufrock*—long considered a work of high culture—that magazine also published Sandburg's sprawling "Chicago" and other poems grounded in urban realism that he later published in book form as *Chicago Poems*. Likewise, *The Little Review* published James Joyce's *Ulysses*, a work of high modernism but also fiction and articles by Midwestern writers, such as Sherwood Anderson, Floyd Dell, Theodore Dreiser, Ernest Hemingway, and many others. Another Midwestern journal that participated in the cultural revolution was the St. Louis-based *Reedy's Mirror*; Masters' *Spoon River* poems began appearing there in the spring of 1914, with editor William Marion Reedy's encouragement, before they were collected in book form the following year.

The era that ushered in the revolt against the conventions of high culture and Victorian values also saw political reform movements gain momentum. The roots of this tradition can be found as far back as the eighteenth century in the language of the 1787 *Northwest Ordinance*, which encouraged education, guaranteed trial by jury, and abolished slavery in the Northwest Territory. Building on this solid foundation of human rights, a strong tradition of radicalism and reform emerged in the Midwest. This tradition, in turn, spawned nineteenth-century rebels such as feminist Voltairine de Cleyre and David Ross Locke. The latter, adopting the persona of Petroleum V. Nasby, functioned as a nineteenth-century Stephen Colbert, whose platform performances and newspaper columns dealt with equal rights for women and African Americans. The abolition and temperance movements had strong roots in Ohio, where the American Anti-Slavery Society flourished, and Personal Liberty laws were passed to protect free Negroes and defy the national Fugitive Slave Law. Ohio also saw the founding of the Women's Christian Temperance Union in Cleveland in 1874 and the Anti-Saloon League in Oberlin in 1893. Earlier in the century, in 1835, Oberlin College claimed the distinction of being the first institution of higher learning in America to admit African Americans and women.

Midwestern radicalism and reform movements also had roots in the post-Civil War Populism of orator Robert Ingersoll and journalist Ignatius Donnelly, who advocated that all humans are equal in dignity and worth and crusaded against the power of big corporations, usurious loan sharks, and monopolies. The populist organizations of the 1880s and 1890s, such as the Free Silver Party, the Greenback-Labor Party, the National Farmers' Alliance, which eventually became the People's Party—its members known as Populists—also furthered the progressive causes. These organizations sought government regulation to free farmers from the snares of the Gold Standard, land speculators, high-interest mortgages , and railroad-manipulated freight rates, all of which left many unable to earn enough from their crops to pay their mortgages.

These problems are reflected in Hamlin Garland's story, "Under the Lion's Paw" from his collection *Main-Travelled Roads* (1891), which relates the experiences of the Haskins family who settle on a rented farmstead, work hard, invest in improvements to the property, and achieve a measure of success. Instead of being rewarded with the ownership of the farm they worked hard to improve, they are punished by an unscrupulous landlord, a loan shark who now wants to charge them twice as much as he originally asked for the farm because the Haskins have doubled its value.

In the Midwest, proponents of progressive reforms became increasingly successful, as in Wisconsin, where Robert LaFollette, governor from 1901 to 1906 advocated the following political reforms, which put government in the hands of citizens rather than railroads and corporations: the primary election, the referendum, the recall, and the initiative. During this period, Upton Sinclair's *The Jungle* was published to convert workers to socialism; however, its impact was one of reform rather than revolution, as its notoriety helped build support for the passage of the Pure Food and Drug Act.

During the 1920s, a successful Russian Revolution created a political climate that was conducive to leftist movements, while the economic collapse at the end of the decade further motivated people to look to Socialism and Communism for solutions. At the beginning of the decade, women won the vote with the passage of the Nineteenth Amendment, a battle chronicled in Janet Ayer Fairbank's suffrage novel, *Rich Man, Poor Man* (1936). Women thereafter began to take their places in colleges and businesses, as seen in Edna Ferber's Emma McChesney stories, which trace the career trajectory of a traveling saleswoman from road trip to corporate office. Other early twentieth-century works of fiction that reflected the era's feminist ferment and introduced the New Woman to Midwestern literature are Elia W. Peattie's *The Precipice* (1914), Susan Glaspell's *Fidelity* (1915), and Edna Ferber's *Fanny Herself* (1917). In 1921, Zona Gale became the first woman to win the Pulitzer Prize for Drama for *Miss Lulu Bett*, which she adapted from her 1920 novel of the same name. The central character, dependent upon her married sister for her livelihood and thus a virtual servant in her household, exposes the humiliations and indignities that a patriarchal social order imposed on the American single woman of that time.

Throughout the 1920s, '30s, and '40s, Midwestern regional painters, the best known of whom are Grant Wood, John Steuart Curry, and Thomas Hart Benton, produced populist works of art firmly rooted in the lives of ordinary Midwesterners. At the same time, radical publications like *The Left*, *The Anvil*, and the *Haldeman-Julius Weekly* were edited in Davenport, Iowa; Moberly, Missouri; and Girard, Kansas, respectively. This populist cultural milieu facilitated the rise of the Midwestern proletarian novel, which celebrated the worker and exposed the exploitative and dehumanizing social conditions, in which he worked and lived.

Edward Dahlberg took the latter for his subject in his 1929 novel *Bottom Dogs*, set in Kansas City and Cleveland. In addition to his editing *The Anvil* through thirteen issues, Jack Conroy wrote *The Disinherited*, a 1933 novel of coal miners turned migrant workers; similarly, Thomas Boyd's 1935 work, *In Time of Peace*, depicts the radicalization of a Chicago factory worker. While journalist and fiction writer Meridel LeSueur reported the effects of the Great Depression on the people of the Midwest, Willard Motley and Nelson Algren exposed the social conditions that produce criminals and addicts in Motley's *Knock on Any Door* of 1947 and Algren's *The Man with the Golden Arm* of 1949.

The works of World War II-era Midwestern authors reflected America's mid-century status as a world power and resulting positive self-image. Ernest Hemingway, in his 1940 novel *For Whom the Bell Tolls* affirms the indomitability of the human spirit and the primacy of the human community; fourteen years later, Hemingway was awarded the Nobel Prize for Literature. Ross Lockridge's prize-winning 1948 *Raintree County* has been read as an affirmation of American idealism, vitality, and power in its tale of John Wickliff Shawnessy's mythic quest for the life-giving raintree in rural Indiana. James Jones's account of World War II in Hawaii in the 1951 novel *From Here to Eternity* and his story of a veteran's difficult adjustment to civilian life in his Midwestern home town in *Some Came Running* of 1957 are more realistic novels of that period.

However, the postwar era also saw the publication of *Dangling Man* in 1944, the first novel of a young Chicago writer who would go on to win the Nobel Prize for Literature in 1976. In this novel, as in much of his fiction, Saul Bellow captured the existential dilemma of postmodern man in his protagonist Joseph's plight. Waiting to be called up in the draft, Joseph is in limbo, caught between two worlds, unable to make meaningful choices and move forward in his life while he is trapped in his unresolved situation. Bellow's 1953 *The Adventures of Augie March* gives us a modern-day urban Huckleberry Finn in Augie March, whose peripatetic life and quest for love and freedom take him from the streets of Chicago to Mexico and Europe. Like Joseph, Augie is a man perpetually in transition.

America at mid-century was smug and self-satisfied; America ten years later was in turmoil and strife as the Civil Rights Movement, followed by the peace and feminist movements, pierced the veil of material comfort that disguised social inequality and oppression due to race, class, and gender. The Equal Pay Act of 1963, the Civil Rights Act of 1964, and the Voting Rights Act of 1965 were laws passed to address these inequalities. Much of the Midwestern literature of the last half of the twentieth century reflects the strength, visibility, and success of these social movements.

The Women's Liberation movement, led by Ohioan Gloria Steinem and Illinoisian Betty Friedan was in full swing by the time the nation celebrated its 200th birthday. Women writers found new places to publish their work with the founding of feminist journals such as *Primavera* and *Black Maria* in Chicago. The "mad housewife" novels of the 1960s, '70s, and '80s replaced the "madcap housewife" books of the 1950s. For example, Ohioan Alex Kates Shulman's 1972 *Memoirs of an Ex-Prom Queen* called into question patriarchal expectations and roles for women. Nebraskan Meridel Le Sueur's *The Girl*, written decades earlier, but first published in 1978, celebrates female community and sisterhood. Since the early 1980s, Sara Paretsky's female detective V. I. Warshawski has exemplified a woman in a nontraditional career, who fights both crime and the prejudices of the criminal justice community in a series of novels set in Chicagoland.

As the twentieth century moved into its final quarter, Midwestern literature felt the influence of the environmental movement. From early on, there had been a strain of Thoreauvian respect and regard for nature in Midwestern literature. One of the earliest Midwestern voices raised in protest against capitalistic exploitation of the land was that of Meridel Le Sueur in her 1931 short story, "Corn Village." Aldo Leopold's *Sand County Almanac* of 1949 is a classic text of environmentalism that advocates human stewardship of our natural resources by proposing a land ethic in which people function as members, not exploiters or commodifiers, of an ecosystem with the moral obligation to preserve its delicate balance, and a land aesthetic, in which the environment is valued for its historical and ecological significance as well as its natural beauty.

Following in this tradition, Scott Russell Sanders, in numerous books but especially in *A Conservationist Manifesto* of 2009, promotes responsible stewardship of the environment by preserving areas such as the Loblolly Swamp in Indiana. Sanders advocates a conservationist culture, opposing it to the dominant consumerist culture that threatens to deprive future generations of the kind of quality of life that we enjoy today. Many Midwestern poets of place have written in this tradition: Robert Bly, Lucien Stark, James Wright, Theodore Roethke, Ted Kooser, William Kloefkorn, Jim Harrison, and a host of others.

Jane Smiley's 1991 Pulitzer Prize–winning novel, *A Thousand Acres* joins environmentalist with feminist concerns in its story of an Iowa farm family whose patriarch, Larry Cook, has violated both the land ethic and the incest taboo: he has used drainage tile that has allowed poison to leach into the water supply and he has sexually abused his daughters. With its plot based on that of King Lear, *A Thousand Acres* is the quintessential ecofeminist novel, chronicling the disintegration of a family whose normal, prosperous appearance belies habits of dishonesty, oppression, selfishness, and greed. Rose's cancer and Ginny's miscarriages result directly from their father's misuse of his farmland, symbolizing the ugly fruits of Larry Cook's disregard for any ethic except his own need for power, control, and wealth.

A Thousand Acres depicts not only a family, but also a region in distress. Many factors contributed to the farm crisis of the 1980s, among them the US decision to stop selling wheat to Russia, high interest rates that forced farm foreclosures and devalued farm land, and government policies that enacted a free-market approach to agricultural production. A combination of these and other factors threatened the Midwestern family farm, historically a symbol of the region's identity. Novels such as David Rhodes's 2008 *Driftless*, one story line of which exposes a corrupt dairy industry that exploits farmers, and *A Map of the World* of 1994 by Jane Hamilton reflect the problems faced by Midwestern family farmers. Like her Iowa counterpart, Jane Smiley, Hamilton writes about Midwesterners who have lost their connection to the land and the spiritual, emotional, economic, and social consequences of that loss. In *A Map of the World*, the Wisconsin community that dairy farmers Alice and Howard Goodwin reside in has abandoned its roots in the land and become commercialized and suburban. Ironically, the Goodwins—forced to sell their farm through a combination of difficult circumstances—have become the Other that the community persecutes—a comment on how alienated Midwesterners have become from their roots in the land, which represents the foundation of the Jeffersonian dream.

The smokestack industries in cities such as St. Louis, Cleveland, and Detroit were another part of the Midwestern economy that was badly damaged during the last quarter of the twentieth century. As the United States shifted its economic emphasis from industry to the service and information technology sectors, corporations furthered weakened the Midwestern industrial base by using government tax breaks to move their factories overseas and close those at home. Among the Midwestern authors who wrote during this period was the late Steve Tesich, whose 1982 novel *Summer Crossing* is a coming-of-age story set in East Chicago, Indiana that records the beginning of the decline of the Midwest's steel mills and foundries.

Also at this time, diversity and multiculturalism became increasingly important social values, a legacy of the protest movements of the '60s and '70s. African American, Hispanic, and Asian writers moved increasingly into the Midwestern, as well as the national literary forefront, along with writers of other ethnicities formerly less visible. In many of these novels, identity becomes a major theme, as characters attempt to reconcile their ethnic affiliations and values with American and Midwestern ones. In Bharati Muhkerjee's *Jasmine* (1989), the protagonist's crisis of identity is conveyed through the various names by which she is called—Jyoti by her Indian family, Jasmine by her first husband, Jase by her Manhattan employer, and Jane by her second husband, an Iowa banker whose friends and family confront Jasmine with her Otherness several times a day in their well-meaning but clueless questions and comments about her ethnicity. Similarly, Sandra Cisneros's *Caramelo* (2002) explores a young girl's struggle to establish an identity when her life is split between Mexico and Chicago, a fact attributable to her family's annual migration between the two countries. It also examines the psychic confusion of the girl's elderly grandmother when the woman moves to Chicago after her husband dies.

Perhaps the multiplicity and diversity of the Midwest are most directly reflected in the number of different names we have for it. While the South is simply the South, and the same is true for New England and the West, we call the twelve-state region in the middle of the country by a variety of names, including the Midwest, the Middle West, Mid-America, Middle America, the Middle Kingdom, the Middle Border and, of course, the Heartland. Indeed, there are many Midwests, and many different voices speak in Midwestern literature. Our hallmark is diversity, and our diversity is our strength.

Works Cited

Algren, Nelson. *The Man with the Golden Arm*. 1949. Ed. William J. Savage Jr. and Daniel Simon. New York: Seven Stories Press, 1999.

Anderson, Sherwood. *Poor White*. 1920. New York: New Directions, 1998.

_____. *Tar: A Midwestern Childhood*. New York: Boni and Liveright, 1926.

_____. *Winesburg, Ohio*. New York: B.W. Huebsch, 1919.

Arnow, Harriette. *The Dollmaker*. New York: Macmillan, 1954.

Bellow, Saul. *The Adventures of Augie March*. 1953. Greenwich, CT: Fawcett, 1953.

_____. *Dangling Man*. 1944. New York: Signet, 1965.

Boyd, Thomas. *In Time of Peace*. New York: Minton Balch Putnam, 1935.

Bromfield, Louis. *The Green Bay Tree*. New York: Frederick A. Stokes, 1924.

Brooks, Gwendolyn. *A Street in Bronzeville*. New York: Harper & Brothers, 1945.
Cather, Willa. "Neighbour Rosicky". 1932. *Collected Stories*. New York: Vintage Books, 1992. 231-61.

_____. *O Pioneers!* Boston: Houghton Mifflin, 1913.

Cisneros, Sandra. *Caramelo*. New York: Knopf, 2002.

Conroy, Jack. *The Disinherited*. New York: Covici-Friede, 1933.

Dahlberg, Edward. *Bottom Dogs*. London: Putnam, 1929.

Darrow, Clarence. *Farmington*. Chicago: A.C. McClurg, 1904.

Dreiser, Theodore. *An American Tragedy*. New York: Doubleday, Page & Company, 1925.

_____. *Jennie Gerhardt*. New York: Doubleday, Page & Company, 1900.

Eggleston, Edward. *The Mystery of Metropolisville*. New York: O. Judd, 1873.

Fairbank, Janet. *Rich Man, Poor Man*. Boston: Houghton Mifflin, 1936.

Farrell, James T. *Studs Lonigan: A Trilogy*. New York: Library of America, 1935.

Ferber, Edna. *Fanny Herself*. New York: Frederick A. Stokes, 1917.

Ferber, Edna. *So Big*. New York: Doubleday, Page & Company, 1924.

Gale, Zona. *Friendship Village*. New York: Macmillan, 1908.

_____. *Miss Lulu Bett*. New York: D. Appleton & Company, 1920.

Garland, Hamlin. *Main-Travelled Roads*. 1891. New York: Signet Classics, 1962.

Gjerde, Jon. *The Minds of the West: Ethnocultural Evolution in the Rural Midwest, 1830-1917*. Chapel Hill: U of North Carolina P, 1997.

Glaspell, Susan. *Fidelity*. New York: Small, Maynard, and Company, 1915.

Grierson, Francis. *The Valley of Shadows*. London: Constable, 1909.

Hallwas, John, E., ed. *Edgar Lee Masters Spoon River Anthology: An Annotated Edition*. Urbana: U of Illinois P, 1992.

Hamilton, Jane. *A Map of the World*. New York: Anchor Books, 1994.

Hemingway, Ernest. *For Whom the Bell Tolls*. New York: Charles Scribner's Sons, 1940.

Howe, Edgar Watson. *The Story of a Country Town*. Atchison, KS: Howe, 1883.

Howells, William Dean. *A Boy's Town*. New York: Harper & Brothers, 1890.

Hughes, Langston. *Not Without Laughter*. New York: Knopf, 1930.

Imlay, Gilbert. *The Emigrants*. 1793. New York: Penguin, 1998.

Jones, James. *From Here to Eternity*. New York: Scribner's, 1951.

_____. *Some Came Running*. New York: Scribner's, 1957.

Kirkland, Joseph. Zury: *The Meanest Man in Spring County*. Boston: Houghton Mifflin, 1887.

Krause, Herbert. *Wind Without Rain*. Indianapolis: Bobbs-Merrill, 1939.

Le Sueur, Meridel. *The Girl*. Cambridge, MA: West End Press, 1978.

_____. "Corn Village." *Scribner's* (Aug. 1931): 133-40.

Leopold. Aldo. *Sand County Almanac and Sketches Here and There*. New York: Oxford UP, 1949.

Lewis, Sinclair. *Main Street*. 1920. New York: Harcourt, Brace and Howe, 1920.

Lockridge, Ross. *Raintree County*. Boston: Houghton Mifflin, 1948.

May, Henry F. *The End of American Innocence: A Study of the First Years of Our Own Time, 1912-1917*. New York: Knopf, 1959.

Motley, Willard. *Knock On Any Door*. New York: D. Appleton-Century, 1947.

Muhkerjee, Bharati. *Jasmine*. New York: Grove Weidenfeld, 1989.

Peattie, Elia. W. *The Precipice*. 1914. Urbana: U of Illinois P, 1989.

Rhodes, David. *Driftless*. Minneapolis: Milkweed Editions, 2008.

Riley, James Whitcomb. *Home-Folks*. New York: Braunworth, Munn & Barber, 1900.

Rølvaag, Ole. *Giants in the Earth*. 1927. New York: Harper & Brothers, 1929.

Sandburg, Carl. *Chicago Poems*. New York: Henry Holt and Company, 1916.

_____. *Cornhuskers*. New York: Henry Holt and Company, 1918.

Sanders, Scott Russell. *A Conservationist Manifesto*. Bloomington: Indiana UP, 2009.

Shortridge, James R. *The Middle West: Its Meaning in American Culture*. Lawrence: UP of Kansas, 1989.

Shulman, Alix Kates. *Memoirs of an Ex-Prom Queen*. New York: Knopf, 1972.

Sinclair, Upton. *The Jungle*. New York: Doubleday, Page, & Company, 1906.

Smiley, Jane. *A Thousand Acres*. New York: Knopf, 1991.

Suckow, Ruth. *New Hope*. New York: Farrar & Rinehart, 1942.

Tarkington, Booth. *The Magnificent Ambersons*. New York: Doubleday, Page, & Company, 1918.

_____. *The Midlander*. New York: Doubleday, Page, 1923.

_____. *The Turmoil*. New York: Harper & Brothers, 1915.

Tesich, Steve. *Summer's Crossing*. New York: Random House, 1982.

Turner, Frederick Jackson. *The Frontier in American History*. New York: Henry Holt, 1920.

Wright, Richard. *Black Boy*. New York: Harper & Brothers, 1945.

What is "Middlewestishness"? The Evolution of Midwestern Literary Studies

Sara Kosiba

In his preface to the collection *Transatlantic Stories* (1926), Ford Madox Ford reflected on the content and quality of the writing he read through as he edited the little magazine *the transatlantic review* in Paris during the 1920s. He stated that the quality of "Middle Westishness" was not unique to the middle region of the United States but instead contained a global quality:

> It is in fact a world movement, the symptom of an enormous disillusionment . . . and an enormous awakening. In England it is produced by a disillusionment with regard to education and to the past; in the United States it is produced by a disillusionment with regard, precisely, to the other Wests in the world, by a sudden conviction that the world—even the world as seen in the central western states of North American—is a humdrum affair. (Ford, Preface xxi)

Later, in his reminiscences of that time, Ford noted the large number of submissions from the Midwestern region of the United States and declared about those pieces, "a great proportion of them were obviously biographical in conception and all of them local in scene. But a just perception of one's surroundings and of one's own career form the first step towards a literature that shall be great in scope" (*It Was* 338-39). The early twentieth century was, indeed, a time of first steps for identifying Midwestern literature as a regionally specific product and yet one that had national and international implications.

Ford's comments are reflective of the great search for a definition of Midwestern literature that has taken place throughout the twentieth and continued into the twenty-first century. The search has involved everyone—from native Midwesterners defending and defining their region to non-natives, like Ford and others—questioning the region's characteristics and trying to place those qualities in a national or international literary framework. This overall discussion has been characterized more by debate than consensus. While writers, critics, students, and scholars have noted points of commonality within Midwestern writing, the interpretations resulting from those observations have often differed greatly. At its core, this debate has thus encouraged confining stereotypes when individuals have latched onto the same ideas. Moreover, the debate has continually used narrow definitions, and yet argued for reassessment, when individuals have delved deeper into the layers of social and cultural diversity within the Midwest.

Even though the roots of what would become the Midwest go back as far as the Northwest Ordinance of 1787, a formal study of Midwestern literature would not begin until the twentieth century. As geographer James Shortridge has noted, "Middle West came into its own as a major regional term about 1912" (24), and studies focused on the literature of the region would start to solidify and flourish during that decade. Before 1912, the region of the country that would become known as the Midwest was known more generally as the West or the Old Northwest, as evidenced by one of the earliest anthologies of what might be considered "Midwestern" literature, William T. Coggeshall's *The Poets and Poetry of the West*, published in Columbus, Ohio in 1860. Few, if any, of the participants in Coggeshall's anthology would be familiar to contemporary readers, with the exception perhaps of Alice and Phoebe Cary and William Dean Howells.

Book–length studies began appearing in the 1920s, which defined Midwestern literature as a cohesive regional literary form. Two notable examples are Ralph Leslie Rusk's two-volume *The Literature of the Middle Western Frontier* (1925) and Dorothy Anne Dondore's *The Prairie and the Making of Middle America: Four Centuries of Description* (1926). Rusk's study focuses entirely on the frontier period of Midwestern literature and writing. He notes in the preface to the first printing of his study that he "arbitrarily" chose the end of 1840 to mark the end of the pioneer period in the Midwest (vii). Dondore's study is equally impressive in scope because she discusses the region from its origins all the way up to the time of her collection's publication. She observes in the book's "Foreword" that her research will prove "this section has been the subject of numerous and varied interpretations which have reflected all stages of its life" (vii).

Both Rusk and Dondore expand their examination of Midwestern literature beyond purely artistic definitions of poetry, drama, and prose to include other genres of writing like political pamphlets, journalism, and other forms of non-fiction writing. These early studies are indicative of a trend not only in Midwestern regionalism but also in American regional writing as a whole. Regional studies of the time emphasized that the region's history and legacy are an essential component to any study of the literature.

Midwestern literature, particularly of the early twentieth century, would also be forever marked by an observation made by literary critic Carl Van Doren in 1921. Writing in *The Nation*, Van Doren highlighted several novels and short story collections by Midwestern writers that he felt were not:

> "faithful to the cult of the village, celebrating its delicate merits with sentimental affection and with unwearied interest digging into odd corners of the country for persons and incidents illustrative of the essential goodness and heroism which, so the doctrine ran, lie beneath exciting surfaces." (407)

Sinclair Lewis, Sherwood Anderson, and F. Scott Fitzgerald were among the writers discussed in Van Doren's article, all of whom already had a great deal of literary notoriety and were known for their Midwestern roots. Van Doren applauded the efforts of these writers to break away from a sentimental past to critique hypocrisy and capture irony where they saw it occurring. This commentary regarding the "revolt against the village" would inspire widespread discussion and debate, becoming a common theme in discussions of Midwestern writing. Dondore mentions it in her discussion of Midwestern literature, demonstrating the phrase's early accommodation into the genre a mere five years after Van Doren's article. Van Doren's comments would serve as the basis for literary criticism, divided into two major groups: those who agreed that Midwestern literature tended toward idealism and sentimentality, particularly when treating the subject of the small town or family farm, and those who defended Midwestern literature as a complex genre, filled with social diversity and contradictory—as opposed to homogenized—ideas. The debate has continued throughout the twentieth and into the twenty-first century, as later publications, like Anthony Channell Hilfer's 1969 book *The Revolt from the Village, 1915-1930* and those of other scholars, have continued to use Van Doren's critique to define that era (and even later works) in Midwestern literature.

The work of Professor John T. Flanagan serves as a notable contrast to the perspective of a bland or sentimentalized Midwestern literature and represents a point of view that embraces the region rather than revolts against it. Flanagan published a significant number of critical articles in the mid-twentieth century , which reflected the depth of possibility in Midwestern literature. Covering everything from historical novels, farm novels, origins, and European influences in his examinations of Midwestern writing, Flanagan made a substantial contribution to defining the scope of both a modern and historical discussion of the region. In his article "A Half-Century of Middlewestern Fiction," Flanagan provided a historical overview that he stated would establish "the amazingly diversified subject matter of the middlewestern fiction of the last five decades" and show "the increased sophistication of the fiction, the more skillful handling of the basic elements of the novel, and the promise which this technical mastery seems to hold for the future" (18). Flanagan was not alone in his arguments for the merits of Midwestern literature, but he was one of the loudest twentieth century voices in exploring the region's literary merit. Explorations like these would inspire later Midwestern literary scholars to continue to embrace and explore the diversity and sophistication of the region.

Midwestern literature, however, has never quite fought off the confining perceptions of many critics. Despite advances by scholars like Flanagan, mid-twentieth century publications examining the Midwest were still forced to argue for the value in regional perspectives. There have been a number of books and articles published that debate the "myth or reality" of the Midwest. In one example, a collection of symposium papers titled *The Midwest: Myth or Reality?* (1961), literary scholars, economists, historians, and political scientists addressed the questions surrounding regional definition. Professor John T. Frederick, a Midwestern writer and scholar most known for his editing of *The Midland*, a Midwestern literary magazine published from 1915-1933, stated in his closing remarks:

> The Midwest is real, we have decided. We have agreed to strike out the word 'myth' and the question mark, and leave 'The Midwest: Reality.' But we have also agreed that this Midwest is largely an unknown reality. [. . .] We have seen the Midwest as waiting for its social scientists and its historians, for its writers and painters and musicians, of the region that it is now and is becoming; waiting for the men and women who can become its leaders of the mind and heart. (95)

For a region still struggling to find its regional identity and to make a strong case for itself in the larger American culture as something more than just a bland, largely rural "middle," comments like those made by Frederick would inspire a surge of interest in the region in the late twentieth century.

One of the important advances in the study of Midwestern literature and culture was the founding of The Society for the Study of Midwestern Literature (SSML) in 1971. From the founding to the present day, the organization has promoted both the study and creation of Midwestern literature and culture through conferences, awards, and publications. In the process, the group has further professionalized the study of Midwestern literature and culture and continued to explore the diversity of the region. Founding SSML member David D. Anderson advocated that any true definition of the Midwest would be found in embracing the region's complexity and contradictions rather than in oversimplifying its history and status:

Much of the reality of the Midwest today, of the paradoxical Midwestern mind that produced such ideological disparity and continuity, can be explained in mythical as well as historical terms; equally clear as a result is the reality of the Midwestern mind at once diverse and unified, consistent in its paradoxical nature, and, in its own sometimes not so quiet way, as forceful in the life of the Republic in the last half of the twentieth century as it was in the last half of the nineteenth. (9)

Rather than a region strictly in revolt or engaged in sentimentality, Anderson's words demonstrated that the region was capable of both qualities and encouraged the exploration of that contrast. The tensions that existed in the region's political, social, and historical development, extending to the current day, were indicative of the rich diversity and perspective that the Midwest contained.

The late twentieth- and early twenty-first centuries have produced more books and articles analyzing Midwestern literature and history than ever before. Many have responded to calls, like that of John T. Frederick, to be "leaders" in exploring the Midwestern "mind and heart." Some of this scholarship built on previous work, even as it attempted to break new ground. Ronald Weber's *The Midwestern Ascendancy in American Writing* (1992) is a strong discussion of the significant role Midwestern writers played in shaping modern American literature during the early twentieth century. While Weber's examination explores key Midwestern writers from Hamlin Garland to Ernest Hemingway, his discussion is also limited by a few argumentative distinctions. Weber sees the "Midwestern ascendancy" as coming to an end in 1930 with the awarding of the Nobel Prize for Literature to Sinclair Lewis and believes that that the era he describes "produced only a few works of unquestioned quality—works important for aesthetic reasons rather than social or historical reasons" (3). The 1930 cut-off date for Midwestern literature's height of productivity seems rather arbitrary, as several writers continued to produce works well after that time (although an argument could be made for diminished productivity during the 1940s, due to an increasingly unified national identity inspired by the struggles surrounding World War II). Weber also never really engages in the politics of canon-formation or value, and he never examines why some writers have had their work classified as 'unquestioned quality' while others have languished. However, Weber's study is an important one in establishing a clear sense of Midwestern regional importance amidst a broader American literary perspective.

Despite contemporary perspectives of a politically conservative Midwest, explored in books like Thomas Frank's *What's the Matter with Kansas?: How Conservatives Won the Heart of America* (2004), the Midwest actually has a rather radical political history. As Frank notes about the region's past, "Certain parts of the Midwest were once so reliably leftist that the historian Walter Prescott Webb, in his classic 1931 history of the region pointed to its persistent radicalism as one of the 'Mysteries of the Great Plains.' Today the mystery is only heightened; it seems inconceivable that the Midwest was ever thought of as a 'radical' place, as anything but the land of the bland, the easy snoozing flyover" (14-15). While scholars, like John T. Flanagan, had briefly delved into collective discussions of radical voices from the Midwest earlier in the century, the 1990s brought forth several discussions of the radical literary history of the region. Douglas Wixson's *Worker-Writer in America: Jack Conroy and the Tradition of Midwestern Literary Radicalism, 1898-1990* (1994) is the most comprehensive of these studies. In his thorough discussion of various Midwestern radical writers, including Conroy, Meridel Le Sueur and others, Wixson speculates on the tradition of thought in the region:

> Midwestern indigenous radicalism has appeared in numerous varieties: anarchists, atheists, populists, Debsian socialists, and right-wing survivalists. If there can be said to exist any underlying pattern, it is probably antiauthoritarianism. An anti-ideological current runs through the various radicalisms, as if the midwestern mind functions according to contingency and not principle. The ideological sources of midwestern literary radicals [. . .] derive from indigenous radical traditions of protest—expressed in earlier

manifestations such as the Farmer's Alliance, the People's Party, the Non-Partisan League, the IWW [International Workers of the World], certain unions, and various infusions of immigrant liberalism such as the free-thinking Forty-Eighters. Their legacy was grass-roots democratic expression, a spirit of egalitarianism, and individualism-neighborliness that seemed at times at odds with the demand for revolutionary change. (149)

The observance of the grassroots expression in many examples of Midwestern radicalism being "at odds" with true revolutionary change is borne out in the fact that few of the movements, both in the Midwest and elsewhere, ever gained a lasting legacy. However, for a region often characterized by idyllic farm scenes and a sense of isolated, small-town thinking, these writers exist as evidence that there was a greater diversity of political thought and action in the Midwest.

Many contemporary scholars have delved back further than the twentieth century to try and understand the evolution of Midwestern culture. John Gjerde's 1997 book, *The Minds of the West: Ethnocultural Evolution in the Rural Middle West 1930-1917*, is another valuable contribution to the study of the 'mind' of the Midwest, as invoked by Frederick and others. While not exclusively literary in scope, Gjerde's examination of both the evolution of American culture and the ways it was influenced and affected by an infusion of immigrant beliefs still draws connections to Midwestern authors as diverse as Ole E. Rølvaag, Ruth Suckow, and Herbert Quick, among others. Narrowing the scope of his study to the Upper Middle West, which Gjerde states had a greater contrast of American-born and immigrant settlers, he explains, "the vast tracts of land that contained the promise to transform the migrant simultaneously possessed the potential to nurture former cultural patterns" (4). It is this intersection of ideas that Gjerde believes provides a better understanding of the way Midwestern culture developed and how immigration contributed to a complex American identity.

Examinations of Midwestern literature in the late twentieth and early twenty-first centuries have mirrored developments in the study of American literature as a whole, with a greater focus on ethnic diversity and an increased use of contemporary critical and theoretical frameworks. One innovative contemporary study uses postcolonial theory to examine the early development of the region. The Midwest does not lend itself to common definitions of colonized spaces. Typically, when we study a "colonial" society in American or World history, places like the initial American colonies (colonized by Britain, France, and others) or the history of countries like India come to mind. However, in *An American Colony: Regionalism and the Roots of Midwestern Culture* (2002), Edward Watts establishes a persuasive argument for the marginalization of regional cultures while the United States was still establishing and developing a national identity. Watts states,

> This book argues that the primacy of the Northeast and the marginality of other regions in the Nation is the product of the nineteenth-century colonization of its provinces. As early as 1828, however, Old Northwesterners had began to resist and redirect these sticky misrepresentations. The result was a series of aggressive efforts to localize self-determination and to decentralize the nation's cultural identity. This book suggests that such efforts represent the beginning of the ongoing quest for a 'culture of our own' in resistance to 'the colonial spirit' which kept and still at times keeps the region marginal. (xvii)

Not many individuals would think of approaching the Midwest through this postcolonial lens, but as Watts' study shows, examining the region in this way provides insight into the struggles of developing a regional culture in the midst of a powerful national identity.

Despite the progress that has been made, it seems that the Midwest may be faced with perpetually arguing for its own regional significance. While other major regions of the United States are also debated and discussed, there is something about their core identity that often remains unquestioned. While Southern literature may undergo examination for its particular qualities or be debated over what author or literary work merits inclusion or exclusion, there is often little disagreement about whether a "Southern" literature exists. Midwestern literature has never truly been at rest as a defined concept. Even as scholar David Pichaske notes the merits of Midwestern literature of the past in "Where Now 'Midwestern Literature'?" (2006), he also questions the sustainability of those styles, influences, and themes in writing of the future:

> Writers who spend more time in front of a video screen than on the gravel roads of Lincoln County, who read the *New Yorker* and *APR* more carefully than *The Midwest Quarterly* or *Great River Review*, who spend much of their time 'at a conference in New York,' who live their lives insulated physically by glass and concrete walls and mentally by the words and theories of the academy, who never quite forgive Marshall, Minnesota, for being Marshall, Minnesota, are especially separated from place. (113)

Pichaske admits that he doesn't know what the future holds but expresses dismay if writers, particularly Midwestern writers, actually do move away from an authentic, connected sense of place. Similarly, in her call for a more detailed examination (and therefore understanding) of personal narratives and turning points in Midwestern history, Ginette Aley states that that the Midwest is "a ghost among regions" and that even recent scholarship fails to gain it significant attention. The perseverance of concerns and opinions such as these demonstrates that there is still much ground to explore and many arguments to be made regarding Midwestern literature and culture.

The one thing many scholars agree on is that research into American regionalism and the Midwest is still well worth exploring, despite modern concerns. As Timothy R. Mahoney and Wendy J. Katz state in the introduction to their 2008 collection *Regionalism and the Humanities*, even while acknowledging the prevalence of globalization as an imposing twenty-first century force, many people still "recognize, as many others have, that in the face of all these forces people still understand themselves from the perspective the place in which they live and may want to do so more, rather than less, as material and physical life becomes more and more similar around the world" (xxiii). As a result, hopefully scholars will continue to explore innovative theoretical approaches to studying Midwestern texts, delve further into the ethnic and cultural diversity of the region, and explore established writers, lesser-known voices, and new authors for their contributions to a complex and evolving definition of Midwestern literature.

Works Cited

Aley, Ginette. "Dwelling within the Place Worth Seeking: The Midwest, Regional Identity, and

Internal Histories." *Regionalism and the Humanities*. Eds. Timothy R. Mahoney and Wendy J. Katz. Lincoln: U of Nebraska P, 2008. 95-109.

Anderson, David D. "Notes Toward a Definition of the Mind of the Midwest." *MidAmerica* 3 (1976): 7-16.

Coggeshall, William T. *The Poets and Poetry of the West*. Columbus: Follett, Foster and Company, 1860.

Dondore, Dorothy Anne. *The Prairie and the Making of Middle America: Four Centuries of Description*. 1926. New York: Antiquarian, 1961.

Flanagan, John T. "A Half-Century of Middlewestern Fiction." *Critique 2* (1959): 16-34.

Ford, Ford Madox. *It Was the Nightingale*. Philadelphia: J.B. Lippincott, 1933.

_____. Preface. *Transatlantic Stories*. New York: Dial, 1926. vii-xxxi.

Frank, Thomas. *What's the Matter with Kansas?: How Conservatives Won the Heart of America*. New York: Picador, 2005.

Frederick, John T. "A Summing Up." *The Midwest: Myth or Reality?* Ed. Thomas T. McAvoy. Notre Dame: U of Notre Dame P, 1961.

Gjerde, Jon. *The Minds of the West: Ethnocultural Evolution in the Rural Middle West 1830-1917*. Chapel Hill: U of North Carolina P, 1997.

Hilfer, Anthony Channell. *The Revolt from the Village, 1915-1930*. Chapel Hill: U of North Carolina P, 1969.

Mahoney, Timothy R. and Wendy J. Katz. "Regionalism and the Humanities: Decline or Revival?" Introduction. *Regionalism and the Humanities*. Eds. Mahoney and Katz. Lincoln: U of Nebraska P, 2008. (ix-xxviii).

Pichaske, David. "Where Now 'Midwestern Literature'?" *Midwest Quarterly* 48.1 (2006): 100-19.

Rusk, Ralph Leslie. *The Literature of the Middle Western Frontier.* Vol.2 (1925). New York: Frederick Ungar, 1962.

Shortridge, James R. *The Middle West: Its Meaning in American Culture*. Lawrence: U of Kansas P, 1989.

Van Doren, Carl. "Contemporary American Novelists: The Revolt From the Village: 1920." *The Nation* 12 Oct. 1921: 407-12.

Watts, Edward. *An American Colony: Regionalism and the Roots of Midwestern Culture*. Athens: Ohio UP, 2002.

Weber, Ronald. *The Midwestern Ascendancy in American Writing*. Bloomington: Indiana UP, 1992.

Wixson, Douglas. *Worker-Writer in America: Jack Conroy and the Tradition of Midwestern Literary Radicalism, 1898-1990*. Urbana: U of Illinois P, 1994.

Complicated Grief, Mourning and Melancholia: Reading the Novel of Godfrey St. Peter's Compounded Losses in Willa Cather's *The Professor's House* _____

Sarah Warren-Riley

> "In great misfortunes," he told himself, "people want to be alone. They have a right to be. And the misfortunes that occur within one are the greatest. Surely the saddest thing in the world is falling out of love – if one has ever fallen in." (Godfrey St. Peter, in Cather's *The Professor's House* 250)

In "The Novel Démeublé," written in 1922, Willa Cather discusses novels as being "over-furnished," alluding to the fact that she viewed many contemporary novels as too full of surface-level detail (5). She considers the role of the artists to be "to interpret imaginatively the material and social investiture of their characters; to present their scene by suggestion rather than by enumeration" (6). In this paper, she expresses her appreciation of the use of "emotional penumbra of the characters themselves" in works by authors like Tolstoy (6). By definition, penumbra is either a partial illumination, "a space of partial illumination (as in an eclipse) between the perfect shadow on all sides and the full light" ("Penumbra", def. 1a), or "something that covers, surrounds, or obscures" ("Penumbra," def. 4). She continues to explain this concept by stating:

> Whatever is felt upon the page without being specifically named there – that, it seems to me, is created. It is the inexplicable presence of the thing not named, of the over-tone divined by the ear but not heard by it, the verbal mood, the emotional aura of the fact or the thing or the deed, that gives high quality to the novel or the drama, as well as to poetry itself. (6)

Cather's 1925 novel *The Professor's House* tells the story of a middle-aged college professor, Godfrey St. Peter and the emotional struggle brought on by an impending move to a new house. St. Peter resists the move, continuing to rent the old house for a year after his family moves, and he experiences a steady emotional decline throughout the story. The inability of St. Peter to relinquish the house can be seen as symbolic of his inability to relinquish a past that was more promising to him than what the future may be.

In reading *The Professor's House,* one can sense the "presence of the thing not named" as the presence of Godfrey St. Peter's emotional state. Professor Godfrey St. Peter tells us himself that he has fallen out of love, but fallen out of love with what? And given Cather's desire to present characters' emotional states as what is felt and not explicitly stated, what does it mean? Has St. Peter fallen out of love with his wife, his family, his career, or perhaps out of love with life itself?

Cather's novel was written in 1925. Given the dominant culture of American Freudianism that was the rage in the late 1910s through the 1920s, it is impossible to ignore how the novel may have been perceived through a Freudian lens. One of the main themes that runs through the work is loss; therefore, Freud's work on *Mourning and Melancholia*, published in 1917, seems fitting as a means of literary analysis. By exploring the narrative of *The Professor's House* through Freud's *Mourning and Melancholia*, the attempt here is to discern what the "thing not named" about St. Peter is.

Critical History

The narrative of *The Professor's House* has been interpreted in a variety of a ways. It has been referenced as social criticism of the materialistic culture of the 1920s and as "a critique of modernity" (Wilson 64). The novel has also been viewed in terms of opposing binaries: as a novel that pits the old versus the new, the past versus the present, and the material versus the aesthetic.[1] The novel has been read as harkening back to a primitive, more natural world against the setting of the materialistic anti-aesthetic world, in which St. Peter finds himself .[2] Some critics have even interpreted the novel as homoerotic, finding the Professor's relationship with Tom Outland as a thinly veiled disguise for an unnamed love.[3]

St. Peter's emotional disintegration in the novel has also been interpreted in a variety of ways. Several Cather biographers have discussed the novel and its relationship to Cather's own emotional state and ideological views.[4] Some have viewed St. Peter's emotional condition as that of a midlife crisis that reveals Cather's own struggles at the time. Others view it as representative of her ideological issues. Biographer Hermione Lee views St. Peter's emotional state as related to *accidie*, a Middle Ages form of "spiritual sloth," brought on by his disillusionment with his life (Harbison 66).

On Cather's works as a whole, another biographer, Guy Reynolds, "describes the structure of Cather's fiction as inconsistent, disrupted, fractured, and moving towards ever-increasing formal disintegration" (Bell 424). He regards this movement as evidence that Cather could not reconcile contradictory elements of American culture: "Unable to unravel the dilemma of progress, Cather accreted various answers rather than resolving the central issues" (Bell 424). Hermione Lee contends that "Cather's work gets its energy from the contraries" (Harbison 65). Lee sees Cather's own emotional life as essential to understanding her works and the use of "doubleness" as central to her art (Harbison 65).

Godfrey St. Peter's Grief

In exploring the novel through the theme of loss, it seems that the thing not named is Godfrey St. Peter's grief. The impending loss of the old house (and particularly, the loss of his study and gardens) triggers a form of deferred mourning in Godfrey St. Peter that is directly related to the loss of Tom Outland, his one brilliant student and friend who died in the Great War. In the depths of this mourning, St. Peter recognizes and contemplates the compounded losses that he has suffered in other areas of his life. His unfinished grief for Tom Outland is complicated by additional losses he recognizes (his daughters, his wife, his inspiration, etc.). The ensuing and overwhelming psychological distress from these compounded— and yet to be relinquished— losses results in St. Peter entering a depressive, or melancholic, state.

By refusing to give up the house, in particular his study and garden, which are so central to his remembrances of Tom and consequently to his compounded losses, St. Peter prolongs his mourning. Finding himself in a deepening depressive state, St. Peter begins to withdraw from his family and eventually experiences somewhat of a break with reality, during which he reverts to his childhood. In the end, St. Peter experiences a brush with death, which could be interpreted as suicidal. After surviving, he relinquishes something that he could not have "consciously" done. But just what it is that St. Peter relinquishes is not made clear.

Freud's Mourning and Melancholia

Freud's original paper, "Mourning and Melancholia," published in 1917, describes the characteristics of mourning and further differentiates it from the state of melancholia. According to Freud, "mourning is regularly the reaction to the loss of a loved person, or to the loss of some abstraction which has taken the place of one, such as one's country, liberty, an idea, and so on" (243). Freud goes onto to explain that that the:

> distinguishing mental features of melancholia are a profoundly painful dejection, cessation of interest in the outside world, loss of the capacity to love, inhibition of all activity, and a lowering of the self-regarding feelings to a degree that finds in self-reproaches and self-reviling, and culminates in the delusional expectation of punishment. (244)

Freud then posits that all of the traits of melancholia are present in mourning other than "the disturbance of self-regard" (244).

Freud's theory contends that mourning involves the struggle to accept loss, specifically (object loss), and that recovery requires giving up the love object; in melancholia, the individual cannot give up the love object and then turns the feelings back onto himself. In the process of mourning: "[e]ach single one of the memories and expectations in which the libido is bound to the object is brought up and hyper-cathected, and detachment of the libido is accomplished in respect to it" (244).

To further differentiate between the states of mourning and melancholia, Freud says: "In mourning it is the world which has become poor and empty; in melancholia it is the ego itself. The patient represents his ego to us as worthless, incapable of achievement and morally despicable; he reproaches himself, vilifies himself and expects to be cast out and punished" (246). Melancholia is described as "object-loss which is withdrawn from consciousness, in contradistinction to mourning, in which there is nothing about the loss that is unconscious" (245). "The melancholic displays something else besides which is lacking in mourning – an extraordinary diminution in his self-regard, an impoverishment of his ego on a grand scale" (245).

Freud's concepts can be difficult to understand. In mourning, the world around the subject becomes dark. By contrast, in melancholia, this sense of darkness is directed towards the self. The mourner faces a known object loss, while a melancholic suffers from an unconscious struggle against object loss. In either case, the object must be relinquished in order to recover from the loss. If we view St. Peter's emotional descent in terms of mourning and melancholia, there are many questions to be answered.

Is it that St. Peter's delayed mourning for Tom is finally triggered by the impending loss of the house and the gardens and study that he and Tom had spent so much time in? Is it the mourning that colors St. Peter's view of the rest of the world, so that he sees those who move on around him in a dark and negative light? Or is St. Peter more melancholic—clinically depressed—more darkly disturbed by his inability to recognize his grief and, therefore, release Tom? And what of the ambiguous ending? Does St. Peter relinquish Tom or just his melancholic depression?

Cather and Freud

In many respects, it would seem doubtful that anything that Freud produced would influence Cather's work. In an article in *Cather Studies*, John N. Swift even stated "[i]t is easy to follow the threads of relationship between Willa Cather and Sigmund Freud: there are almost none" (1). It is Swift, however, who goes on to explore a potential connection between the unlikely pair. To Swift, it was nearly impossible that Cather was unaware of Freud's theories, whether or not she gave them any credence. He discusses her life in Greenwich Village during the 1910s and 1920s and some of the friendships that she had with figures such as Carl Van Vechten, Floyd Dell, and Mabel Dodge Luhan. Swift uses these relationships to make the case that she was likely very aware of his work.

Swift finds that the main contradiction between Cather and Freud lies in something, fundamental to American Freudianism:"voluntary, profuse confession—the therapeutic transformation of symptomatic unhappiness into liberating language" (4). By comparison, Cather was a "champion of classical restraint, control, and suggestion in art, and she extended these values to human relations as well" (Swift 4). Despite this, Swift finds Cather and Freud himself (as opposed to Freudianism) to have an unlikely common interest, that of "*anti*modern zeitgeist of nostalgia" (6).

Swift "doubts that Cather ever read Freud (although she must have read a good deal about him and his ideas)" (5). He explains, however, that upon reading his first Cather novel, *The Professor's House*, he "felt at once that [he] had come upon a writer who had both access to the great unconscious world that Freud had disclosed" (Swift 6). Moreover, Swift found that through the novel he "could glimpse the psychoanalytic world" (6). "But most important, not only did Cather's work seem to me to *exemplify* the various processes and contents of psychic representation postulated by Freudian psychoanalysis, it also appeared to be *aware* of this itself" (Swift 6).

Against Floridity

In light of this Freud/Cather connection, it could be said that the narrative of *The Professor's House* alludes to the Freudian need to recover whatever is lost, but the narrative also avoids Freud's confessionary necessity. As a man who proclaims "floridity" to be distasteful, the proper Professor Godfrey St. Peter would never openly make large emotional displays (36-37). Cather herself is clearly opposed to such things. Yet, the subtlety of the Professor's emotional turmoil remains present throughout the novel.

The Professor may not be as even-keeled as he perceives himself to be. Repeatedly, his wife Lillian makes reference to his attitude, his mental state, and the way he presents himself to others, which make it appear that he is grumpy or short tempered. His own demeanor is apparently something he is unaware of. Lillian calls him "intolerant" and after one particular instance, where he defends himself against her accusations, she says: "Oh, Godfrey, how can you be such a poor judge of your own behavior?" (25). At dinner the night before, when his son-in-law Louie Marcellus blurts out that the couple has decided to name their new house "Outland" as a sort of memorial to Tom, St. Peter "expressed his emotion only by lifting his heavy, sharply uptwisted eyebrows" (30). Lillian's statement the following morning leads one to believe that he was ruder than he remembers (37, 38). At minimum, it is clear that his family has sensed a change in him and has begun to register his withdrawal.

St. Peter's Losses

St. Peter experiences Tom Outland's literal loss through death, the result of which is that St. Peter loses both a friend and a source of inspiration. The effect of the loss is complicated and, while not openly expressed, profoundly felt. St. Peter cannot allow his memory of Outland to be diminished, yet he also cannot fully express Outland's personal value. He says at one point of Outland, "I've encountered just one remarkable mind, but for that, I'd consider my good years largely wasted" (50). When his daughter Rosamond offers monetary compensation out of her inheritance from Tom, St. Peter is appalled. He says:

> ... there can be no question of money between me and Tom Outland. I can't explain just how I feel about it, but it would somehow damage my recollections of him, would make that episode in my life commonplace like everything else. And that would be a great loss to me...my friendship with Outland is the one thing I will not have translated into the vulgar tongue. (50)

The complexity of this loss and the Professor's emotional state regarding it is emphasized when his son-in-law Scott admits that he is starting to forget Tom, saying, "You know, Tom isn't very real to me anymore. Sometimes I think he was just a – a glittering idea" (94). The Professor immediately retreats to his study and works at "recalling as clearly and definitely as he could every incident of that bright, windy spring day when he first saw Tom Outland" (95). He seems intent on maintaining the connection to Tom through ideal and memory. Later, when visited in his attic study by his daughter Kathleen, a brief exchange takes place that makes him sense that she remembers Tom in the way that he does. He attempts to get her to stay and reminisce with him a little longer. When she leaves, he stands at the top of the stairs, "motionless, as if he were listening intently, or trying to fasten upon some fugitive idea" (113).

Besides the actual physical loss of Tom Outland, the Professor contemplates other losses throughout his life. He expresses a sense of loss regarding his daughters, as he recognizes the many ways that they have changed over time. He is particularly saddened by the loss of their youth, repeatedly equating their youth with happier times in his life. He remembers the lure of holidays and its relation to "pretty little girls in fresh dresses" (84). He laments: "When a man had lovely children in his house, fragrant and happy, full of pretty fancies and generous impulses, why couldn't he keep them?" (107).

In addition to the loss of their youth, he has also lost his daughters to marriage and to their changed adult selves. His youthful image of his daughters has to be reconciled with the adult women that they have become. His disturbance over these changes (one becomes materialistic, the other jealous) haunt him one night as "two faces at once rose in the shadows outside the yellow circle of his lamp: the handsome face of his older daughter, surrounded by violet-dappled fur, with a cruel upper lip and scornful half-closed eyes, as she had approached her car that afternoon before she saw him and Kathleen, her square little chin set so fiercely, her white cheeks actually becoming green under her swollen eyes" (74). Later, it is clear that he sees his daughter Rosamond as a person who has no real generosity (109).

St. Peter recognizes that, in some senses, he has lost his wife as well. He feels distant from her and describes how she seems to have hardened over time. He discusses the loss of his wife as her devotion and attentions are now focused on her son-in-laws (85). "The thing that struck in his mind constantly was that she was growing more and more intolerant, about everything except her sons-in-law; that she would probably continue to do so, and that he must school himself to bear it" (25).

Additional losses experienced by St. Peter are evidenced throughout the book. It is possible that St. Peter has lost his inspiration. In acknowledging the joy that pursuing his major accomplishment (an eight-volume history, entitled *Spanish Adventurers in North America*) had given him, he tells his wife Lillian, "If with that cheque I could have bought back the fun I had writing my history, you'd never have got your house" (23). With his major life work completed, he now suffers from a form of pervasive boredom. He seems to find losses in general societal decline—as evidenced by his perception of the backsliding university standards, aesthetic loss, and the materialistic culture of the time.

St. Peter's Depression

Despite all of these compounded losses, there is one thing that St. Peter has not yet lost, and that is his old home. St. Peter clings to the old house, unwilling to relinquish it. He spends a growing amount of time in the attic study, fueled by his ever-increasing need for isolation. His refusal to let go of the old house, even the sewing forms in the attic, speaks to his declining emotional state and a need to hold onto something that he cannot express. Evidence that St. Peter is falling into a deepening depression is found throughout the text. What starts as a mild indifference toward things and desire for isolation eventually leads to a need to be completely alone and total disinterest in all activities outside his attic study.

St. Peter's apathy begins with a disinterest in social activity with his own family. Family dinners and excursions become a chore to him; he would prefer to stay isolated in his study. There is a growing sense that his family is aware of this departure. Finally, his wife Lillian questions him on his withdrawal from the family saying, "Two years ago you were an impetuous young man. Now you save yourself in everything. You're naturally warm and affectionate; all at once you begin shutting yourself away from everybody" (142). In response, St. Peter cannot explain to her what he is experiencing. All he can muster is "… I seem to be tremendously tired. One pays, coming or going. A man has got only just so much in him; when it's gone he slumps" (143).

St. Peter's indifference and withdrawal continues to the point that he can barely endure the family obligations that had once been dear to him. Encountering St. Peter upon his return from a trip to Chicago with his daughter—a journey he had dreaded taking in the first place—his son-in-law Scott "sat down beside him and tried to interest him in one subject after another, without success. It occurred to him [Scott] that he had never before seen the Professor when he seemed absolutely flattened out and listless" (133). Enduring the trip to Chicago had been difficult, and the professor returned worn out. In a final and most crucial withdrawal from his family, St. Peter refuses to take a trip with his family to Europe.

With his family away, St. Peter begins the work of editing Tom Outland's diary, only to find that he accomplishes very little over a period of months. During this time, he falls into a state of self-described "mental dissipation," which involves incessant daydreaming and fond reminiscences of his childhood (239). He develops a routine of lying for hours on the beach dreaming about his childhood. He expresses the belief that through this return to his more "primitive" state of childhood, he feels much wiser. While in this state, he wanders around appreciating nature and uttering "that is it" and "that is right" with the sense that he is "dumbly, deeply recognizing" the truths of the world (241).

It is within this time that St. Peter is overwhelmingly confronted by an urgent sense of mortality and the certainty of his impending death: "Along with other states of mind which attended his realization of the boy Godfrey came a conviction (he did not see it coming, it was there before he was aware of its approach) that he was nearing the end of his life" (243). He consults with his doctor, who performs various tests only to conclude that there is nothing actually wrong with the professor. He never confides in his doctor his concern that he senses he will be dying soon.

Later, when he does nearly die as a result of being overcome by gas fumes from his malfunctioning attic heater, he contemplates what his culpability in his own death would be if he does not act to prevent his own death. In this moment, he considers a suicide. The family's sewing lady appears and rescues him by opening a window. Therefore, whether or not St. Peter has taken action to prevent his own death remains a mystery. After recovering from the gas poisoning, he remains firm in his thoughts, saying that although "he had been low-spirited all summer, he told the truth when he told Dr. Dudley that he had not been melancholy... Yet when he was confronted by accidental extinction, he felt no will to resist, but had let chance take its way, as it had done with him so often" (257-258). Later he elaborates that his temporary release from consciousness seemed to have been beneficial. "He had let something go – and it was gone: something very precious, that he could not consciously have relinquished, probably" (258).

Mourning Beyond Melancholia: St. Peter's Ongoing Grief
In "Mourning Beyond Melancholia: Freud's Psychoanalysis of Loss," Tammy Clewell discusses Freud's theories on mourning and melancholia in light of the changes that he incorporated in 1923 and along with more recent theories of mourning. Most interesting in this article is the way she discusses literary critics and their persistent use of Freud's theories to "evaluate narrative representations of death, loss and bereavement" (Clewell 48). She points specifically to Peter Sacks' book *The English Elegy: Studies in the Genre from Spenser to Yeats*, where she states that he "has argued that the elegy from Spenser to Yeats basically reflects a Freudian economy, where consoling substitution becomes the central aim" (Clewell 48). Clewell goes on to discuss how "Sack's study does more than simply show how poets and their contemporaries found comfort in fictions that transcend and outlast death; it demonstrates how the elegy itself emerges as a consoling substitute for the lost one" (48); "the lost

one has transcended death by achieving aesthetic immortality in a timeless literary artifact" (Clewell 49).

In recognizing Freud's changes to his theory on mourning and melancholia—most consequentially in terms of the extended period of personal mourning that he experienced following the death of his own daughter—Clewell finds that Freud recognized that there are times when letting go is not related to punishing the self for the loss of the love object. She finds that the revisions Freud made allow for an endless mourning unencumbered by the "self-punishment entailed in blaming the lost one for our own contingency" (Clewell 65).

When reading *The Professor's House*, it is impossible not to sense the weight of loss on Professor St. Peter without considering whether he experiences what Freud would term mourning (even if it has been delayed) or melancholia. It is likely that he has experienced both. St. Peter may be seen as a man who, through an extended period of mourning, faces a period of melancholia, in which he is unable to recognize specifically the love object that he must relinquish in order to recover. As a result, he enters a deep depression, or melancholic state, wherein he performs the task of editing Tom's diary. This ultimately takes on the form of an elegy and creates a "timeless literary artifact" of what it is he cannot relinquish.

Whether the work that St. Peter takes on by creating the artifact serves as either a form of preserving Tom in perpetuity or as a means of releasing St. Peter's mourning cannot be known. Perhaps this is the sense of "emotional penumbra," the partial illumination, which Cather has provided for the reader. All we know is that, at the end, he feels a profound sense that he has lost something of himself, something that can never be recovered and that he will never be the same. He says:

> He doubted whether his family would ever realize that he was not the same man that they had said good-bye to; they would be too happily preoccupied with their own affairs. If his apathy hurt them, they could not possibly be so hurt as he had been already. (258)

In this way, St. Peter can be seen as a man whose mourning takes on a melancholic state. Once he has preserved the literary artifact of Tom's diary and nearly dies himself, he releases his melancholy only to return to a state of perpetual mourning for a past he cannot recover.

Notes

1. See Hermione Lee's biography of Cather, titled *Willa Cather: Double Lives*, referenced in the bibliography.

2. For more on this interpretation, please see Hermione Lee's biography of Cather, titled *Willa Cather: Double Lives* and Annie Wilson's "Canonical Relations: Willa Cather, America, and *The Professor's House*", both referenced in the bibliography.

3. For more on this interpretation, please see Annie Wilson's "Canonical Relations: Willa Cather, America, and *The Professor's House*" and John P. Anders' *Willa Cather's Sexual Aesthetics and the Male Homosexual Literary Tradition*, both referenced in the bibliography.

4. For more on this interpretation, please see Hermione Lee's biography of Cather, titled *Willa Cather: Double Lives* and Guy Reynolds' *Willa Cather in Context: Progress, Race, Empire*, both referenced in the bibliography.

Works Cited

Anders, John P. *Willa Cather's Sexual Aesthetics and the Male Homosexual Literary Tradition*.Lincoln, NE: U of Nebraska P, 2001.

Bell, Alice. Review of *Willa Cather in Context: Progress, Race, Empire*, by Guy Reynolds. *American Literature*. Vol. 69, No. 2 (1997): 423-424. *JSTOR*. Web. 30 Nov. 2012.

Cather, Willa. "The Novel Démeublé." *The New Republic* 30 (12 Apr. 1922): 5-6. *Writings*. The Willa Cather Archive, Sept. 2013. Web. 22 Nov. 2012. <http://cather.unl.edu/nf012.html>.

Cather, Willa. *The Professor's House*. New York: Vintage, 1990.

Clewell, Tammy. "Mourning Beyond Melancholia: Freud's Psychoanalysis of Loss." *Journal of the American Psychoanalytic Association* 52.1 (2004): 43-67. *Pubmed.gov*. Web. 26 Nov. 2012. Forter, G. "Against Melancholia: Contemporary Mourning Theory, Fitzgerald's *The Great Gatsby*, and the Politics of Unfinished Grief." *Differences* 14.2 (2003): 134-70. *Project MUSE*. Web. 25 Nov. 2012.

Freud, Sigmund. "Mourning and Melancholia." *The Journal of Nervous and Mental Disease* 56.5 (1922): n. pag. *JSTOR*. Web. 23 Nov. 2012.

Harbison, Sherrill. Review of *Willa Cather: Double Lives*, by Hermione Lee. *Legacy*, Vol.9, No.1 (1992): 65-69. JSTOR. Web. 23 Nov. 2012.

Lee, Hermione. *Willa Cather: Double Lives*. New York: Knopf Doubleday,1991.

Lucenti, Lisa Marie. "Willa Cather's "The Professor's House": Sleeping with the Dead." *Texas Studies in Literature and Language* 41.3 (Fall 1999): 236. *JSTOR*. Web. 25 Nov. 2012.

"Penumbra." Def. 1a. *Merriam-Webster.com*. Merriam Webster, n.d. Web. 25 Aug. 2013. <http://www.merriam-webster.com/dictionary/penumbra>.

"Penumbra." Def. 4. *Merriam-Webster.com*. Merriam Webster, n.d. Web. 25 Aug. 2013. <http://www.merriam-webster.com/dictionary/penumbra>.

Reynolds, Guy. *Willa Cather in Context: Progress, Race, Empire*. New York: Palgrave Macmillan, 1996.

Swift, John N. "Cather, Freudianism, and Freud." *The Willa Cather Archive* 7 (n.d.): 1-11. Web. 30 Nov. 2012.

Wilson, Annie. "Canonical Relations: Willa Cather, America, and *The Professor's House*." *Texas Studies in Literature and Language*, 47.1 (Spring 2005): 61-74. *JSTOR*. Web. 30 Nov. 2012.

For Those Non-Midwestern, Midwestern Writers: Richard Powers, Toni Morrison, and the Midwest *Topos* _____

Patricia Oman

This is an essay about non-Midwestern, Midwestern writers—that is, writers who often set their writing in the Midwest, but who are not typically considered regional writers. The Midwest poses a particular challenge in this respect because even though the concept of region relies on difference, the Midwest's most unique characteristic in the late twentieth and early twenty-first centuries is paradoxically its lack of difference. Today's Midwest is the location of that ordinary, middle-of-the-road section of the United States sometimes called "Middle America." Today's Midwest is the rural, geographic, and emotional center of the country known as the "Heartland." In other words, today's Midwest is really just a synonym for average America. Defining the literature of this region is thus a difficult task because Midwest literature does not always identify itself as Midwestern. The focus here is on two novelists, Richard Powers and Toni Morrison, who do not write about typically Midwestern subjects, but who nevertheless use the Midwest's unique regional qualities to their advantage.

Powers, who was born in Illinois, sets many of his novels in Illinois and the larger Midwest, but he is not often called a Midwestern writer because of his propensity for engaging with difficult scientific and philosophical ideas. His 1988 novel *Prisoner's Dilemma,* for instance, is set in DeKalb, Illinois, but deals with the historical effects of the atomic bomb on American culture. His 1998 novel *Gain* is set in Lacewood, Illinois and addresses the potentially dangerous effects of chemicals in everyday products. Despite the clear Midwestern setting of many of his novels, however, many critics and readers still have trouble seeing Powers as a Midwestern writer. In fact, one interviewer once remarked to Powers, "I'm curious about what it means to be a Midwestern novelist and to write the kinds of books that you do. I guess the clichéd image that people have of the Midwest is that it's not a place intellectuals are necessarily drawn to" (Miller n.p.). Even Powers himself expresses confusion about being a Midwestern writer when he argues in the same interview:

> My books are not Midwestern in the sense that they plumb the Midwestern psyche in the way that Southern writers get to a real precise regional sense of their culture. Or New Yorkers do for their culture. Or the western does for another whole American narrative. I don't know what the Midwestern narrative is really. (Miller, n.p.)

Like Powers, Morrison sets many of her novels in her home state, but she is not interested in "the Midwestern psyche" either. Her novels *The Bluest Eye* (1970), *Sula* (1973), *Song of Solomon* (1977), and *Beloved* (1987) are all set in Ohio and address the struggles of the African American community, but Morrison does not see these experiences as specifically Midwestern. In fact, she argues, in a 1983 interview, that Ohio is an important state for the African American community because it was a road from slavery to freedom in the nineteenth century and "a Mecca for black people [after the Civil War]; they came to the mills and plants because Ohio offered the possibility of a good life, the possibility of freedom" (Tate 119). However, she argues in the same interview that "Black people take their culture wherever they go. If I wrote about Maine, the black people in Maine would be very much like the black people in Ohio" (Tate 119). Morrison, therefore, seems to be interested in the Midwest as a backdrop for the larger historical experiences of the black community.

The novels of Richard Powers and Toni Morrison thus pose a difficult question for scholars of Midwest literature: how does one talk about a writer or discuss a text as 'Midwestern' if the writer is not interested in the Midwest *per se*? As I argue in this essay, the problem is not with the texts or the writers, but with how we define the Midwest in the first place. Powers' comment that he does not "plumb the Midwestern psyche" assumes a definition of region that is very common with regional scholars—that a specific geographic place can be identified by the unique psycho-social characteristics of its residents. However, this is not always the most productive critical orientation a scholar can adopt when studying a region, especially the Midwest. The first two sections of this essay—"The Midwest as Geographic Place" and "The Midwest as Way of Life" —describe the most common ways of defining the Midwest and why these definitions are problematic. The third section, "The Midwest as *Topos*," outlines a way to talk about those Midwestern authors who do not seem to fit under traditional definitions of the Midwest.

The Midwest as a Geographic Place

The Midwest has not always been the Midwest. This may seem like common sense, but it is important to recognize that the area we now call the Midwest has a long history of shifting borders and names. Today, there are about twelve states that often fall under that regional label—Ohio, Indiana, Illinois, Michigan, Wisconsin, Minnesota, North Dakota, South Dakota, Iowa, Missouri, Nebraska, and Kansas—but that list is not a stable one, nor has it ever been.

James R. Shortridge, for instance, argues that the term "Middle West" first appeared in popular literature in the 1890s to refer to Kansas and Nebraska ("Emergence" 212). At that time, Ohio, Indiana, Illinois, Michigan, and Wisconsin were known as the "Old Northwest" and Minnesota and the Dakotas were known as the "New Northwest" (Shortridge, "Emergence" 210). By 1912, the term "Middle West" included all of these states (Shortridge, "Emergence" 212). In a 1980 study of college students from 32 states, however, Shortridge found that the Midwest was not the stable region that many assumed it to be. In fact, when he asked these students to identify the borders of the Midwest, he found two general, but differing, responses. For most respondents, the Middle West "was focused on the central plains, usually in south-central Nebraska" (*The Middle West* 86), which happens to be the near geographic center of the United States. However, he found that "[r]espondents from eight states (Illinois, Iowa, Kansas, Missouri, Nebraska, North Dakota, South Dakota, and Wisconsin) saw themselves at the center of the Middle West" (*The Middle West* 85–86). In other words, respondents from some traditionally defined Midwest states generated maps that placed their state at the center of the Midwest and challenged the idea of a single geographic region known as the Midwest.

Historian and cartographer Bill Rankin found even more disparate results in his 2013 study of the Midwest. Rankin, who compiled a map of the Midwest from 100 different maps he found through a Google search, writes, "One important thing to note here is that even though Illinois emerges as the most Midwestern state, there is no area that was included on every map...The sum of all possible Midwests...is incredibly vast, stretching from Newfoundland to New Mexico and Idaho to Georgia" (n.p.). Like Shortridge's project more than 30 years earlier, Rankin's project demonstrates the difficulty of defining the Midwest as a geographic place. If defining the borders of the Midwest itself is difficult, defining the borders of Midwest literature is just as difficult.

The Midwest as Way of Life

Two conflicting images have dominated popular thought about the Midwest for the last century: the Midwest as agrarian ideal and the Midwest as provincial backwater. Shortridge, for instance, argues that in the early twentieth century, the Midwest came to represent the national agrarian ideal imagined by J. Hector St. John de Crèvecoeur and Thomas Jefferson in the eighteenth century and therefore came to represent America as a whole ("Emergence" 214–16). Even with the rise of cities such as Chicago, Cleveland, and Detroit in the twentieth century, Shortridge found in his 1980 survey of college students that the agrarian myth still dominated conceptions of the Midwest (*The Middle West* 76). Alongside the agrarian myth, however, is the equally strong myth of the Midwest as culturally backward, a phenomenon first described in Anthony Channell Hilfer's 1969 book *The Revolt from the Village*. These two images of the Midwest still dominate discussions of Midwest literature.

While it is true that much of the Midwest is rural, the myths of the agrarian ideal and the cultural backwater have become so prevalent that it is sometimes difficult for scholars to see the Midwest as anything else. In fact, one scholar argues that a recent anthology of poetry called *Illinois Voices* is "no more Illinois than the New York Yankees" (Pichaske 21) because it includes such varied topics as "didacticism, modernism, Imagism, Surrealism, Objectivism, Deep Imagism, Confessionalism, feminism, Afro-American, Latino/ Latina, and Asian American voices, gay and lesbian poetry, New Narrativism, New Formalism, language and 'performance' poetry" (Pichaske 21). This laundry list of supposedly non-Illinois topics suggests that the scholar identifies avant-garde literature and -*ism*s, including multiculturalism, with cities like New York, not with supposedly rural states like Illinois. Such an assumption is patently untrue, however.

These myths can make scholars forget that the Midwest includes immigrants, gays, intellectuals, and non-whites. This is why black writers who set their works in the Midwest—such as Toni Morrison— are often classified as African American, not regional writers. This is the same reason that writers such as Richard Powers who write about "intellectual" subjects are not identified as Midwestern, even when their novels are set there. The agrarian and backwater myths can thus limit the study of Midwest literature. The common image of the Midwest as rural is certainly accurate for some, but not for all. The Midwest is just too big, too diverse, and too changing to be characterized by only one myth or narrative. In other words, there is no definitive "Midwestern psyche." That is why scholars of Midwest literature need to seek other ways to define the region.

The Midwest as *Topos*

Despite the difficulties outlined in the previous sections, it is possible to define the Midwest in a way that is inclusive of all Midwest narratives. Roberto Dainotto, for instance, argues in *Place in Literature: Regions, Cultures, Communities* that "regionalism is not a literary genre . . . but a way of reading" (30). This definition allows us to understand the term 'Midwest literature' not just as a collection of texts, but as a critical lens. He cites the ancient Roman rhetorician Quintilian in defining region as a *topos*, "'the place in which arguments and demonstrations' about the existence of a cultural identity . . . 'are stored, and from which they can be retrieved'" (19). The *topos* is a very useful critical tool for defining the Midwest because it acknowledges that regions exist primarily in the realm of language, thus getting around the problems of unstable geographic boundaries and overgeneralized statements about regional culture.

The Midwest, therefore, is not just a place where people live but a rhetorical place where specific possibilities for American identity are stored as tropes (i.e., figures of speech). In other words, a *topos* is a collection of all the tropes of a region, that is, all the figurative and symbolic ways that people talk about, write about, and represent that region. While the Southern *topos* might include the trope of the romantic plantation, for instance, the Midwest *topos* includes tropes such as the frontier, the prairie, the heartland, and Middle America. By defining the Midwest as a *topos*, the traditional images of the Midwest as agrarian and as a cultural backwater are thus revealed as just *two* tropes among many.

In this essay, I want to focus on a common Midwest trope of the second half of the twentieth century: emptiness. When people refer to the Midwest as "fly-over country," they are implying that it is empty, just the unimportant space that people have to fly over to get from one coast to the next. Like the trope of cultural backwardness, this trope is derogatory, but it actually provides writers with fertile figurative possibilities. Clearly, the Midwest is not actually empty, but thinking of the region as figuratively empty can be useful in literature. Both Toni Morrison in her 1987 novel *Beloved* and Richard Powers in his 1988 novel *Prisoner's Dilemma* rely on this trope.

Powers' use of the Midwestern trope of emptiness is quite self-conscious. In fact, in the same interview mentioned earlier in this essay he argues, "The Midwest is such a tabula rasa. . . . It's useful to me as a kind of Everyman setting. There is that sense of omnipotential, unwritten, blank page to it" (Miller n.p.). The Midwest functions similarly for Morrison when she argues in a 1983 interview with Claudia Tate, "Black people take their culture wherever they go. . . . You can change the plate, but the menu would still be the same" (Tate 119). Like Powers, therefore, Morrison sees the Midwest as a blank slate, an interchangeable "plate" on which culture is expressed. More important, however, Morrison sees the Midwest, especially Ohio, as a useful setting for novels about black people because it "offers an escape from stereotyped black settings. It is neither plantation nor ghetto" (Tate 119). In other words, the Midwest *topos* provides figurative possibilities that the plantation trope of the southern *topos* and the ghetto trope of the urban *topos* do not.

Powers' novel *Prisoner's Dilemma* demonstrates the trope of emptiness explicitly in both form and content. The story is told in two, alternating narratives, and the protagonist, Eddie Hobson, Sr., is a high-school history teacher who suffers a mysterious and debilitating illness. One narrative, the "reality" narrative, takes place in De Kalb, Illinois, in the late 1970s and is narrated by the adult children of the Hobson family. The second narrative, the fantasy narrative, is an imaginative and fictional account of Walt Disney's attempt to create a nationally unifying propaganda film in De Kalb, Illinois, during World War II. It is not clear until the end of the novel that the Disney narrative is actually Eddie Sr.'s imaginative project to create an ideal world, which he calls *Hobstown* and that this project is recorded onto an audio tape. Readers also discover at the end of the novel that the two narratives actually occupy the same physical space when Eddie Sr.'s oldest son erases the Disney narrative and begins recording a new story, the "reality" narrative that readers have been following all along. In other words, readers discover at the end of the novel that the two alternating narratives they have been reading are actually recordings made on the same audio tape. This tape is a literal rendering of what Powers calls the "omnipotential, unwritten blank page of the Midwest."

The novel takes inspiration from an actual 1939 film—*The Middleton Family at the New York World's Fair*—which was shown at the fair and produced by Westinghouse as an hour-long advertisement. The film follows a wholesome Midwestern family as they marvel at all of Westinghouse's newest technologies at the fair. The Middletons, as their name implies, represent the middle-class, middle-brow family of Middle America. In the fantasy narrative of

Prisoner's Dilemma, Eddie Sr. visits the fair and strikes up a life-long friendship with the fictional Bud Middleton, who is about the same age. Disney originally wants the all-American Bud to star in his peace propaganda film, *World World*, but Eddie Sr. ends up taking the role. The references to the Westinghouse film indicate that the Midwest is vital to Eddie Sr.'s fictional project, however. The film he imagines Disney creating, the film that will save the world, will thus try to harness the trope of the all-American Midwest as well.

The all-American trope is shown to be closely linked to the emptiness trope when Disney chooses to film *World World* in DeKalb because of the seemingly limitless opportunities it offers. He argues that it is a "vast, flat, empty, infinitely pliable, blank slate of land cordoned off with wire. They can make of it anything they choose" (183). His desire to create a better, alternate reality can be seen in his groundbreaking speech, in which he tells his workers "to look at this evacuated place and imagine it filled with *the perfect world*. Think one step beyond verisimilitude. Do not stop at the goal of creating a replica 'just like real life,' but imagine a finished product that fleshes out real life and improves on it" (183). Disney's reference to a world that is better than real life indicates explicitly that his goal is to fix the real one. To do that, however, he has to ignore the Midwest's agrarian trope. In the first promo for the film, for instance, "the camera pans across the enormous, living ordnance survey map of unsuspecting, frozen Midwestern cornfields" (213) before the narrator labels the landscape as totally empty: "From out of this absolute absence of features,' the voice resonates, 'this flat, empty tabula rasa, this blank slate of nothingness, can come anything at all, anything that a majority of folks agrees to put here" (213). The description of the cornfields as "empty" and "frozen" explicitly rejects the region's association with agrarianism, and the emphasis on the will of "a majority of folks" implies that people can choose which characteristics of the Midwest *topos* they want to see. In other words, as a writer, Powers has consciously chosen which tropes of the Midwest are appropriate for his novel.

Eddie Sr.'s illness is at the heart of the novel and explains why he feels the need to create a better, alternate reality. At the end of the novel, we learn that his mysterious ailment is likely caused by radiation sickness, which he acquired as a young man while stationed at an army base in Alamogordo, New Mexico, during WWII. After witnessing the first test of an atomic bomb, he was exposed to its radiation, and the strange episodes he intermittently encounters for the rest of his life always start with a short period of paralysis where he seems to stare at something very bright and intense, like an atom bomb. During these episodes of sickness, he becomes unconscious for a while and then works on his Hobstown project, having no memory of the episode he just suffered. In addition to the physical ailments, Eddie Sr. also seems to suffer from an emotional ailment much like post-traumatic stress disorder because the memory of the atom bomb testing is always the trigger of his episodes. His pet project, therefore, seems to be both a symptom of his sickness and an attempt to cure it.

In many ways, the atomic bomb is a parallel metaphor to the emptiness trope because it represents the shattering of previous conceptions of time, space, and materiality. Quantum theory relies on an understanding of materiality not as carefully contained objects but as potentially amorphous collections of energy. Instead of focusing on the borders between objects—say, the borders between a chair and the floor it sits on—quantum theory focuses on the spaces between subatomic particles. Objects (and people) thus become masses of energy that could be molecularly reorganized at any time. According to quantum theory, there is no separation between a chair and the floor it sits on at the subatomic level. There is no *there* there. *Prisoner's Dilemma* thus suggests that the trope of Midwest emptiness is both the effect and potential cure for the atomic bomb's psycho-social effect on U.S. culture. In other words, the Midwest *topos* contains the figurative possibilities for addressing the effects of the atomic bomb on a cultural level.

In fact, the novel may even suggest that the atomic bomb is partly responsible for the creation of the Midwest's emptiness trope. When Artie and Rachel are discussing their father's illness while driving from DeKalb to Chicago, for instance, the landscape seems to reflect their grief and general malaise. The lingering effects of the bomb are suggested in the description of the setting sun as "the last, sourceless light scatter[ing] across vacancy, running opposed all the way to the horizon" (171), and this light forces the siblings to interpret the landscape as "an endless, fenceless detention camp of openness where nothing—not rage, not native contrarity, not even their father's fatal illness—could ruffle this Euclidean perfection" (171–72). Their internal emotions are explicitly connected to this voided landscape when they wonder, "Why was it so impossible, these days, to experience anything, to look out the window and *feel*?" (170). This description of the Midwestern landscape as devoid of feeling is a direct contrast to the traditional agrarian trope, which contains rich emotional undercurrents. The agricultural fields of the Midwest would normally inspire feelings of contentment and security, but Artie and Rachel feel that " the basic four-chambered heart and the standard two-chambered brain," symbols of the natural world, " were not designed to live in the kind of place they had made of the world" (170). The implication is that the atomic bomb has created the empty landscape before them and destroyed the traditional image of the Midwest (i.e., America).

Morrison's novel *Beloved* also imagines the Midwest landscape of Ohio as both a sickness and cure because it provides a place of escape for several former slaves and also prevents them from confronting that traumatic past. The novel is set in the nineteenth century and follows the story of Sethe, an escaped slave who lives in a little gray house in Ohio with her four young children and her mother-in-law, Baby Suggs. When her former slave master tracks her down, she decides to kill her children rather than let them be taken back to the South as slaves and succeeds in killing one of her daughters. The house then becomes haunted by the baby, which forces Sethe's two sons to run off as soon as they are old enough. Her daughter Denver is the only living child who remains at the house until several years later when a young woman appears at the door claiming to be named Beloved, which is the only word inscribed on the tombstone of Sethe's dead daughter. Sethe believes that the undeniably supernatural Beloved is the grown-up ghost of that child.

Sethe's nondescript house in Ohio is a literal rendering of the trope of Midwestern emptiness. The "gray and white house" (3) is not even referred to as a house in most places in the novel, just as a number: "124 was spiteful" (3); "124 was loud" (169); "124 was quiet" (239). Its anonymity is reinforced by the fact that it does not have a name, in contrast to the beautiful and terrifying southern plantation, on which Sethe was a slave—a plantation ironically named "Sweet Home." The Ohio house, therefore, is a blank slate, and the anonymity of the house allows it to be a blank canvas for its occupants' emotions and traumas, just as the Midwest is a blank slate for Powers in *Prisoner's Dilemma*.

The necessity of this blank slate becomes apparent when Beloved appears as a young woman. She behaves like a child and has only vague imagist memories of her life before appearing at Sethe's house. She remembers specific characteristics about Sethe, including her face and her earrings, but she also recalls being on a slave ship, something neither Beloved nor Sethe ever experienced. She remembers specifically the "dead man on [her] face" (210), "men without skin" (210–212), a "little hill of dead people" (211), and her mother jumping overboard (212). There is some evidence that Beloved's memories on the slave ship could be the experiences of Sethe's mother, whom Sethe never really knew, but Beloved's memories could also represent the unknowable story of slaves on the middle passage. When Stamp Paid visits the house, for instance, he hears numerous voices ringing the house, not just the voices of the three women who live there, and "he believed the undecipherable language clamoring around the house was the mumbling of the black and angry dead" (198). Whether Beloved is actually Sethe's dead daughter or the embodiment of a larger historical narrative, she seems to make a once suppressed and invisible history a part of the real world again. The stories of black slave women almost never make it into the historical record, but the novel makes that possible by projecting them onto the blankness of the Midwest.

Beloved thus takes as a cultural assumption Walt Disney's (fictional) argument in Powers' *Prisoner's Dilemma* that the Midwest is a tabula rasa, from which " can come anything at all, anything that a majority of folks agrees to put here" (213). In her 1992 book *Playing in the Dark*, Morrison argues that American national identity has always relied on the presence of racial darkness, against which to define itself, but in *Beloved*, Midwest regional emptiness is the background against which black identity can be recognized as American. In other words, the lost stories of illiterate slaves can find their way into American history through the trope of Midwestern emptiness. Because the tropes of the southern *topos* do not allow for those stories to be told, they can be made visible only through the Midwest *topos*.

The many references to color in the novel demonstrate the many, sometimes conflicting, possibilities afforded by the trope of Midwest emptiness. On the one hand, color is a sign of the depressing emptiness of the Midwest. When Baby Suggs is dying, for instance, her only desire is for color. The two orange squares on her quilt, which "looked wild—like life in the raw" (38), symbolize the yearning that she and Sethe feel for their family. Sethe grieves for her husband and Baby Suggs for her sons, who died as slaves. On the other hand, color is also a sign of trauma or pathology in the novel, as evidenced by Sethe's unhealthy obsession with gaudy colors when Beloved arrives. Beloved's presence eventually brings about a total excess of color in 124, as Sethe quits her job, uses her life savings to buy gaudy bright fabric for new dresses, and gives over her entire life to pleasurable, childlike play with her children. This new interest in pretty things is much like Eddie Sr.'s Hobstown project in *Prisoner's Dilemma*. While Eddie Sr.'s trauma is the atomic bomb, Sethe's is slavery. As in *Prisoner's Dilemma*, then, the Midwestern trope of emptiness in *Beloved* provides a figurative space where a character can hide out to escape a historical trauma, but also a place where that trauma becomes visible.

Sethe's concept of 'rememory' is actually quite similar to the concept of the *topos*. Her definition of rememory becomes clear when she tells Denver, " If a house burns down, it's gone, but the place—the picture of it—stays, and not just in my rememory, but out there, in the world" (36). The idea that rememory could relate specifically to region is revealed when she refers to the plantation where she was a slave, arguing that Sweet Home is:

> ...never going away. Even if the whole farm—every tree and grass blade of it dies. The picture is still there and what's more, if you go there—you who never was there—if you go there and stand in the place where it was, it will happen again; it will be there for you, waiting for you. (36)

In other words, because a regional *topos* is the repository for all possibilities for cultural identity, beautiful, horrible places like Sweet Home are always possible. Rememory is one way that these horrors can still exist in the world without an individual having to carry them around. *Beloved* thus demonstrates how repressed histories can nevertheless be made visible through the regional *topos*.

Conclusion

As the preceding comparison of Powers' *Prisoner's Dilemma* and Morrison's *Beloved* demonstrates, the *topos* is a powerful critical tool for regional scholars. These novels do not represent the Midwest in its traditional forms, as agrarian or as culturally backward. In fact, thinking of the Midwest as a "blank slate" seems to contradict the concept of region altogether. But when we think of the region not as a geographic place or a way of life but as a *topos,* a repository for all of the rhetorical and figurative possibilities of the term "Midwest," we see that these novels are, in fact, Midwestern. To understand Richard Powers and Toni Morrison as Midwestern writers, therefore, we have to change the way that we define the Midwest.

Works Cited

Dainotto, Roberto M. *Place in Literature: Regions, Cultures, Communities.* Ithaca: Cornell UP, 2000.

Hilfer, Anthony Channell. *The Revolt from the Village: 1915–1930.* Chapel Hill: U of North Carolina P, 1969.

Miller, Laura. "Richard Powers: The Salon Interview." *Salon.com.* Salon, 23 July 1998. Web. 20 Aug. 2013.

Morrison, Toni. *Beloved.* New York: Knopf, 1987.

———. *Playing in the Dark: Whiteness and the Literary Imagination*. Cambridge: Harvard UP, 1992.

Pichaske, David R. *Rooted: Seven Midwest Writers of Place*. Iowa City, U of Iowa P, 2006.

Powers, Richard. *Prisoner's Dilemma*. New York: Perennial, 1988.

Rankin, Bill. "The Midwest." *Radical Cartography.net*. Radical Cartography, 2013. Web. 20 Aug. 2013.

Shortridge, James R. "The Emergence of 'Middle West' as an American Regional Label." *Annals of the Association of American Geographers* 74.2 (June 1984): 209–220.

———. *The Middle West: Its Meaning in American Culture*. Lawrence, Kansas: UP of Kansas, 1989.

Tate, Claudia. *Black Women Writers at Work*. New York: Continuum, 1983.

CRITICAL READINGS

Patricia Hampl, Minnesota, and *The Florist's Daughter*: Memoir as History _____

Marilyn Atlas

Too often, the Midwest exists in the world's mind as a mythically safe and rather nondescript space. For instance, in Mario Vargas Llosa's *Feast of the Goat* (2000), a novel about the 1961 fall of Rafael Trujillo, the Dominican Republic's powerful and perverse dictator, the reader finds that one of Trujillo's henchman, Agustin Cabral, had a daughter, the novel's main character, Urania. Not accidentally, she was educated as a young teen in Adrian, Michigan.[1] Why Adrian, Michigan? Why the Midwest? T. S. Eliot was born in St. Louis, Missouri,[2] but we never hear about the Midwest's influence on his art. *Poetry* magazine began in Chicago and its first editor Harriet Monroe was a lifelong Chicagoan, dedicated to her art and to that exceptionally creative city,[3] and yet, when readers think of the Midwest, of the literary Midwest, they think of a place in-between two coasts, "flyover" country. Well, the Midwest as a literary space is worth a second, third, and fourth look; but even a writer as famous a memoirist as Patricia Hampl, who makes her intellectual life in the Midwest, sometimes wonders if indeed that is the place she should have remained, if perhaps her career and her art would have been even richer had she made her home elsewhere in America or in the world.

Patricia Hampl, born in 1946 in Minnesota, had and still has great ambitions to be a writer and intellect, and she is also a daughter who decided to stay in the Midwest for personal and familial reasons. Like Louisa May Alcott, author of *Little Women* (1868), she had the ability to make the ordinary extraordinary. As a MacArthur Fellow; a writer nominated for the National Book Critics Circle Award for General Nonfiction; author of the powerful, beautifully crafted and moving memoir, *The Florist's Daughter* (2007); and a writer whom Pat Conroy claims "writes the best memoirs of any writer in the English language,"[4] Hampl should perhaps even be better known than she is. And perhaps she is correct, that were she more clearly connected to New York, her books might be on the best-seller lists. That is not to diminish the fact that she is a recipient of the prestigious Guggenheim Foundation Fellowship and has had a long career teaching literature and creative writing at the University of Minnesota, but her craft outranks her popularity. As the author of brilliantly written and well reviewed books, including *Woman Before an Aquarium* (1978); *A Romantic Education* (1981); *Resort and Other Poems* (1983); with Steven Sorman, *Spillville* (1987); *Virgin Time: In Search of the Contemplative Life* (1992); *I Could Tell You Stories* (1999); and *Blue Arabesque: A Search for the Sublime* (2006), she would have perhaps even more "name recognition" had she made her life as a writer on the East Coast.

As readers, we can't know that, but it is clear and no clearer anywhere than in *The Florist's Daughter* that the ethnicity and geography of Minnesota have shaped her.[5] Hampl, by documenting her story, has given the world a taste of Czech St. Paul and Irish Catholic Minneapolis. In *The Florist's Daughter*, she reveals and brilliantly documents a good deal of what she experienced as an artist who spent the majority of life in Minnesota even as she wonders who she might have been had she left her family and lived elsewhere.

Her older brother, Peter, an oral-surgeon, gave himself permission to practice medicine in the West and had a minor role in his aging parents' care, but Hampl, as a daughter, thought her parents required her presence and she stayed. *A Florist's Daughter* possibly demonstrates that because she stayed in the Midwest— because she documented her life in the Midwest—she has become a major chronicler of life in Minnesota. Hampl makes the ordinary extraordinary, and we see life in St. Paul/ Minneapolis through the eyes of a woman caught between the dreams of her Czech father and Irish mother, the dreams of home and of flight. Who knows if she would have been able to create Minnesota as brilliantly as she did had she left the state, is she had taken her heart elsewhere?

What is "Midwesterness"? In *A Florist's Daughter*, Hampl tells us that fortitude, tolerance, and prudence are Midwestern virtues

(19). What is it not? Possibly, Hampl suggests, the Midwest is not "just" (19). Is it safe? Is it kind? Is it a place where art can be created? There are conventional views and stereotypes about the Midwest, and some of them, like Midwesterners' ability to self-deceive, are not particularly favorable, but what this essay attempts to examine is the notion that the late Michigan State University professor and Midwest literary scholar, David D. Anderson, repeated rather often: "all places are bad." What he meant was there was no reason to find this particular stand point any worse or better than any other. Patricia Hampl, in this memoir, demonstrates that though she is ambivalent/resistant, finally she agrees. And yet what she experienced and what many Midwest writers experience is a type of "internalized oppression," the sense that one is less because one is in the "wrong" place. By the end of the memoir, Hampl completes her examination of this internalized oppression and decides to banish it. But early in her memoir and recurrently, Hampl has little confidence in the region's ability to support art—not to the extent that Paris, or New York support art—and this perspective must affect her writing because it must exacerbate her sense of isolation, undermine her confidence, color and diminish what Minnesota has to offer her. But stay in Minnesota she does, even though she lets the reader know she had always planned to leave (10), and her craft and her storytelling remain aesthetically and culturally significant regardless of this ambivalence. She learns, through her own craft, that sometimes oppression is an illusion—and lets the illusion go. In the middle of her memoir, Hampl considers her perspective of the Midwest and tries, rather unsuccessfully, to make peace with her place in the world:

> The Midwest. The flyover, where even the towns have fled to the margins, groceries warehoused in Wal-marts hugging the freeways, the red barns of family farms sagging, dismantled and sold as 'distressed wood for McMansion kitchens, the feedlots of agribusiness crouched low to the prairie ground. Of all the American regions, the Midwest remains the most imaginary, ahistorical but fiercely emblematic. It's Nowheresville. But it's also the Heartland. That weight again; the

innocent middle. Though it isn't innocent. It's where the American imagination has decided to archive innocence.[6]

Hampl lets the reader know—without apology—that the Midwest in not innocent; that America wants it to be innocent; that innocence is "archived" there; and that, in reality, it is no more and no less angelic than damned—but that it is hers—in all its complexity. This memoir becomes, for Hampl, a way to process, as well as to document, the Midwestern myth and her Midwestern reality. Patricia Hampl's mom, in the last few paragraphs of this memoir, tells her daughter that she needs a copy of this memoir for "the Archive" (227), the archive of her daughter's creative life, an archive no longer of Midwestern innocence or resistance, but of Midwestern self–love and acceptance. Mother and daughter are sitting by the big nursing-home aquarium and her mother verbalizes pleasure when she hears the topic of the memoir: Hampl's Midwestern life explored and finally accepted and offers approval as she drinks one of her last glasses of Chardonnay: "*I like it here*, she said. *The view*" (author's italics 227). Mother and daughter are momentarily on the same page: finally, Hampl is accepting the view as well—a little realism, a little magic:

> We settled back in our deck chairs. Just sat there. Side by side, taking in the bracing salt air, and faced without dismay the gauzy hinge, between sea and sky, the limitless horizon dividing the elements, the disappearing point where we were headed. (227)

Hampl accepts the Midwest, and the pleasure and pain of living on this earth—and departing from it. She ends her memoir with herself and her mother, together, happy enough, mentally out of doors. And in reality, metaphorically, the ocean isn't all that far away: even the aquarium can transport one; even the aquarium can somehow be enough. Documenting one's life, becoming a good citizen in one's world, is a process, and Hampl, by the end of her memoir, has arrived and has documented this Midwestern journey toward acceptance of self and acceptance of place.

Hampl, the artist, has always been conscious that creative writing is about process, but it is also, she demonstrates in this memoir, about who the author is or wants to be in the world. In an interview published in *The Writer's Chronicle* in 2010,[7] Hampl explains to Katherine Jamieson, the person interviewing her, that for her, memoir writing is never just about form:

> We don't have a place for thinking politically in our literary culture, and this is very odd given the example of Whitman. Literary culture, since I've been publishing, has largely been interested in talking about process. Nuts and bolts, and sometimes about theory. But we don't seem to have a way to take a position as a citizen. (22)

In this interview, Hampl examines and explores her ambivalent and contradictory need to belong and to remain an outsider, to share what she sees and not simply what she feels and what she believes the role of beauty and art is in the writing of significant memoirs. In this seven-page interview, Hampl explains that she sees memoirs as documentaries that happen to be aesthetic and adds that even unaesthetic documentaries are valuable as documentaries. For her, art is amazing, important, but Hampl never forgets that citizenship matters, explaining that she is consciously a historical memoirist: "'I'm interested in memoir largely as a feature of history, so that I'm interested in reading and writing works that somehow fill out the bigger picture." She continues, referring directly to *The Florist's Daughter:*

> . . . the book that I just did is most highly personal, about my family, which is inevitably psychological. However I clung to my beliefs about memoir having to do with history by really seeing us as features of a middle-class family, in the middle of the country, in the middle of the century. That middle-ness and that ordinariness were what I was trying to reveal. I couldn't have written it if I didn't believe there was that bigger context. (22)

At a certain point, she explains, a memoirist doesn't need to write about the self. And she iterates—perhaps facetiously—that as a writer living in "flyover "country, part of her doesn't feel significant or that there is any history. But her documentation of her own family history belies that she feels the Midwest is "no place," and she knows that she is attempting, in her memoir, to capture the zeitgeist the spirit of her time, and the spirit of ethnic, mid-century Minnesota. In this memoir, she brilliantly captures a spirit of ambivalence, beauty, strife, and loss. And she captures not only what it is to be a writer in the Midwest, but a woman and a daughter as well. Hampl thinks back through her St. Paul/ Minneapolis childhood and her own presence in the "flyover" region, trying to understand space, place, and the formation of identity in relation to geography. Hampl did not, like F. Scott Fitzgerald, get out of the Midwest, but like him, she spends much of her creative life thinking about "home"[8] and like him, she has documented a Midwest reality that no careful reader of *The Florist's Daughter* will soon forget.

Perhaps because her story is so emotionally complex, Hampl chooses a complex narrative form: rather than linearly narrating her story, Hampl meanders through her life evoking the texture of her parents' world, recreating the various ethnic neighborhoods of St. Paul, rethinking her family relationships and what they meant to her as a daughter, granddaughter, niece, and writer.

Her memoir is framed around the hours surrounding her mother's death. Holding her mother's hand, writing her mother's obituary, she simultaneously works out a story filled with images of her family home, her father's flower shop and greenhouses, her mother's Minneapolis anchovies and kitchen table stories, her family bungalow on Linwood, her Czech grandmother's attitude toward reading and the values floating through her childhood and adulthood.

Hampl reveals to us in the memoir that she was not safely separate from her childhood family, nor was she safely in the middle—as her mother thought the location of Minneapolis and of being middle class provided for her. According to Patricia's third grade teacher, she was neither brilliant nor stupid, and her mother responded with approval: "'You're in the middle,' she said with obvious relief. The best place to be: the middle. No harm done there.

That's us: smart enough, middle-class, Midwestern, midcentury—middle everything. Safe, safe" (20).

But throughout this memoir, Hampl demonstrates that she is anything but simply ordinary: she is funny, confused, furious, and scared—a writer trying to figure out whether it was her father's love of earthly beauty, of perishable things, that had made her the artist she is, or whether it was the love of words, the irony, the careful order and analysis bequeathed to her from her Irish mother that had made her that person.

During the last hours of her mother's life, Hampl imaginatively wanders through her hometown and her childhood. Here, in her fifth memoir, she finds her version of St. Paul/ Minneapolis and family life. As her mother tells her: "'Reach for the stars, sweetie—and stay, stay right here'" (20) and Hampl ambivalently obeys the request and the requirement.

Hampl proves that Minneapolis and St. Paul are no less central to the world than Nantucket and that as a Chicago planetarium guide indicates, "All seats provide equal viewing of the universe."[9] The personal becomes political, the ordinary anything but ordinary as Hampl, who remains in Minnesota tells her story sometimes with wonder and sometimes a bit more acerbically, explaining, defamiliarizing the reader with the stereotype of the Midwest that "An ordinary middle-class Midwestern family . . ." is also a ". . . cozy setting for heartlessness" (18). We come to know this family and this writer, but Hampl surprises the reader, makes us think and feel, refusing to allow the middle to be a soulless place.

Hampl clearly does not believe in the myth of Midwestern innocence; and she frequently demonstrates that she is not a believer in the "blameless middle" (51). But blameless or not, it is this middle that she sometimes lovingly and sometimes sardonically, but always provocatively, portrays. It is Minneapolis and St. Paul in the middle of the century, which creates the writer, the lifelong Midwesterner and the creative writer and citizen that she is. But the outside world remains as part of the package, the geographical cards she and her father have not been dealt. Her father, too, yearns for a larger world. She recalls a game she played with him:

For years at night before bed my father took a volume off the shelf, reading at random about far-flung places and moments in history, scientific discoveries, and wild beasts. Fiji and Bhutan, Napoleon on Elba, Einstein and Freud, the gar fish, the hundred-year aloe. It's how he ended his day, roaming the world. But the World stayed in its Book. And we stayed in St. Paul, playing the geographic card we'd been dealt. (65)

Like all self-loving individuals, Hampl discovers that life is not elsewhere and that the myths and realities of lives, the exterior and the interior, can never really be—nor should they be—separated. We are the sum of our complex experiences and the place and space where these experiences happen. In this memoir, Hampl, a conflicted daughter, observer par excellence, makes a temporary peace with Minnesota. For her, geography is destiny and that is ultimately okay because what is, is good. Patricia Hampl, always the artist, balances, loses her way, shocks herself and others as she discovers the essence of her Minneapolis and St. Paul, the shadow of the cathedral near her home, the nuances of her family, their disappointments and secrets, and her position in it all.

In chapter one of twelve chapters, Hampl wittily informs the reader: "Nothing is harder to grasp than a relentlessly modest life" (16), and yet she is determined to grasp it and recreate it in layers of photographs and images, *Red Book* encyclopedia volumes, and post-it notes. We experience, along with her, just how these people—who have been among the essential backdrops and markers of her life— came to be and who they were to each other and to her.

The Florist's Daughter was recognized in the Midwest as an important, worthy book: it was a Minnesota Book Award finalist in the category of Memoir & Creative Nonfiction, and it was also listed in the *Chicago Tribune* as one of the Best Books of 2007. But why isn't it more famous outside the Midwest? Dan Cryer in *Newsday*'s "Our Favorites of 2007" clearly adores her writing and sees her place in the world as interfering with her reputation:

If Patricia Hampl had written memoirs chronicling her days in New York or Los Angeles, her name would be on every American reader's lips. Hailing from flyover country, Minnesota, she has fewer readers than she deserves. Still, *A Romantic Education* and *Virgin Time* demonstrated her bountiful evocative gifts. Now comes The *Florist's Daughter* (Harcourt) to summon her parents back to vivid life. Hampl's mother, a feisty Irish-American storyteller, and father, a tenderhearted Czech-American florist who catered to St. Paul's elite—Truth and Beauty, indeed!—endowed their daughter with a writer's essential credentials. Hampl's prose is delightfully fluid, artful without being arty, ever attuned to ambiguity. She is unquestionably, one of the finest stylists we have."[10]

So while Patricia Hampl is famous, she may well be less famous than what she would be if the world she were exploring was not St. Paul, Minnesota but a larger urban space.

The Florist's Daughter opens with death, but it is very much about living, becoming an artist and discovering that her mother, too, would have liked to be a writer. To enjoy this memoir one needs to follow the voice, the images, the internal exploration and accept than the travel here will be mostly interior and non-linear and that one must stop craving action or adventure in order to experience how these flowers—and characters—grow. And one must come to understand that flowers—beautiful ones—grow in the Midwest.

One can get a kick out of St. Paul history, with its Irish and Czech worlds. Here is a rendition of how one family was formed in the shadow of the Depression, navigated the pecking order of neighborhoods. Yet also depicted is the contrast between parents, the love and betrayal, the silences and empty spaces, and the layers of these fascinating lives. Mary, the mother, is suspicious; Stan, the father, embraces life's beauty. He enters its wonder and finds the world enchanting and benevolent as he serves the elite of St. Paul. He works hard to maintain Patricia Hampl's innocence and is upset when he finds he cannot: Patricia Hampl feels oppressed by her father's wish for her innocence. After he retires, he paints a picture of her, entitling it "Patricia's Garden", and she stuffs it in her closet (70). It is a picture that panics her. For her the picture represents who she doesn't care to be: "She's her father's angel, her mother's dutiful daughter. She's staying 'till it's over. An indentured innocent. Everything is contrived—the vines and blossoms, the wall high as a monastic enclosure, the constricting obscuring dress, and the gaze trained on the itty-bitty bookette—it's the hex of love" (71). And so the memoir honors and despises love: ambivalent, trapped, self-trapped.

There is never a moment in this memoir where the images are stable or unremarkable. Hampl weaves and unravels her story of humor, confusion, and pain as she tries to understand what is lost and what is gained with love, art, and loyalty to people or places. *The Florist's Daughter* opens with a remarkable image of her sitting in her mother's hospital room after her mother has suffered a terrible stroke. There, Hampl and the doctors agree that treating her like a sixteen-year-old, who has just had a terrible motorcycle accident, no longer benefited anyone. In Hampl's lap lies a yellow notepad, and she is composing her mother's obituary. The nurse—Hampl projects—minds this activity and finds it a rather disrespectful gesture. However, Hampl quickly reassures the reader that her mother, if she were conscious, would not in the least be offended. Mary, her mother, honored writing and breathed the need to write into Hampl's unconscious—with Hampl ever suspecting that her mother's and her dream of becoming a great writer were the same. Hampl, as her earlier memoirs demonstrate, has always dealt with life's contradictions and complexities through writing.

The *Bookreporter* also notes this: "writing a mini-biography of her mother, even as the woman lay dying, seems a fitting image."[11] It becomes the central image of this memoir: a daughter losing a mother and finding a mother; a daughter accepting her solo flight in life and internalizing the love that will always follow, even when her lovers/parents are no more. *A Florist's Daughter* is a new, creative obituary honoring time, space and place, honoring a family and the lives they lived—simultaneously ordinary and everything—the microcosm becoming the universal.

While the memoir is entitled *The Florist's Daughter*, Hampl clearly wants the reader to understand that her mother frames the entire memoir as well. Hampl's mother was a biography-reading, Midwestern library clerk, practical and pragmatic on the outside, exact and exacting.

As her mother dies, Hampl and her readers ponder how art and craft happen. Is it a gift of nature, a vision, a drive? How is art related to place, to market economy, to ethnicity, to happiness? How is it that difficult people can be charming as well? How is it that a woman like her, who dreams of escape, ends up spending her life in St. Paul, Minnesota?

What to do with the setting? Hampl suggests that, in the Midwest, it is bad form to be a drama queen; "here" lives are meant to be little and only weather allowed to be big. But if everyone west of Ohio and east of Nebraska knows that drama is all just weather, we readers don't really know that. Drama, Hampl demonstrates, is for the geographical and the human, for the construction and the constructed, for the flower arrangements and the legal/financial battles. Everything counts; everything is part and parcel of the whole.

Norah Piehl demonstrates in her writing that she understands that this memoir works as a weaving: "In *The Florist's Daughter* this setting, family history and personal memoir intersect to make for a rich, rewarding meditation on how we become the people we are, why we end up where we live, why we make the choices we do" ("Rev. of *Florist's Daughter*" n.p.). Piehl is correct—this memoir is a meditation, a reflection on what it means to be the child of one's parents. Poetry and prose, cakes—the lilac nostalgia—and streets come to life. Hampl hurts and turns this hurt to beauty and wonder—like her mother and like her father.

Another review, this one published in *The New York Times* by fellow memoirist Danielle Trussoni, author of *Falling Through the Earth*, praises this memoir, partially because in it, Patricia Hampl confronts so many demons and learns to accept that, often, the material closest to home is the richest. Trussoni responds to the title's modesty:

And, in a way, playing down her most intense, brilliant book, with a soft title makes sense: Hampl is a memoirist almost completely devoid of ego. She once wrote that good autobiographical writing is less about self-absorption than about the individual's interaction with the world. Memoir, she claimed, 'begins as hunger for a world, one gone or lost, effaced by time or a more sudden brutality.' Like the best memoirists, Hampl has used her own experiences to understand what is exterior, amorphous, longed for. She has written about herself to understand what shaped her, but also about the ways desire has pulled her beyond the self. Her tireless ambition to rise above her own limitations—in art, in g-d, in escape from her home—has always been best served through a voice that is highly suspicious of glorifying the self."[12]

The Florist's Daughter is amazing in its "tempest in a teapot" fashion. Hampl's mother is dying: when, then, is she obsessing about geography? Perhaps it is an ordinary diversion and perhaps it is a metaphor. Hampl needs to accept her life so that she can accept her mother's death. Because the memoir is so ordinary, it also becomes so special. Readers are required to pay attention as images argue with one another, mushroom into something quite different than where one thinks they are going. An almost rape becomes a rape, the impossibility of an affair becomes the likelihood of one. Hampl creates for us a self that feels authentic and worth comprehending, an artist, a writer, who is at once a conflicted daughter, a begrudging Midwesterner, and a person who really doesn't even get what she thinks she understands, proving that nothing is richer than St. Paul, than family dramas.

At the end of the memoir, framed by the death of her private, epileptic mom, Mary Catherine Ann Terese Eleanor Marum Hampl, at once royalty and the artist, Patricia Hampl is no longer a daughter. Her last parent is gone. So many years spent living a life where she could walk from her family home to her adult home was irrevocably ending. No matter which direction she turned—towards the water or downtown, toward the Cathedral, or the old Czech neighborhood— she could not turn from being an orphan and from the reality that her parents were gone. Stuck in the "blameless middle," Hampl tries to sort out her life through this memoir and ends up doing more than sorting. She creates beauty.

Her other memoirs might be romantic, but this one examines the real, unsentimental, unsolvable story where ultimately there is no solace. Hampl has successfully and self-consciously narrated one Midwestern life and has found a Midwest for herself and for history. No matter how hard we try to escape our past, our place, no matter how hard we try to keep them stable, time passes as do humans, and we go solo. Like Ishmael, we are all orphans with different and important tales to tell of how we survived when the ship and the captain went down.

This tale is beautifully told. and it continues the story of how one woman—marked by the Midwest, by the 1960s, by the world of words and flowers, by stability and mutability—becomes the driven and gifted memoirist that she is: a Midwestern memoirist, a historian, a documenter of a specific time and place.

Notes

1. Mario Vargas Llosa, *Feast of the Goat*, translated from the Spanish by Edith Grossman New York: Farrar, Straus and Giroux, 2000, 146. Even in the Dominican Republic, Llosa proves that innocence has been archived in the Midwest.

2. T.S. Eliot is seldom thought of as a Midwest Poet, but he is born in the Midwest and, not to take that into account, is to miss how the child's experience informs the man's.

3. Harriet Monroe became one of the major participants in the now famous Chicago Renaissance. *Poetry* magazine began in 1912 during the height of this phenomenon.

4. Pat Conroy, New York Times best-selling novelist and memoirist, is quoted as saying this on the cover of the hardbound first edition of *The Florist's Daughter*.

5. A version of this essay was presented at the January 2011 Los Angeles, California Society for the Study of Midwestern Literature/ Modern Language.

6. Patricia Hampl. *The Florist's Daughter*. New York: Harcourt. 2007. 125. All further quotations to this edition will be noted internally.

7. Katherine Jamieson, "An Interview with Patricia Hampl." *The Writer's Chronicle*, 43, 2 October 2010, 22 -28. Hampl clarifies that for her memoir writing is never mainly about the self, but rather about documenting history.

8. F. Scott Fitzgerald's *The Great Gatsby* has often been read as a Midwest novel, where the central character, Jay Gatsby, an outsider, perhaps a Midwest Jew, attempts to leave home, but imaginatively and obsessively returns to the place that formed him.

9. Hayden Planetarium Guide, Chicago, Illinois, no date.

10. Dan Cryer, "Book We Like Best in 2007," Newsday, December 29, 2007. <http://www.newsday.com/entertainment-2.822/entertainment-2.822fanfare-2.828/entertainment2.822fanfare-2.828our-favorites-of-07-1.495324>.

11. Nora Piehl, *Bookreporter*. Review. January 22, 2011. http://www.bookreporter.com. Piehl stresses in her review that Hampl's mother has the gift of remembering details and has a "writer's eye," even if she isn't herself a writer.

12. Danielle Trussoni, "The Hopelessness of Escape, *New York Times Book Review*, October 7, 2007 <http://www.nytimes.com/2007/10/07/books/review/Trussoni-t.html?_r=0&ref=books&pagewanted=print>. This review focuses on Hampl's rejection of the Midwest and her coming full circle, ending her illusion that elsewhere would have given her more of what she needed as a writer or a woman.

Works Cited

Ackroyd. Peter. *T.S. Eliot: A Life*. New York: Simon & Schuster, 1984.

Cryer, Dan. "Book We Like Best in 2007," *Newsday*, 29 December 29 2007. <http://www.newsday.com/entertainment-2.822/entertainment-2.822fanfare-2.828/entertainment2.822fanfare-2.828our-favorites-of-07-1.495324>.

Fitzgerald, F. Scott. *The Great Gatsby*. New York: Scribners, 1996.

Hampl, Patricia. *The Florist's Daughter*. New York: Harcourt, 2007.

Hayden Planetarium. *Hayden Planetarium Guide*. Chicago: Hayden Planetarium,, n.d..

Jamieson, Katherine. "An Interview with Patricia Hampl." *The Writer's Chronicle*. 43, 2 October 2010, 22 -28.

Llosa, Mario Vargas. *Feast of the Goat*. Transl. Edith Grossman. New York: Farrar, Straus and Giroux, 2000. 146.

Monroe, Harriet. *A Poet's Life: Seventy Years In a Changing World*. New York: Macmillan, 1938.

Piehl, Nora."Review of *The Florist's Daughter*." *Bookreporter*. 22 January 2011. <http://www.bookreporter.com>. 12 Nov. 2013.

Trussoni, Danielle. "The Hopelessness of Escape." *New York Times Book Review*. October 7, 2007. <http://www.nytimes.com/2007/10/07/books/review/Trussoni-t.html?_r=0&ref=books&pagewanted=print>. 12 Nov. 2013.

'Your Homeland Is Where You Live and Where You Work': Challenging Midwestern Pastoral(ism) in Tomás Rivera's ... *And the Earth Did Not Devour Him* _____

William Barillas

As many scholars have observed, the Midwest figures in the popular imagination in relation to rural and agrarian life and landscape.[1] Fields of corn, wheat, and other crops; orchards and dairy farms; wooded lots and large oak trees lining the fencerows between properties; red wooden barns, timber-frame farmhouses, and one-room schools; small towns built on railway lines, with downtown business districts consisting of late nineteenth- and early twentieth-century brick storefronts: such are the scenes most commonly associated with the Midwest in mass media, as well as canonical early twentieth-century, Anglo-American literature. These images embody Midwestern pastoralism, the region's "defining ideology: the pastoral vision of a peaceful agrarian kingdom between (and away from) the extremes of eastern urban sophistication and the moral license of unsettled western frontiers" (Barillas 24). The essentialized Midwesterner inhabiting that mythic space is the archetypal yeoman farmer, a white, rural, agrarian, heterosexual male as the representative figure of Midwestern cultural identity.

The pastoral myth, of course, belies the modern and contemporary reality of the Midwest, with its large and medium-size cities and long-standing industrial sector, with most people engaged in the service and production industries rather than agriculture. The myth also overlooks ethnic and racial diversity, which always has been central to Midwestern life. Native Americans; immigrants from eastern and southern, as well as northern Europe; African Americans; and many other peoples are as significant in Midwestern history and culture as Anglo Americans. Midwestern writers have long recognized these cultural complexities, even when writing works of pastoral literature, including fiction, poetry, and essays about people and places in the rural parts of the American heartland.

As written in *The Midwestern Pastoral: Place and Landscape in Literature of the American Heartland* (2006), Midwestern pastoral writers "view tradition critically, questioning the assumptions of Midwestern pastoralism as they know it through personal experience and from the region's history and literature" (Barillas 9). Issues related to social class, race, imperialism, violence, and environmental destruction are treated with increasing forthrightness in their writing, so much so that in the work of Jim Harrison, an important contemporary figure in this literary tradition, the darker side of American history is often foregrounded as the central theme (8).

Yet the writers on whom I focus in that book, from Willa Cather to Jim Harrison, are all Anglo Americans; all (with notable exceptions like James Wright and Paul Gruchow) came from middle-class backgrounds. Despite their empathy for working-class Midwesterners and people of color, Midwestern pastoral writers tend to write about, and for, relatively privileged people. The central characters in their novels, the speakers in their poems, and the personae in their essays, are, more often than not, both white and middle-class, if not wealthy. Many are rural landowners, farmers and ranchers with a spiritual, even mystical sensibility when it comes to nature. They are good stewards of the land and fair employers to their hired hands. But they are privileged nonetheless. A richer, more nuanced view of Midwestern rural life must consider the experience of laborers, non-landowners, and people of color—all those who are not celebrated or elevated as regional archetypes in Anglo-American cultural myth or literature.

For such a view, we may look to the writing of Tomás Rivera (1936-1985), whose fiction about Mexican American migrant workers in the mid-twentieth century challenges the perspectives and values expressed in Anglo Midwestern pastoral. Whereas pastoral writers in the tradition of Willa Cather generally focus on owners and employers and express a fundamentally Romantic view of people and nature, Rivera concerns himself with laborers who do not own the land they work, who lack leisure time to contemplate natural beauty, and who are generally treated by Anglo farmers and townspeople not as part of the broader community, but as racially, culturally, and economically *Other*. Rivera's writing calls into question archetypes and stereotypes of Midwestern cultural identity and rural experience from a point of view, which is working-class rather than middle-class, naturalistic rather than Romantic, and family and community-centered rather than individualistic.

Born in a south Texas town to Mexican immigrants, Tomás Rivera spent his early years with his family, engaged in migrant labor. They lived and worked half of the year in Texas, over the winter months, and half of the year in the upper Midwest, wherever field work was available. In late spring or early summer, they joined the stream of migrants coming by truck and automobile to plant, tend, and harvest crops in Iowa, Minnesota, North Dakota, Wisconsin, and Michigan. Like other migrant children, Rivera went to school whenever possible, his education being frequently interrupted by his family's need for his labor during the fall harvest season. He went on to college and graduate school, eventually becoming a professor of Spanish and chancellor of the University of California, Riverside. He was first Mexican American to hold that office in the University of California System. While this distinguished career meant less time for his writing, Rivera produced stories; poems; scholarly essays; and, most notably, one novel, . . . *y no se lo tragó la tierra* / . . . *And the Earth Did Not Devour Him* (1971), now a classic of Mexican American, and more broadly, Latino/Latina literature of the United States.

Written in Spanish and published with accompanying English-language translation, it was the first major novel of the Chicano Literary Renaissance, a movement that accompanied and supported the Chicano Civil Rights Movement of the 1960s and 1970s. Drawing on the author's early experiences, . . . *And the Earth Did Not Devour Him* portrays Mexican American migrants in the late 1940s and 1950s, a time before Chicano labor unions, political activism, and cultural nationalism, when migrant laborers faced harsh working conditions, poor pay, discrimination, and even violence from employers and other Anglo Americans. Although it is set fifteen to twenty years before the Chicano Civil Rights Movement, . . . *And the Earth Did Not Devour Him* contributed to that movement, according to Julián Olivares, "not only [by] documenting the migrant workers' experience but also as a form of protest against the conditions that permitted such an existence. . . . Rivera saw the migrant workers . . . as precursors of the struggle of the *movimiento* for social and political justice" (25-26).

One fundamental way that Rivera's writing problematizes Midwestern pastoral ideology and the conventions of Midwestern pastoral literature is the complexity of its regionalism. Pastoral writers typically portray life in one location, with an attachment, both practical and spiritual, to the landscape and history of that place. Rivera's characters, however, including the adolescent boy who provides the central and recurring consciousness in . . . *And the Earth did Not Devour Him*, have a more complicated sense of place. They have a homeland in Texas, which was a Hispanic, specifically Spanish-speaking, region, first as part of the Spanish Empire and then as Mexican territory, for nearly a century and a half before its conquest by Anglo Americans. Because they live and work half of the year in the upper Midwest, however, the migrants are at least as Midwestern as they are *tejano* (Mexican Texans). The Midwest is as much their homeland as Texas, even if most Anglo Midwesterners in Rivera's narrative do not consider the migrants to be locals, or treat them as such.

That Rivera rarely names the setting in his stories underlines the idea that the Chicano homeland is not limited to Texas or the U.S. Southwest. In some cases, the setting simply cannot be known with certainty, suggesting that the events being narrated are representative of migrant experience in the Midwest, as well as in Texas. Discrimination, for example, occurs in both locations, as in the untitled vignette that begins "It was an hour before," in which a barber refuses to cut the boy's hair. No geographical reference is given. In other stories, the setting is implied by reference to circumstances like weather. In "The Children Couldn't Wait," for example, the severe heat in April, along with the tyrannical attitude of the Anglo foreman, indicates that the events take place on a Texas farm. A reference to cactus toward the end of "First Communion" places that story in Texas as well.

More specific references to location are sometimes keyed to the characters' seasonal migration—from Texas to the Upper Midwest in early summer, and back down again in autumn. The narrator tells us in "The Night before Christmas" that the boy's parents "had to save money every week to pay for the trip up north. Now they charged for children too, even if they rode standing up the whole way to Iowa" (131). While a reader may have already correctly assumed that December would find the migrants in Texas, this reference confirms the story's setting, while emphasizing the migrant life as one of dual residence and regional identity.

One convention of pastoral literature is an intense focus on individual experience in a beloved landscape. In the U.S. literary tradition, this is in keeping with Romantic individualism, which celebrates psychological development, intellectual freedom, and a mystical spirituality of nature and place. Alexandra Bergson, the protagonist of Willa Cather's 1913 novel *O Pioneers!* personifies these characteristics. Given charge of the family by her father on his deathbed, Alexandra turns their frontier-era Nebraska homestead into an orderly and prosperous farm. She does so not through physical force or by financial dealings alone, but through empathy and vision. "A pioneer should have imagination," the narrator tells us, "should be able to enjoy the idea of things more than the things themselves" (48). Cather characterizes Alexandra as a Romantic artist and visionary, a prairie Transcendentalist whose empirical observations about trends in land use are confirmed by a mystical epiphany of place—an archetypal occurrence in pastoral—that causes her to feel "a new consciousness of the country," a love for the place that now seems like home (70).

After the Bergson family's initial struggles, the novel portrays the consequences of success, with Alexandra becoming estranged from her increasingly "bigoted and self-satisfied" brothers, Lou and Oscar (237), and her youngest, educated brother losing himself in a secret and illicit romantic affair. Family is deeply problematic in this novel; the marriages appear to be empty or, at best, companionate, and familial relations are maintained or broken over issues of property and social status. Constant, however, through loneliness and loss is Alexandra's independent selfhood. She remains as she appears in the novel's first chapter, her character fully formed as "a tall, strong girl" who "walked rapidly and resolutely, as if she knew exactly where she was going and what she was going to do next" (6).

The sense of self that emerges in... *And the Earth Did Not Devour Him*, by contrast, is contextual to family and community. The boy's psychological development is related to his growing comprehension of the migrant workers' plight as a social injustice. "By discovering who he is," Olivares argues, "this adolescent becomes one with his people. Through his quest, he embodies and expresses the collective conscious and experiences of his society" (13). Rivera leads the reader to an appreciation of that socially-defined selfhood through narrative form and technique. Although the first story, "The Lost Year", and the last, "Under the House", occur after the stories in between and frame the book as a retrospective of the previous year in the boy's life, the stories are sequenced to emphasize theme rather than chronology. Rivera never names his protagonist, a narrative trope that makes his experiences more representative than unique. Some of the stories do not directly involve the boy; they tell of other migrant workers, people the boy knows, or at least knows of. Such is the case in "The Little Burnt Victims," about a migrant couple who loses two children in a fire, after leaving them at home "when they went to work because the owner didn't like children in the fields doing mischief and distracting their parents from their work" (120). In "The Children Couldn't Wait," a boy is shot dead by a Texas farmer when he goes to a water tank for a drink on a hot day. The farmer, who had told the workers to stay away from the tank, intends to scare the boy, but accidentally shoots him in the head.

Rivera's placement of "The Children Couldn't Wait," as the third narrative in the book creates a crucial dramatic irony. The two previous narratives—"The Lost Year" and the untitled vignette about the boy's mother placing a glass of water under his bed every night to appease the spirits—establish the boy as the protagonist. While reading "The Children Couldn't Wait," a reader may understandably assume that the unnamed boy, working in the fields with his father, is the same character. When that boy is killed, and the narration switches to a dialogue between two unnamed migrant workers, one is startled into reassessing that assumption. The boy shot by the Texas rancher cannot be the protagonist, who is said in "The Lost Year" to be thinking back on the previous year, when the events in subsequent stories occurred. Yet, he could have been in the same situation; he could have been shot by a farmer, since he does the same work as the boy who died. Like the protagonist remaining unnamed and like the stories that do not directly involve the boy, this dramatic irony—meaning, the reader is briefly led to believe the protagonist has died—emphasizes identity as situated in community and family rather than individual desire or private property. The boy's emerging sense of self is not individualistic in the Anglo American sense; it encompasses solidarity with other Mexican American workers and their families. "The Children Couldn't Wait" implicitly links utilitarian individualism—a primarily economic outlook that emphasizes ownership, efficiency, order, and social prestige—with violence.

There is some continuity between Rivera's portrayal of small Midwestern towns and rural communities and those by the canonical writers of what critic Ronald Weber calls "the Midwestern ascendancy in American writing," most notably, Hamlin Garland, Sherwood Anderson, Edgar Lee Masters, Willa Cather, and Sinclair Lewis.[2] Like those early twentieth-century writers, Rivera rejects unexamined assumptions about rural life, revealing hypocrisy, avarice, lust, and other faults among people that sentimental varieties of pastoralism present as uniquely virtuous and open-hearted. It is not such a leap from Garland's scheming landlords, Anderson's grotesques, and Lewis's small-town philistines to some of the people Rivera sketches: the white barber who refuses to cut the boy's hair, the minister's wife who runs off with the man who came to teach the migrants carpentry, the thieving Mexican, or Mexican American couple who murder the undocumented worker. The difference is that Rivera portrays these transgressions from the point of view of a person whom Anglo townspeople do not consider as a member of their community, but as the *Other*, an outsider because of his or her ethnicity and status as migrant. Through fragmentary glimpses of the boy's family and experiences at school and elsewhere, Rivera illustrates the worth and dignity of Mexican American migrant culture and labor, setting up dramatic ironies that place the failings and bigotry of Anglo locals in a light so intense that no commentary or exposition is needed.

A strong example of this narrative technique occurs in "It's That It Hurts." The story finds the boy walking through the country, likely down a road in rural Iowa. In Anglo Midwestern pastoral, this scene would provide an opportunity to portray a Romantic solitary figure finding solace and spiritual uplift in nature. Rivera's protagonist, however, is coping with injustice and exclusion: he has just been expelled from school for fighting. He is mature enough to perceive the unfairness of his expulsion, but young and naïve enough to hope, throughout the story, that he will be allowed back in class: "Maybe they didn't expel me from school. Maybe it ain't so, after all. Maybe it's not. *Sure it is!* It is so, they did expel me. And now what do I do?" (92). Rivera sets up the dramatic irony by having the boy recall certain events before telling of the fight and his subsequent expulsion. He remembers being embarrassed by the teacher and the school nurse, who were looking for lice, a symptom of inadequate housing provided by employers. He remembers his father escorting him to school and worries about his parents' reaction when they learn he has been kicked out. He then recalls the event that got him expelled: defending himself when cornered in the bathroom by a bully who taunted him with racist slurs before hitting him.

By first making readers aware of these events, Rivera prepares them for an immediate recognition of naked prejudice and ignorance in the school principal. Only the principal's end of the phone conversation is given. He is identifiable as the principal because of his authority to expel students, and because of the subservient tone with which he speaks, the principal is almost certainly talking to the school superintendent. (The voice on the line is represented by inclusive quotation marks, which suggests that the boy overhears the principal, but cannot make out what the other person is saying). "The Mexican boy got into a fight and beat up a couple of our boys" (94), the principal says, effectively banishing the boy from the local community, which figures here as "*our boys*" as opposed to "*the Mexican boy*." National and ethnic or racial identity are collapsed, so that "Mexican" means "foreign" and "outsider," regardless of citizenship status, just as "American" apparently implies white and Anglophone. The reader infers that the principal is referring to the boy's parents when he rationalizes his decision—"they could[n't] care less if I expel him. . . They need him in the fields"—instantly recognizing the principal's assumption as ignorant and untrue (94). The boy's parents, as we have seen and as Rivera goes on to emphasize, are deeply concerned about his education and economic advancement. The figuratively and literally one-sided conversation between the principal and the superintendent contrasts starkly with the story's first dialogue between the boy and his father at the schoolhouse door, and the next, between the boy, his father, and his godfather, in which the father praises the son's aspirations, despite the disparagement of his Anglo boss. "'He's smarter than anything,' the father concludes. 'I just pray God helps him finish school'" (95). Rivera contrasts the self-justifying rhetoric of institutional racism with the Other-directed language of parents and the extended Chicano family, not by means of exposition, but through his arrangement of the story's component narratives.

A situational irony follows the boy's expulsion in "It's That It Hurts" with a scene that raises and then dashes the possibility of a rural idyll or mystical epiphany of place. Halfway home, the boy reaches a country cemetery. The setting is a familiar one in pastoral; cemeteries are sacred places with significance both social and personal. Following precedent in Romantic-era poetry and prose, pastoral writers like Cather and Roethke often write of graveyards, which in the Midwest figure as ironic gardens, green spaces with grass and trees as well as gravestones, where one can contemplate mortality or simply enjoy the earth and sky. The boy likes the place, which he associates with reflection and play, rather than physical labor or the social exclusion he has just experienced at school. Best of all, he finds that unlike the traditional Mexican cemetery he knows in Texas, this Midwestern one is not frightening, but "real pretty. Just lots of soft grass and trees, I guess that's why here when people bury somebody they don't even cry" (95). The boy's adolescent naiveté about grief suggests a moment of relief from his most pressing worry, that his parents will be angry at him for being expelled from school. He feels and expresses a sense of comfort in the rural Midwest, the landscape of which is "pretty" in a pastoral way, unlike arid south Texas. Yet the pastoral idyll is broken as soon as it occurs: "If only they would let us fish in the little creek that runs through here, there's lots of fish. But no, you even need a license to fish, and then they don't even sell us one 'cause we're from out of state" (95). At work, at school, and even alone in nature, the boy is constantly aware because he has been *made* to be aware, of his exclusion from the rural, Anglo construction of Midwestern American identity.

Two climactic moments of the book, having to do with the boy's growing consciousness of himself as a free moral agent and of his selfhood as socially situated, also challenge pastoral conventions. In both instances, the physical setting bears heavily on the action and psychological outcome of the event. Place is crucial in these scenes, the first of which takes place outdoors in the rural Midwest. Neither epiphany, however, fits the Romantic model: in neither is the boy alone and in neither does he come to a mystical sense of oneness with nature or God. His realization, in the first event, centers on a rejection of the religion of his upbringing and, in the second, on the social construction of his family's status as underpaid manual laborers, whose culture and civil rights are disrespected by the Anglo majority.

The first transitional moment occurs in the title story, "…And the Earth Did Not Devour Him," in which the boy's anger over his family's situation comes to a crisis. An aunt and uncle die of tuberculosis, and seeing his grieving mother weep causes the boy to feel "hate and anger . . . because he [is] unable to do anything against anyone" (108). He does not know who or what is to blame for his family's suffering or where to direct his anger. Soon thereafter, his father collapses from sunstroke and is laid up in bed, and the boy becomes even angrier. Until now he has kept private his doubts about supernatural aid—the glasses of water his mother places under his bed for the spirits, her fervent prayers for the return of her older son from war, his testing (in the story "A Silvery Night") whether the devil actually exists. Hearing his father's prayers and moans of pain, however, and observing his mother's religious practice causes the boy to verbalize his anger. Her prayers and devotions strike him as futile: "What's to be gained from doing all that, Mother? Don't tell me it helped my aunt and uncle any? How come we're like this, like we're buried alive? Either the germs eat us alive or the sun burns us up. Always some kind of sickness. And every day we work and work. For what? Poor Dad, always working so hard." Since his intellectual understanding of socioeconomics and class structure is yet unformed, the boy fixes his anger on God: "[W]hy, God doesn't care about us . . . I don't think there even is . . . No, better not say it, what if Dad gets worse. Poor Dad, I guess that at least gives him some hope." For the second time (the first occurred previously, in "A Silvery Night") the boy nearly states that God does not exist, but stops short of completing the thought, again telling himself "Better not say it." The next morning he challenges his mother by reasoning that since his father is good, as were his aunt and uncle, "God has no concern for us" (109).

The climax of the story, and of this conflict in the novel, occurs later that day, when the boy is laboring in the fields with his younger siblings. His nine-year-old brother vomits and then falls unconscious from sunstroke, and the boy must carry him home. As he walks, he repeats his questioning as to why good people suffer:

Each step that he took towards the house resounded with the question, *why?* About halfway to the house he began to get furious. Then he started crying out of rage. His little brothers did not know what to do, and they, too, started crying, but out of fear. Then he started cursing. And without realizing it, he said what he had been wanting to say for a long time. He cursed God. Upon doing this he felt that fear instilled in him by the years and by his parents. For a second he saw the earth opening up to devour him. Then he felt his footsteps against the earth, compact, more solid than ever. Then his anger swelled up again and he vented it by cursing God. (111)

This epiphany is transformative as any in Anglo Midwestern fiction or poetry, yet it comes not as an overwhelming sense of oneness with nature but as a liberating act of defiance against a cosmology the boy has come to see as untenable. In "Silvery Night" he tested the Mexican folk belief that the devil will come if one calls to him at midnight. The devil did not come, the boy reasoned, therefore the devil does not exist. In the short story, "...And the Earth Did Not Devour Him", the boy's cursing of God is an emotional release rather than a rational act, but the result is similar: the boy's ideas change as to how the world works. He knows now that "the earth [does] not devour anyone, nor [does] the sun" (111-12). It is unclear whether the boy now disbelieves in God, but the next day, with the hot weather giving way to cool, and his father and brother recovering, "for the first time he [feels] capable of doing and undoing anything that he pleased" (112). He is beginning to perceive his agency as a moral actor, a person with a degree of control over his life.

The boy's growing skepticism and independent thought reflects cognitive development as outlined by psychologist Claude Piaget. Piaget's theory, as summarized by David Reed Shaffer and Katherine Kipp, characterizes younger children's thinking as concrete-operational, meaning that they think in terms only "of objects, situation, or events that are real or imaginable" (268). Formal-operations, "first seen between the age of 11 and 13 years of age, are mental actions performed on ideas and propositions. No longer is thinking tied to the factual or observable, for formal operators can reason quite logically about hypothetical processes and events that may have no basis in reality" (268). The boy in .

. . And the Earth Did Not Devour Him is precisely at that age and stage of development, struggling to achieve formal-operational thought.[3] The book's first story, "The Lost Year," shows him at the brink, almost but not quite able to achieve a reasonable perspective on the often traumatic experiences of the last twelve months of his life. "He tried to figure out when that time he had come to call 'year' had started. He became aware that he was always thinking and thinking from this there was no way out. Then he started thinking about how he never thought and this was when his mind would go blank and he would fall asleep." The narrative of "The Lost Year" takes place entirely in the boy's mind. There is no description or exposition of character or setting, only the boy's thoughts tending toward conceptualization. Lost in the mental space between childhood and adolescence, he begins to remember the events narrated in the rest of the novel: "before falling asleep he saw and heard many things" (83).

Those "things" are the suffering and sacrifice not only of the boy and his family, but also of others in the migrant community. "[F]ormal operations," argue Shaffer and Kipp, "may pave the way for thinking about what is possible in one's life, forming a stable identity, and achieving a much richer understanding of other people's psychological perspectives and the causes of their behavior" (270). That understanding emerges as a final epiphany in the novel's concluding story, "Under the House," which is set chronologically soon after "The Lost Year," providing a framing device for the novel that relates the boy's maturing sense of self not to utilitarian ambition for money and prestige or to the emotional self-regard of Romanticism, but to social solidarity and empathy. The final story differs from the first in that setting and action are realized, and the boy's thoughts tend not to confusion and uncertainty, but to specificity and ultimately to the conceptual and philosophical depth made possible by formal-operational thinking.

The story is indeed set under a house: not the boy's family's house, but that of a another migrant family in Texas. In the half-dark, bitten by fleas, and afraid of being discovered by his neighbors, he finds that he "could think very clearly in the dark" (148). His thoughts come in a long, italicized stream-of-consciousness sequence, with brief narratives recalling events of the previous year, many of which are familiar stories in the novel. Snippets of conversation recall people like Doña Cuquita, the elderly lady with whom the boy picked the dump, and tragedies, like the shooting of the boy at the water tank. The entire novel seems to repeat itself as the boy remembers and then comes to his realization of himself, of his selfhood, as both independent and responsible to his community: "I would like to see all of the people together. And then, if I had great big arms, I could embrace them all. . . . I like it right here because I can think about anything I please. Only by being alone can you bring everybody together" (151). The sophistication and subtlety of that paradox surpasses anything the boy has previously uttered or thought. He values reflective solitude, but he has found it not in a green open field or along a watercourse, but under a house, with his neighbors—his fellow migrant workers—above and around him. Being philosophical and unconventional distinguishes the boy from others; he is soon discovered by other children, who mistake him for a man (in a sense he *is* now a man, despite his young age) and throw rocks at him until he comes out from under the house. The woman who lives in the house speculates that the boy "must be losing his mind. He's losing track of the years" (152). That final dramatic irony confirms the boy's maturation. The reader knows, as does the boy, "that in reality he hadn't lost anything. He had made a discovery. To discover and rediscover and piece things together. This to this, that to that, all with all. That was it. That was everything" (152).

The reader, too, has had to piece together a perception of the boy as a character and as a developing moral agent. This is due to the fragmentary format of the novel as a collection of stories and vignettes, which, at times, purposefully lack exposition and description. By requiring active collaboration and contemplation, Rivera places the reader into the boy's struggle for meaning and identity. Ethical selfhood includes the imagined Other, as represented in the novel's final five sentences; when the boy climbs a tree in his parents' yard and views a palm tree in the distance, he "imagine[s] someone perched on top, gazing across at him. He even raised one arm and waved it back and forth so that the other could see that he knew he was there" (152). The *Other* could be another migrant worker, or the boy's younger self, and he is waving goodbye. Or, the imagined figure could represent the boy in the future, towards which he now feels more equipped to strive. In any case, the boy's final, happy epiphany expands his sense of self, implying that individual happiness partly depends on social solidarity. Like the author who created him, Rivera's boy is of the generation that will march in the Chicano Civil Rights Movement, and effect institutional changes in society. We cannot know the boy's ultimate fate, but his possibilities are clear.

A final question remains as to the novel's regional perspective and place in U.S. literary history. Critic Theresa Delgadillo points out that while many stories "in which [Rivera's] protagonist/narrator gains insights about himself in relation to a broader community or prevailing knowledge take place in the Southwest," the apparent "emphasis on a Southwestern homeland contained in the established version of Rivera's novel . . . appears to diverge from the author's original vision." Rivera's editors removed from the manuscript four stories set in the upper Midwest: "The Salamanders," "On the Road to Texas: Pete Fonseca," "The Harvest," and "Zoo Island," which were subsequently published in *The Harvest* of 1987. As Delgadillo shows, these "excluded stories [suggest] that Chicano/as might have a homeland outside of the Southwest and that they may succeed in knowing and asserting themselves in the struggle against domination in places other than the Southwest" (35-6). Olivares suggests that "The Harvest," the title story of that later volume, "presents a theme that is absent in . . . *y no se lo tragó la tierra.* By the novel's very title, we note that the land is seen as the worker's antagonist, the struggle against nature. . . . [A]n aspect of Chicano reality is missing in *Tierra*—the campesino's love of the land. In the ideological thrust of the novel, this theme would have been contradictory" (32).

The struggle of Chicanos in the Midwest and their love of the region's landscape are indeed thematically diminished by the absence of the four stories. Yet, "When We Arrive," the next-to-last story in the novel, does develop both themes. Framed by introductory and concluding paragraphs in the voice of an omniscient narrator, the story provides the private thoughts of several migrant workers, who are in the back of a truck that has broken down in Iowa on the way north. They reveal their troubles, both mundane and life-changing, from fatigue and illness to the frustration and self-directed anger of one man, who curses and vows the trip "is the last time I go through this, standing up all the way like a goddamn animal. As soon as we get there I'm headed for Minneapolis" (144). Such workers leaving the migrant life did, in fact, help establish the sizeable Mexican American community in Minneapolis, St. Paul, and communities elsewhere in the Midwest. The thoughts of another migrant in the back of the truck hint at a sense of place in the Midwest, an outlook that Olivares finds lacking in the novel as edited for publication. Among all the migrants that night, amid all those troubled thoughts, one worker thinks, "What a great view of the stars from here! It looks like they're coming down and touching the tarp of the truck. . . . The silence of the morning twilight makes everything look like it's made of satin" (144). The passage does not make Rivera's novel a work of Romantic literary pastoral, but it does portray sensitivity to natural beauty, suggesting that migrant eyes fall on Midwestern landscapes with love and yearning.

. . . *And the Earth Did Not Devour Him* is a classic of Chicano/ Chicana and Latino/Latina literature; it is also an important contribution to Texas and Southwestern literatures. At the same time, it stands as a major text in the evolving Midwestern literary canon, one that challenges Anglo-American myths of identity and regionalism.[4] The notion that twelve-month residence in a place is necessary for one to be considered a local is essentialist and unfair; the Mexican American and Mexican workers that Rivera portrays are as Midwestern as they are *tejano*, as were the real people Rivera based them on. A story Rivera told about his grandfather illustrates this aspect of the migrant experience. His grandfather "would become angered when he heard of people returning to 'nuestra tierra,' ('our native land'). He would say 'Tu tierra es donde vives y donde trabajas' (Your native land is where you live and where you work)."[5] Rivera plainly felt the same way; he felt at home in the Midwest as well as in Texas, just as he felt at home in two languages, Spanish and English, neither of which is a "foreign language" in the United States. He was a Midwesterner as well as a *tejano* in his youth and a Californian in later life. His novel resulted from labor undertaken in all three locations, work that was physical, psychological, intellectual, and ultimately, social in its aims and accomplishments

Notes

1. Important studies of Midwestern pastoral ideology and literature include *The Middle West: Its Meaning in American Culture* (1989) by James R. Shortridge,, *The Midwestern Ascendancy in American Literature* (1992) by Ronald Weber, and *The Midwestern Pastoral: Place and Landscape in Literature of the American Heartland* (2006) by William Barillas.

2. Ronald Weber, *The Midwestern Ascendancy in American Writing.* Bloomington: Indiana University Press, 1992.

3. Piaget's theory also sheds light on the boy's anger and confusion in the book's title story. "Formal operations," Shaffer and Kipp observe, "may also be related to some of the more painful aspects of the adolescent experience. Unlike younger children, who tend to accept the world as it is and to heed the dictates of authority figures, formal operators—who can imagine hypothetical alternatives to present realities—may begin to question everything. . . . Indeed, the more logical inconsistencies and other flaws that adolescents detect in the real world, the more confused they become and the more inclined they are to become frustrated with or even to display rebellious anger toward the agents (for example, parents or the government) who are thought to be responsible for these imperfect states of affairs" (270).

4. Rivera discusses his experiences and Mexican American culture in the Midwest in his essay "The Great Plains as Refuge in Chicano Literature," in *Tomás Rivera, The Complete Works*, ed. Julián Olivares . Houston: Arte Público Press, 1992. 384-97. Significant to Rivera's relationship to Midwestern literary history is his account of reading Ole Edvart Rølvaag's *Giants in the Earth* (1924-25; English translation 1927) as a first-year college student. A narrative about late nineteenth-century Norwegian immigrants settling the Dakota territory, Rølvaag's novel struck Rivera as "a reliving and reconstruction of our own experience: as migrant workers in the forties and fifties, the Chicanos were giants in the earth. It was after reading Rølvaag that I decided I would one day tell the story of the Chicano migrant workers. The land, the people of the plains, and their drive to gain sustenance from the earth became a profound preoccupation" (385).

5. Quoted in Olivares, "Introduction," 13.

Works Cited

Barillas, William. *The Midwestern Pastoral: Place and Landscape in Literature of the American Heartland.* Athens: Ohio UP, 2006.

Cather, Willa. *O Pioneers!* Boston and New York: Houghton Mifflin, 1913.

Delgadillo, Theresa. "Exiles, Migrants, Settlers, and Natives: Literary Representations of Chicano/as and Mexicans in the Midwest." *Midwestern Miscellany* 30 (Fall 2002): 27-45.

Olivares, Julián. "Introduction." Tomás Rivera, *The Complete Works.* Olivares, ed. Houston: Arte Público Press, 1992.

Rivera, Tomás. *. . . y no se lo tragó la tierra / ...And the Earth Did Not Devour Him.* 1971. Houston: Arte Publico Press, 1995.

Shaffer, David R. and Katherine Kipp. *Developmental Psychology: Childhood and Adolescence.* Belmont, CA: Wadsworth, 2007.

"A Place to Fear and Love:" The Imagined Heartland of David Foster Wallace's *The Broom of the System* ⎯⎯⎯⎯

Jurrit Daalder

> "A writer must have a place where he or she feels this, a place to love and be irritated with." (Louise Erdrich, "*A Writer's Sense of Place*")

Considered by many to be the voice of an entire post-postmodern generation, a voice that Don DeLillo described as both youthful and distinctly "American," David Foster Wallace nonetheless spoke with the "hard-earned Rural Midwestern" accent of his Illinois home (DeLillo 24; Wallace, "Authority" 99). Yet, there is a substantial body of critical commentary that has fruitfully examined the author's national contribution to American letters and his general artistic origins in American postmodernism, while a mere handful of critics have tentatively suggested examining Wallace's geographical roots and classifying him as a regional writer, too, albeit a somewhat unusual one. Only recently have scholars begun to conduct sustained research on "Wallace's topography," proposing that Wallace's writing may be an example of a new kind of "American regionalism" (Quinn 87; Giles, *Global* 175).

Taking its cue from these new studies of Wallace's regionalism, this essay will focus very closely on the Midwesternness of the author's debut novel, *The Broom of the System* (1987). The Midwesternness of this first novel is complicated in very interesting ways by both the young Wallace's ambition "to try and sing to the next generation" of all-American readers, on the one hand, and his loyalty to the specific, oft-neglected region of his Midwestern childhood, on the other hand (Wallace, "Westward" 348). Wallace ended up stuck in the middle between literary ambition and regional loyalty, so to speak, which led to a sense of dislocation that manifests itself in *Broom*'s deeply ambivalent portrait of the Midwest. It is this ambivalence that, finally, bears on the prominent theme of geographical and spiritual loneliness that began to take shape in

Broom and runs through all of the author's subsequent works, a loneliness that reflects, at once, Midwestern life as Wallace knew it as well as the existential dread of his all-American reader, whom Wallace dubbed "Joe Briefcase" ("E Unibus" 23). Some insightful biographical comments made by the writer's sister, Amy Wallace, will serve as a useful point of departure into this discussion about the author's imagined Midwest.

In an interview with Paul Quinn and Geoff Ward, Amy Wallace draws attention to her brother's perpetual geographical outsiderness. She explains that, because their parents were transplanted East-Coast academics, she and her brother were never treated as natives by the Midwestern children, with whom they grew up (qtd. in Quinn 95). Strictly speaking, David Foster Wallace was indeed no native Midwesterner. Born in Ithaca, New York, where his father, James Welch, was finishing a PhD in philosophy at Cornell University, he was six months old when the Wallaces relocated to Champaign-Urbana, twin cities in the state of Illinois (Max 1; J. Wallace qtd. in Harris 186). There, the author grew up amid, on the one hand, the cornfields of the towns' rural community and, on the other hand, the academic institution of the University of Illinois at Urbana-Champaign, the flagship campus of the state's most prominent public university (Max 1). Curiously, however, Amy Wallace also notes that, when her brother had eventually moved to the East-Coast to attend Amherst College in Massachusetts, his new classmates saw him as an outsider and "treated him like a hayseed," which finally led the young author to the realization that maybe "he was from a place no one else was" (qtd. in Quinn 95). The novelist's Midwest must have been "*somewhere in the middle*," says Amy Wallace, "*neither here nor there*" (Ibid).

This realization may explain Wallace's inclination to write about an imagined heartland, which, according to his father, was supposed to reflect "a better truth" (J. Wallace qtd. in Harris 186). For instance, in his first article for *Harper's Magazine*, "Tennis, Trigonometry, Tornadoes: A Midwestern Boyhood" (1991), Wallace claimed that he did not grow up in Urbana but in the nearby town of Philo, Illinois, and he maintained this claim even in his posthumous novel, *The Pale King* (2011). This piece of biographical invention has, understandably, found its way into the first wave of Wallace scholarship, where it lingered on until James Wallace, in an e-mail to Charles B. Harris written in 2010, clarified once and for all that "[n] one of us, including David, ever set foot in Philo" (J. Wallace qtd. in Harris 185). In the same e-mail, James Wallace speculates that his son may have considered Urbana too ordinary or unsophisticated a place and may have been attracted to Philo for its ancient Greek place name, which means "love."

But if his father is right, why did David Foster Wallace not opt for the much grander and slightly more biographically correct Ithaca, with its obvious potential for high-cultural, Homeric allusions to "home"? The author's postmodern precursor and fellow Midwesterner William H. Gass certainly had no reservations about making such direct allusions to ancient Greek cities: in the title story of his first collection, *In the Heart of the Heart of the Country* of 1968, Gass exaggerates the backwardness and ordinariness of the rural town of Brookston, Indiana, and contrasts it with the intellectual city of Byzantium as depicted in W.B. Yeats's 1928 poem, "Sailing to Byzantium". Considering that, after Wallace's death in 2008, both Gass's story collection and his 1996 debut novel, *Omensetter's Luck*, were found in the author's personal library, why did he not follow in Gass's footsteps? The short answer is that, according to James Wallace, "Ithaca is a name to conjure with, but David," despite the region's supposed provincialism and cultural insignificance, "felt a very close connection with Illinois" (qtd. in Harris 185). In comparison, Gass has stated in an interview with *The Paris Review* that, "though people try to label me as a local Midwestern writer [, …] I never had roots: all my sources (as a writer) were chosen" ("The Art").

The above comparison between Wallace's views and Gass' is useful for getting a clearer understanding of Wallace's conflicted attitude toward his Illinois home. Unlike Gass, Wallace still seemed, as he wrote of one of his fictional characters, "married to the land" of his Illinois childhood, despite having felt like an outsider there ("Westward" 300). Similar to Gass, however, Wallace did make frequent attempts to adorn or overcompensate for what he feared was his ordinary or unsophisticated Midwestern home. From the earliest stages of his career, Wallace was keenly aware of the Midwestern self-effacement that seemed necessary for reaching a broad American readership, as evidenced by the cover letter he sent to literary agent Bonnie Nadell, who eventually took on *Broom*. Its prominent Midwestern setting notwithstanding, Wallace described his first novel to Nadell by likening it to the popular "new, young writing" of the literary Brat Pack, a group of jaded East-Coasters that was primarily centered on Bret Easton Ellis, Jay McInerney, and Tama Janowitz (qtd. in Max 65). The young novelist was apparently willing to downplay his Midwesternness in exchange for the opportunity to reach the same broad "generation X" audience as these East-Coast writers.

This ambivalent attitude toward the Midwest complicates critics' claim that Wallace's fiction signals a transition to a new American regionalism that entails a different "phenomenology of place," a claim made, most notably, by Paul Giles ("All Swallowed" 10). Giles writes that a new era of post-postmodernist literature has "moved beyond the spatial dialectics" of center and periphery that structured twentieth-century culture ("Sentimental" 327). In particular, he suggests that "David Foster Wallace's work [...] tends to flatten this distinction entirely" and that Wallace "envisages American space as a level playing field" (327, 328). But, as the abovementioned cover letter illustrates, Wallace did not adopt any particular attitude toward the Midwest in order to flatten this center-periphery dialectics. On the contrary, *Broom*, as well as many of his subsequent works, meditate self-consciously on this spatial dialectics and make clever use of the power relations embedded within it.

Like Wallace's non-fiction, *Broom* is a product of the author's first impulse to write about an imagined heartland instead of his real Illinois home. Helen Dudar already identified this inclination in her 1987 feature on the 25-year-old Wallace, then in his final year of the MFA in creative writing at the University of Arizona. In her article for the *Wall Street Journal*, Dudar made the astute observation that

Wallace may have set *Broom* in Cleveland, Ohio, a city that, like Philo, he had never set foot in because "he wanted a heartland city that he could imagine instead of describe" (10). In order to see how such an imagined heartland might match Amy Wallace's description of her brother's Midwest as a location that is neither here nor there, but somewhere in the middle, it is helpful to examine the novel within the biographical context from which it emerged. This should offer especially useful insights, given the author's own description of the book as his "coded autobio" ("An Expanded" 41).

Wallace started *Broom* as one of his two undergraduate theses at his father's *alma mater*, Amherst College, where he majored in both philosophy and English. The fact that Wallace was working on two theses means that there may have been some interesting cross-pollination between his creative and his philosophical writing. Indeed, the presence of the Austrian logical positivist Ludwig Wittgenstein in the novel is commonly ascribed to Wallace's undergraduate work in philosophy. This philosophical presence will be discussed shortly, but first, it is important to take a closer look at Wallace's college life, of which there is now a detailed reconstruction, thanks to D.T. Max's recent biography. The image that emerges from Max's book is that of a mostly quiet and devoted student, an image that is consistent with Wallace's own remarks, made in an interview with *Amherst Magazine*, that Wallace was "cripplingly shy" and, therefore, did not enjoy or "have much to do with the life of the College" ("Brief Interview"). Nevertheless, Wallace would once in a while surprise his roommates by opening their windows in the morning and shouting into the quad, "I love it here!" (Max 17). These bursts of happiness were, however, overshadowed by Wallace's homesickness. The Wallaces remember that their son missed the Illinois farmland of his Midwestern boyhood and once wrote them that "the mountains in Massachusetts were 'pretty' but the terrain wasn't beautiful 'the way Illinois is'" (Ibid).

These mixed feelings about his time at Amherst would eventually find their way into *Broom*, in which one of the main characters, an Amherst alumnus by the name of Rick Vigorous, reflects on his time at Amherst in a journal entry: "I hated it here.

And I have never been as happy as when I was here. And these two things confront me with the beak and claws of the True" (207). But, interestingly enough, Rick also says about his Midwestern childhood that he can remember "being young and feeling a thing and identifying it as homesickness, and then thinking well now that's odd, isn't it, because I was home all the time. What on earth are we to make of that?" (78). What his therapist, Dr. Curtis Jay, makes of this is that Rick is "the watcher, the observer, looking on from a spatial-dash-emotional elsewhere" (344). He tells Rick, "you are intrinsically Outside, here" (Ibid). Of course, Dr. Jay's diagnosis and Rick's comments about his outsiderness bear a striking resemblance to Amy Wallace's description of her brother's not belonging to either his Midwestern rural community or the East Coast academic community of Amherst. It is no surprise, then, that the imagined heartland of *Broom*'s Cleveland setting constitutes Wallace's most direct attempt to reflect on these feelings about the Midwest, its relation to the East Coast, and the author's place within it.

To be exact, Wallace completely invented two other Midwestern geographies for the purpose of this critical reflection, namely the suburb of East Corinth and the man-made Great Ohio Desert. East Corinth is the hometown of the novel's main protagonist, Lenore Beadsman, Jr., a young switchboard operator fresh out of Oberlin College, Ohio, whose family is a major player in Cleveland's corporate game and whose grandfather, Stonecipher Beadsman II, is the actual founder of East Corinth. The novel follows Lenore as she attempts to resolve a series of personal crises that eventually contribute to the *Bildung* that Wallace referred to when he described *Broom* as a "sensitive little self-obsessed *Bildungsroman*" ("An Expanded" 41). The first and most important of these unfortunate events is the disappearance or "mislocation" of Lenore's grandmother, Lenore Beadsman, Sr., from East Corinth's Shaker Heights Nursing Home, whose administrator, a character by the telling name of *David* Bloemker, offers some of the novel's most thought-provoking observations about the Midwest and its ambivalent relation to the rest of the United States (*Broom* 36). The following quotation is from a conversation between Lenore and Mr. Bloemker about the regional roots of the patients or "residents" of the Shaker Heights facility, which, throughout the novel, is significantly referred to simply as "Home" or "the Home" (34, 74, 99):

> 'They are also Midwesterners,' continued Mr. Bloemker. 'As a rule, almost all of them are Midwesterners.' He stared off. 'This area of the country, what are we to say of this area of the country, Ms. Beadsman?'
> 'Search me.'
> 'Both in the middle and on the fringe. The physical heart, and the cultural extremity. Corn, a steadily waning complex of heavy industry, and sports. What are we to say? We feed and stoke and supply a nation much of which doesn't know we exist. A nation we tend to be decades behind, culturally and intellectually. What are we to say about it?' (141-142)

"Both in the middle and on the fringe" is the phrase that is key to understanding how, at the start of his writing career, Wallace mapped the "*cultural* location" of his Midwestern home and feared the insignificance of its cultural and intellectual contributions to the nation (Quinn 95). The author's reflections on the Midwest's in-betweenness are consistent with a general trend in critical thinking about the Midwest as "the nation's middlescape" and about Midwesterners as "being lost in the middle" (Barillas 4; Barlow and Cantonwine 12). Observations comparable to Mr. Bloemker's can be found in many geographical and socio-cultural studies of the Midwestern region. The historian Jon C. Teaford, for instance, writes that the term "Middle West," besides its topographical denotation, also "implie[s] the dual sense of centrality and isolation characterizing the region" (254). What is more, William Barillas remarks that Midwesterners take pride in identifying as "Americans," which, on the one hand, bespeaks a certain level of confidence, while, on the other hand, it "betrays a weak sense of regional identity" (19). The problem for Wallace, then, revolves around the question of how to define himself when the Midwest he grew up in is itself so hard to define.

Wallace anticipates this problem and, again, voices his concerns through the observations of Mr. Bloemker, who believes that "[t]he Midwest: a place that both is and isn't," makes for "truly bizarre [... and t]roubled people," especially when they grow old and become conscious of themselves as "parts of this strange, occluded place" (*Broom* 142). In the company of Lenore and a rather timid character named Brenda, David Bloemker ponders:

> 'How to begin to come to some understanding of one's place in a system, when one is part of an area that exists in such a troubling relation to the rest of the world, a world that is itself stripped of any static, understandable character by the fact that it changes, radically, all the time?' (143)

To drive his point home, Wallace ends the conversation between Mr. Bloemker and Lenore on a "truly bizarre" note. When Lenore is about to leave, she discovers that the overly quiet Brenda is, in truth, an inflatable doll. Still, Mr. Bloemker insists he had no idea: "I thought she was simply extremely shy. A troubled Midwesterner, in an ambivalent relation ..." (144). A Midwesterner made up out of thin air, Brenda is quite literally a prop that Wallace uses to illustrate, *ad absurdum*, Mr. Bloemker's understanding of a troubled and hard-to-define Midwesternness.

The young Wallace nevertheless attempts to define this Midwesternness primarily by emphasizing that the region's identity and national importance are inextricably linked to the distant past. It is no coincidence that the Midwestern "Home" on which Mr. Bloemker bases many of his observations is a home for the *elderly* and that Mr. Bloemker compares the Midwest to "[m]emories: things that both are and aren't" (142). To this, he adds that the "residents, the people who are very old now, have really made our culture what it is" (143). "They were pioneers," says Mr. Bloemker, yet now they have been reduced to "people in wheelchairs with blanketed laps" (144). But David Bloemker is not the only one who implies that the region has gone old and stale. Rick offers at least two noteworthy descriptions of Cleveland as long past its expiry date, so to speak. Early on, he mentions that he lives in "Cleveland, Ohio, between a *biologically dead* and completely offensive-smelling lake [i.e. Lake Erie] and a billion-dollar man-made desert" (57; italics added). Halfway into the novel, on a return flight from Amherst to Cleveland, Rick can even "sense the closeness of Cleveland" (267). He asks, "Can you smell that? A smell like removing the lid from a pot of something that's been left in one's refrigerator a little too long?" (267-268).

In his emphasis on the Midwest's staleness, the author conforms to established, dismissive views on the area. As Robert Whutnow puts it in his recent socio-cultural study of the Midwest, "[t]hat America's heartland is a thing of the past is a long-standing refrain in treatments of the region" (10). An appropriate case in point is Ronald Weber's treatment or, rather, mistreatment of the region's literary tradition: Weber writes that the Midwest had its "day in the literary sun" long ago, from 1890 to 1930, a period that brought forth such literary greats as Sinclair Lewis, Edgar Lee Masters, and Sherwood Anderson, but "was not particularly long lasting" and did not "run particularly deep" either (3). Wallace appears to agree: the Midwest seems a rather unlikely place to find the culturally new and exciting, let alone the literary voice of the next generation of post-postmodern Americans. A character by the Pynchonesque name of Judith Prieth mockingly asks, "'Who ever heard of a publishing house in Cleveland?'" (51). Even so, the novel also includes characters who are more appreciative of the Midwest, characters such as Neil Obstat, Jr., who speaks the memorable words: "Cleveland gets underrated. You guys in the East forget that significant cultural stuff goes on in the Midwest" (301). Wallace's dismissal of the Midwest could, therefore, just as easily be regarded as his first strategic move toward establishing himself as the region's literary rejuvenator. To use the author's own pithy phrase, the exaggeration of the region's anachronistic character may be his first attempt to find in the Midwest "any *garde* of which to be *avant*" ("Westward" 304).

Yet, the novel's most significant *avant-garde* update to the Midwest comes not in the shape of East Corinth, which, as one of the author's more gimmicky pop-cultural adornments, is built as a large-scale reproduction of Jayne Mansfield's head. Rather, it comes in the form of the vast emptiness embodied in the man-made wasteland of the Great Ohio Desert or, simply, the G.O.D. Exactly how central a place the G.O.D. is supposed to occupy in the novel is illustrated by the fact that *Broom* "had begun, at Amherst, as *The Great Ohio Desert*" (Max 71). Wallace even briefly considered the title, *Three Deserts*, which, as he later explained to his editor, Gerry Howard, referred to "Rick, Lenore, and the G.O.D." (Ibid). The latter of these two working titles implies that the desert's emptiness is both geographical and spiritual or symbolic, even though critics have mostly pointed out the desert's symbolic emptiness. Marshall Boswell, for instance, writes that the desert and Wallace's choice of the acronym G.O.D. "see[m] to be poking fun at what Derrida would call a *logocentric* view of language or [...] 'referent-based signification,'" a view that states that at the heart of any linguistic system lies a stable point or object of reference (34). The G.O.D., Boswell argues, is the novel's "primary symbol for the emptiness of [such] logocentric thinking," and he suggests that Wallace opts for the late-Wittgensteinian alternative that is modelled on community-based contextual signification, which posits that "the meaning of a word is its use in the language" (Boswell 50; Wittgenstein par. 43). Boswell's persuasive argument certainly helps to explain the novel's philosophical overtones. After all, Wallace later described *Broom* to David Lipsky as "a conversation between Wittgenstein and Derrida" (*Although* 35).

But this lingua-philosophical interpretation turns the desert into a space that is "all about the head," a space of intellect that the French thinker Henri Lefebvre classified as a "conceived" space (Wallace, *Although* 35; Lefebvre 39). It provides no explanation for the desert's Midwestern location. By cross-referencing the novel's description of the G.O.D. with three of Wallace's later pieces that are explicitly about the Midwest, it is possible to see how *Broom*'s desert also relates to Wallace's general views on Midwesternness. First, in the upcoming passage, which is taken from a meeting between the governor of Ohio, two of his aides (one of whom is Neil Obstat Jr.), and the vice president of Industrial Desert Design, the governor describes the G.O.D. as follows:

Gentlemen, a desert. A point of savage reference for the good people of Ohio. A place to fear and love. A blasted region. Something to remind us of what we hewed out of. A place without malls. An Other for Ohio's Self. Cacti and scorpions and the sun beating down. Desolation. A place for people to wander alone. To reflect. Away from everything. Gentlemen, a desert. (54)

The governor's emphasis on the site's "desolation" and especially his use of the phrase "away from everything" anticipate Wallace's appropriately named essay, "Getting Away from Already Being Pretty Much Away from It All," first published in *Harper's Magazine* as "Ticket to the Fair" in 1994. In this essay about the 1993 Illinois State Fair, the Midwest is repeatedly described as an "empty, lonely" region, in which "[y]ou can go weeks without seeing a neighbor" ("Getting Away" 84). Wallace adds to this description that "[h]ere you're pretty much Away all the time" (108). In particular, he makes the following observation about his Illinois home, which is remarkably similar to the barren wasteland of the G.O.D.: "Rural Midwesterners live surrounded by unpopulated land, marooned in a space whose emptiness starts to become both physical and spiritual" (91). To make this twofold emptiness abundantly clear, Wallace adds that "[i]t is not just people you get lonely for. You're alienated from the very space around you" (91-92). Just as the G.O.D. is an empty Other to Ohio's Self, so too Midwesterners are alienated from their desolate surroundings.

In *Broom*, this physical and spiritual alienation or Otherness is highlighted by the color of the G.O.D.'s sand: in a white state such as Ohio, says one of the governor's aides, "[w]hat better contrast than a hundred miles of black sand?" (55). But the black sand is also Wallace's geographical marker for the Midwest and, more specifically, the state of Illinois. In Wallace's novella-length story, "Westward the Course of Empire Takes Its Way" (1989), the character J.D. Steelritter describes the Central Illinois landscape as "a flat blanket of soil so verdant and black it is one of the only two things he truly fears" ("Westward" 242). The story is full of such descriptions of the empty Illinois land's "ungentle black edges" and its various "rich black fallow field[s]" (281, 342). Add to this Wallace's description of the Midwest as "blank flatness, black land" in his *Harper's* essay, "Tennis, Trigonometry, Tornadoes," and it is not unreasonable to assume that, in addition to its Otherness, the black sand of the G.O.D. also marks the site's Midwesternness (68). This explains why the governor in *Broom* repeats three times to Neil Obstat, Jr. that the construction of the man-made desert is "going to hit *home*" (54; italics added). In other words, the G.O.D.'s geographical and spiritual emptiness also directly relate to the Lefebvrian "lived" space, that is, the Midwestern home that Wallace and his characters inhabit (Lefebvre 39).

With the governor's plans for the construction of the G.O.D., Wallace combines specific regional concerns with broader philosophical ones. The G.O.D. is located "somewhere in the middle" between the geographical emptiness of Wallace's Midwestern lived space and the symbolic emptiness of the intellectual, conceived space that Boswell points out in his study. The character whose sentiments most clearly gesture toward this combination of symbolic and geographical emptiness is the obese businessman, Norman Bombardini. In his speech about his Project Total Yang, which entails the maximization of his Self and the elimination of the Other by grotesquely overeating and growing to infinite proportions, Mr. Bombardini translates his spiritual loneliness into a geographical or spatial emptiness that he tries to fill with his own corpulent body:

> [W]e each ought to desire our universe to be as *full* as possible[. …T]he Great Horror consists in an empty, rattling personal universe, one where one finds oneself with Self, on one hand, and vast empty lonely spaces before Others begin to enter the picture at all, on the other. A non-full universe. Loneliness. (90)

The link that is established here between "vast empty lonely" geographical spaces and existential dread or alienation illustrates Wallace's first attempt to combine his lived experience of the regional Midwestern landscape with the intellectual, all-American literary theme he called solipsism, a philosophical concept he would only occasionally discuss as a technical term. More often, as is the case in *Broom*, it is simply "evoked as a metaphor for isolation and loneliness" (Ryerson 27).

After having laid the groundwork for these ideas about loneliness in *Broom*, the author would go on to develop them in his subsequent works, as one of his college friends, Mark Costello, observes: "one of the big things he matures to [is] talking about why we can't live alone" ("Endotes" 16:10-16:14). Exactly how central a theme loneliness would become for Wallace is underlined by the author's fellow Midwesterner Jonathan Franzen, who said, in his 2008 memorial speech, that he and Wallace had decided that a "'neutral middle ground on which to make a deep connection with another human being' [...] was what fiction was for. 'A way out of loneliness' was the formulation [they] agreed to agree on" (178). For Wallace, a Midwestern author whose imagined heartland was neither here nor there, but somewhere in the middle; whose feelings about that middle ground were somewhere between love and fear, geographical loneliness and existential dread; and whose regional loyalty and literary ambition required him to establish a strong connection between specific regional concerns and broader national ones, fiction could have hardly had a more fitting purpose.

Works Cited

Barillas, William. *The Midwestern Pastoral: Place and Landscape in Literature of the American Heartland*. Athens: Ohio UP, 2006.

Barlow, Philip and Becky Cantonwine. "Introduction: Not Oz." *Religion and Public Life in the Midwest: America's Common Denominator?*. Eds. Philip Barlow and Mark Silk. Walnut Creek: Altamira Press, 2004. 11-16.

Boswell, Marshall. *Understanding David Foster Wallace*. Columbia, SC: U of South Carolina P, 2003.

Dudar, Helen. "A Whiz Kid and His Whacky First Novel." *Conversations with David Foster Wallace*. Ed. Stephen J. Burn. Jackson: UP of Mississippi, 2012. 8-10.

DeLillo, Don. "Informal Remarks from the David Foster Wallace Memorial Service in New York on October 23, 2008." *The Legacy of David Foster Wallace*. Eds. Samuel Cohen and Lee Konstantinou. Iowa City: U of Iowa P, 2012. 23-24.

"Endnotes: David Foster Wallace." *Sunday Feature*. Host Geoff Ward. BBC Radio 3, London, 6 Feb. 2011. Radio.

Erdrich, Louise. "A Writer's Sense of Place." *A Place of Sense: Essays in Search of the Midwest*. Ed. Michael Martone. Iowa City: U of Iowa P, 1988. 34-44.

Franzen, Jonathan. "Informal Remarks from the David Foster Wallace Memorial Service in New York on October 23, 2008." *The Legacy of David Foster Wallace*. Eds. Samuel Cohen and Lee Konstantinou. Iowa City: U of Iowa P, 2012. 177-181.

Gass, William H. "In the Heart of the Heart of the Country." *In the Heart of the Heart of the Country*. New York, Evanston, San Francisco, and London: Harper & Row, 1968. 172-206.

_____. *Omensetter's Luck*. New York and London: Penguin Books, 1997.

_____. "The Art of Fiction No. 65." Interview by Thomas LeClair. *The Paris Review* 70 (Summer 1977). n.pag. Web. 12 Aug. 2013. <http://www.theparisreview.org/interviews/3576/the-art-of-fiction-no-65-william-gass>.

Giles, Paul. "All Swallowed Up: David Foster Wallace and American Literature." *The Legacy of David Foster Wallace*. Eds. Samuel Cohen and Lee Konstantinou. Iowa City: U of Iowa P, 2012. 3-22.

_____. *Global Remapping of American Literature*. Princeton: Princeton UP, 2011.

_____. "Sentimental Posthumanism: David Foster Wallace." *Twentieth Century Literature* 53.3 (Fall 2007). 327-344.

Harris, Charles B. "David Foster Wallace's Hometown: A Correction." *Critique: Studies in Contemporary Fiction* 51.3 (2010). 185-186.

Lefebvre, Henri. *The Production of Space*. Trans. Donald Nicholson-Smith. Oxford: Blackwell Publishing, 1991.

Max, D.T. *Every Love Story Is a Ghost Story: A Life of David Foster Wallace*. London and New York: Viking, 2012.

Quinn, Paul. "'Location's Location': Placing David Foster Wallace." *A Companion to David Foster Wallace Studies*. Eds. Marshall Boswell and Stephen J. Burn. Basingstoke: Palgrave Macmillan, 2013. 87-106.

Ryerson, James. Introduction. *Fate, Time, and Language: An Essay on Free Will*. By David Foster Wallace. Eds. Steven M. Cahn and Maureen Eckert. New York: Columbia UP, 2011. 1-36.

Teaford, Jon C. *Cities of the Heartland: The Rise and Fall of the Industrial Midwest*. Bloomington, IN: Indiana UP, 1993.

Wallace, David Foster. *Although Of Course You End Up Becoming Yourself: A Road Trip with David Foster Wallace*. By David Lipsky. New York: Broadway Books, 2010.

_____. "An Expanded Interview with David Foster Wallace." By Larry McCaffery. *Conversations with David Foster Wallace*. Ed. Stephen J. Burn. Jackson: UP of Mississippi, 2012. 21-52.

_____. "Authority and American Usage." *Consider the Lobster and Other Essays*. London: Abacus, 2009. 66-127.

_____. "Brief Interview with a Five Draft Man." *Amherst Magazine* (Spring 1999). Web. 17 Aug. 2013. <https://www.amherst.edu/aboutamherst/magazine/extra/node/66410>.

_____. "E Unibus Pluram: Television and U.S. Fiction." *A Supposedly Fun Thing I'll Never Do Again: Essays and Arguments*. London: Abacus, 1997. 21-82.

_____. "Getting Away from Already Being Pretty Much Away from It All." *A Supposedly Fun Thing I'll Never Do Again: Essays and Arguments*. London: Abacus, 1997. 83-137.

_____. "Tennis, Trigonometry, Tornadoes: A Midwestern Boyhood." *Harper's Magazine* (Dec. 1991). 68-78.

_____. *The Broom of the System*. London: Abacus, 1997.

_____. "Westward the Course of Empire Takes Its Way." *Girl with Curious Hair*. London: Abacus, 1997. 231-373.

Weber, Ronald. *The Midwestern Ascendancy in American Writing*. Bloomington and Indianapolis: Indiana UP, 1992.

Whutnow, Robert. *Remaking the Heartland: Middle America since the 1950s*. Princeton and Oxford: Princeton UP, 2011.

Wittgenstein, Ludwig. *Philosophical Investigations*. Trans. G. E. M. Anscombe. 2nd ed. Oxford: Blackwell, 1958.

Yeats, William Butler. "Sailing To Byzantium." *Poetry X*. Ed. Jough Dempsey. 14 Nov 2003. Web. 28 Sep. 2013. <http://poetry.poetryx.com/poems/1575/>.

Performing Africa in the American Midwest: Memories of Africa in Toni Morrison's *Beloved* and *Song of Solomon* _____

Maureen Eke

"Abiku: 'Wanderer child. It is the same child who dies and returns again and again to plague the mother.' " (Wole Soyinka, *Idanre and Other Poems*[1])

Africa as reality, myth, or historical ancestral home figures in the works of African Diaspora writers from Olaudah Equiano's *The Interesting Narrative of the Life of Olaudah Equiano the Africa*, to Venture Smith's *A Narrative of the Life and Adventures of Venture, A Native of Africa*, Phillis Wheatley's poem "On Being Brought from Africa to America," Paule Marshall's *Praisesong for the Widow*, and Virginia Hamilton's *The People Could Fly*, to mention a few. Like these writers, Toni Morrison invokes "memories" of Africa in two of her narratives, *Song of Solomon* (1977) and *Beloved* (1988). She calls upon these memories—whether they involve historical reality or place, the Middle Passage, or folklore—and brings them together as part of an African diasporic imagination. I propose that in these novels, Africa (not only as place, but also imaginatively and through its cultural practices, memorialization, and history) is negotiated and recast or reconstructed in what I call a "performance of memories" of Africa.[2] Thus, by examining such performance in these novels set in the American Midwest, Morrison recuperates a collective "Africanness" or blackness in the Midwest.[3] I use the word "performance" broadly in this essay to refer to any act that signifies the participatory nature of experience and/or the presence of an audience, either real or imagined. In fact, Morrison has stated that her works are participatory and that meaning is achieved through "the participation of the reader and the chorus" (Morrison 2289).

In her essay "Rootedness: The Ancestors as Foundation," Morrison states that in her works, "there has always a choral note"

(2288) and this can be "the 'I' narrator of *The Bluest Eye*," the "town" in *Sula*, or the "community" in *Song of Solomon* (2288). For Morrison, these features mark her work as "Black, because it uses the characteristics of Black Art" (2288). Indeed, Morrison's deployment of elements or memories of an African (black) cultural and artistic presence in her works is itself a performance because of the participation of her readers, an observant audience, chorus, or community. As such, her novels can be seen as double, if not multiple, performances, since several characters in these novels engage in various levels of performance. In particular, this essay will explore Morrison's re-figuration of Africa through the deployment of oral and folkloric narrative strategies, African spiritual beliefs, myths, and cultural practices. In *Song of Solomon*, the focus is primarily on the sections that are associated with the Midwest.[4]

In her essay, "Home", Morrison asserts that the "forced transfers" of Africans to the new world is the "defining event of the modern world" (qtd.in Zauditu-Selassie 1). Indeed, the journey of millions of Africans to the Americas is important not only because their survival as Zauditu-Selassie claims "represents a journey of remarkable resiliency" (1), but also because such survival through the cultural productions of the group would alter the nature of new world cultures. Zauditu-Selassie also suggests that for diasporan Africans, the endurance of their culture in the new world "became a way to physically survive" (1). Scholars such as Lorenzo Turner and Joseph Holloway have provided strong scholarship that supports the endurance of African cultural elements in the Americas. In his book *Africanism in America*, Joseph Holloway cites various studies, including those by Lorenzo Turner and W.E.B. DuBois, which point to African retentions or "carryovers in American society" (x). Holloway also indicates that Carter G. Woodson, for instance, listed "several major African survivals—technical skills, arts, folklore, spirituality, attitudes toward authority, a tradition of generosity— and called attention to African influences in religion, music, dance, drama, poetry, and oratory" (xi). Indeed, oral folk art, such as African work songs and folk musical structures, including slaps, clapping, call-and-response, and hollers, inform African American music from the spirituals to the blues, rap, spoken word, soul, hip-hop, and rap. Documentary evidence in the film *The Language You Cry In* (1998) establishes linguistic, cultural, and historical connections between Gullah people of the Georgia and South Carolina coasts and the Mende of Sierra Leone, dating back to the eighteenth century.[5] African language, musical, and spiritual influences are traceable too in other art forms and cultural practices of the Americas. Morrison is a product of this rich cultural tradition, and her works also help to sustain these continuities or presences.

In her novels *Beloved* and *Song of Solomon*, Toni Morrison recreates various aspects of African cultural practices, these memories of Africa, especially its orature and spirituality through several performances. In *Beloved*, for example, these performances include Baby Suggs' laying of hand (88-89); the collective expiation, or making amends, at the end of the book, when the community comes to help Sethe; communal cleansing through singing, chanting, or invocation of the spirit (ancestors) and healing at the end of the book; ancestor worship and reincarnation, symbolized by Beloved, whom Sethe believes is (an *abiku* or *ogbanje*), the physical embodiment of the spirit of her dead "crawling-already" child returned to visit her; and Beloved's recasting or retelling of the traumatic memory of the Middle Passage as Morrison narrates the effects of slavery on African American psyche. In *Song of Solomon*, Morrison recuperates the West African tradition of *griot*, or male oral historian, in the figure of Pilate, who sings to heal the sick and dying or tells Milkman the story of his ancestry, thus, setting him on his quest of self-(re) discovery. In addition, the myth of the flying Africans is a central element in the novel, which Morrison invokes at the beginning of the novel and which Milkman interprets as an important component of his ancestral narrative. The myth also reconnects this novel to a large African and Black literary and cultural tradition.

Like a West African *griotte*, praise singer, or Zulu *imbongi* (praise poet), Morrison draws on African orature, deploying narrative elements such as calls, shouts, repetitions (talk-think— *iche-uche* in *Beloved* 38) to create stories that address individual and collective anxieties and experiences. Multiple literary influences inform Morrison's works and the diversity of African cultures, as well as the danger of homogenizing Africa. But, in this essay, Gay Wilentz's contention that the use of a "collective term," like African, is possible because of the "intermingling of cultures from west and central Africa during the slave trade" (qtd. in Jennings 1) will become the central focus.

The essay, therefore, explores Morrison's reconstruction, or reimagining, of a collective African presence in *Beloved* and *Song of Solomon* as a performance of memories, sometimes incomplete, sometimes reconstituted or recuperated from a (submerged) past through story-telling, songs, myths, incantations, and other elements. An example of such performance occurs in *Beloved*, when Sethe attempts to describe or explain "rememory" to Denver. In response to Denver's question, "'Can other people see it [rememory]?'" Sethe says, "'Oh, yes. Oh, yes, yes, yes. Someday you be walking down the road and you hear something or see something going on. So clear. And you think it's you thinking it up. A thought picture. But no. it's when you bump into a rememory that belongs to somebody else'" (36). Sethe's description here is performative, an act of storytelling, signaled by the phrase "someday," as if to mark the beginning of the story, which she tries, but fails to tell Denver. The latter's anticipation of her mother's divulging of the secret of Sethe's past is articulated in Denver's subsequent comments: "'You never told me all what happened. Just that they whipped you and you run off, pregnant. With me'" (36). But, the performance is ruptured by Sethe's hesitation or reluctance to share her past. The orality of the performance is underscored by Sethe's repetitions or stuttering: "'Oh, yes. Oh, yes, yes, yes'" and "'you think it's you thinking it up'" (igbo *iche-uche*: "thinking thinking" or "thinking thought") as if the speaker were engaged in a double thinking. Also, Sethe's notion of "'bump[ing] into a rememory'" (36) underscores the orality of Morrison's novel.

Giving Voice: Invoking the *Griotte*, Invoking the Ancestors
As stated earlier, in the tradition of the West African *griottes* and Zulu *imbongis*, Morrison invokes African ancestors and spirits

by returning to the storehouse of memory, to the past as source. Consciously or unconsciously, she excavates various African myths and narrative practices and structuresto reconfigure the past. In her essay, "Memory, Creation, and Writing," she underscores the centrality of black identity in her literature. "I simply wanted to write literature that was irrevocably, indisputably Black, not because its characters were, or because I was, but because it took as its creative task and sought as its credentials those recognized and verifiable principles of Black Art" (qtd. Zauditu-Selassie 4). Zauditu-Selassie suggests that "these verifiable principles" "correspond to a compendium of culturally constructed deliberations imagined, sculpted, and fashioned from the shared memory of spiritual culture" (2). But, while Zauditu-Selassie limits these principles to "spiritual culture," it seems that Morrison's "black" credentials extend beyond spirituality to include the larger body of African narrative and artistic strategies, cultural practices, histories, and experiences, all of which inform and are sometimes foregrounded in her works.

In *Song of Solomon* for instance, Mr. Smith's flight from the roof of Mercy Hospital into communal history is accompanied by a singing voice, which acts as if it were conjuring up Smith's action or consciousness into existence. The singing woman serves as *griotte*, or praise singer, a living ancestor guardian, even a blues singer, whose voice accompanies Mr. Smith's action from its beginning to its end. According to Morrison, the singing woman (Pilate), "[h]er head cocked to one side, her eyes fixed on Mr. Robert Smith, … sang in a powerful contralto:"

O Sugarman done fly away
O Sugarman done gone
Sugarman cut across the sky
Sugarman gone home. . . . (6)

Call this a praise song, dirge, blues, or sorrow song. It had several effects, including providing a brief distraction for the gathering crowd; soothing Mrs. Smith (who must jump in the midst of the crowd's nervousness), and announcing Milkman's birth, for Ruth goes into labor during this incident. In fact, Morrison presents two parallel stories in this moment—one in which a life is lost or threatened, that is, Mr. Smith's, and the other in which life is renewed, that is, the (re)birth of Ruth and her baby, Milkman. Morrison seems to suggest that only the singing woman, a prescient Pilate, gifted with alternative vision, noticed Ruth's labor pains, for "[t]he singing woman quieted down and, humming the tune walked through the crowd toward the rose-petal lady, who was still cradling her stomach" (9). Then, the singing woman whispered to the "rose-petal lady:" "'[y]ou should make yourself warm'. . . touching her lightly on the elbow. 'A little bird'll be here with the morning'" (9). Within an African cosmology, it would not be inconceivable to read the two events as spiritually linked. Here, the supernatural and the real merge and Pilate, or the singing woman, protects both. In this case, Ruth's son, born the day after Mr. Smith's incident would represent a returned ancestor. The Yoruba of Nigeria would have called him *Babatunde* (father has returned) were he to be related to the dying Mr. Smith.

But, the filial connections may not be as important as the spiritual and racial/communal connections Morrison finds between the two incidents. Did Mr. Smith's spirit reincarnate as the newborn little boy, who "at four" would learn "the same thing Mr. Smith had learned earlier—that only birds and airplanes could fly..." (9)? Both events are connected temporally, spatially, and through the singing woman (Pilate), who seems to conduct the two lives to their destination. As Morrison states, "Pilate is the ancestor" (Morrison 2289), and she provides a balance in the novel and in the lives of the characters, guarding the past, present, and future. She is "a natural healer," who could "[mediate] a peace that lasted a good bit longer than it should have" (*Song of Solomon* 150). It is Pilate, who gave birth to herself, who carries (symbolically and literally) the past memories of her family and people, carrying her father's bones, who is mentored by her father through dreams, who transmits knowledge about her family to Milkman, initiating his search for his roots. It is also Pilate who shields Milkman even before his birth and with her life when it is threatened later by Guitar. Truly, within an African cultural context and for Morrison as well as the people in Pilate's community, Pilate is the living ancestor, the protector of their memories and their voices and the link to their past, present, and future.

Without Mother (or) Tongue

Language serves as a medium for communicating cultural knowledge and history and plays a role in identity construction. As a storyteller, Morrison weaves a narrative of cultural loss represented by the loss of the tongue, the inability to speak, and really, the loss of language or trauma. Sethe, in Morrison's *Beloved*, is constantly confronted with moments of speechlessness, moments when her tongue is stuck, and she seems to lose control of her body. For instance, when she first sees the face of the adult Beloved, Sethe's body experiences shock and her "bladder filled to capacity" and she "void[ed]" "endless" water in front of the door of the outhouse (51). As a child, Sethe's loss of her tongue signifies a symbolic displacement, her loss of community or her un-rootedness. In other words, it symbolizes her inability to communicate in the language of her mother. Sethe has no mother tongue because she did not inherit one from her mother and what she had learnt from Nan, she has forgotten. As such, Sethe is unable to transmit the story of her people effectively within this Midwestern landscape; she cannot recreate or reproduce her past or Africa effectively. Indeed, Sethe communicates little about her mother or her people before Sweet Home. In a painful but poignant moment of reflection, Sethe recalls her maternal history, and only briefly, tells Denver about her experience of disconnection, loss, shame and unbelonging. She recalls her desire to belong to a community: "'but how will you know me? How will you know me?'" she asked her Maam, pleading, "'Mark me too . . . Mark the mark on me too'" (61). As a child, Sethe felt she did not belong because she did not carry the physical scar of Trans-Atlantic slavery. Although her mother is branded with what appears to be a cross or circle, indicating that she is claimed by another, the child Sethe reads this mark as representative of her belonging to a people. The irony of the accuracy of Sethe's interpretation is powerful, for the mark, indeed, brands her mother with a unique identity—slave—associated with a group, whose members have died, leaving her as its sole survivor. Thus, for Ma'am, the mark represents an insignia by which Sethe can recognize her. Although the young Sethe felt betrayed and severed from community, she did belong to one, for she was claimed by Nan, who taught her the language of her people, giving her a mother tongue, which the adult Sethe has lost.

Like Pilate in *Song of Solomon*, Nan serves as the bridge between Sethe and her African ancestors. She is the *griotte*, a living ancestor, a guardian of both the past and Sethe's present. In teaching her the language of Africans and telling her the story of her mother, Nan inducts Sethe into her community, sharing the story of the Middle Passage with her. Again Morrison writes:

> Nan was the one she knew best, who was around all day, who nursed babies, cooked...And who used different words. Words Sethe understood then but could neither recall nor repeat now...What Nan told her she had forgotten, along with the language she told it in. The same language her ma'am spoke, and which would never come back. But the message—that was and had been there all along. (62)

In her act of rememory, Sethe tries to pick "meaning out of a code she no longer understood" (62) and all she could recall is Nan's instructions: "'Telling you. I am telling you, small girl Sethe'" (62). In this telling, Nan reconstructs the violence of slavery writ on the bodies of black women: "She told Sethe that her mother and Nan were together from the sea. Both were taken up many times by the crew" (62). But, Sethe's Ma'am claimed agency by rejecting the products of such violence, refusing to mother them and throwing them "away on the island" (62). She kept and named only one: Sethe, her child with a black man because "[she] put her arms around him" (62).

Whereas Sethe is reluctant to speak her own story or that of her mother or that of those lost at sea, Morrison incorporates these stories in a layered narrative rendered through what seems to be the consciousness of Beloved. "I am Beloved and she is mine. . .

she was about to smile at me when the men without skin came and took us up into the sunlight with the dead and shoved them into the sea" (214), the narrative begins, as if engaged in total recall. It also repeats part of the story Nan told Sethe. Then, in a trancelike chant, the narrative voice recounts the story of slavery from the Middle Passage to Beloved's presence. The latter section of the recall is then rendered like a conversation between two parties, transforming it into a performance of "hurts" whose naming dislodges the wounds of their potency:

> Tell me the truth. Didn't you come from the other side?
> Yes. I was on the other side.
> You came back because of me?
> Yes.
> You rememory me?
> Yes. I remember you.
> . . . .
> If they put an iron circle around your neck I will bite it away. (215)

In this performance, too, Morrison reconstructs the familiar call-and-response, generally associated with African (black) oral and folk performance traditions and found in cultural practices from folktales to the African American spirituals, blues, soul, gospel, rap and other performance forms. Although the narrative appears as if it were the garbled thoughts of one consciousness, it is, however, layered, a collage of various voices, rearticulated through a traumatized consciousness, which repeats the story of the wounding. While the narrative consciousness may be unclear, or seems to be Beloved's, the language succeeds in communicating the power of the act, the rememory, which culminates in a conscious assertion of ownership: "you are mine. You are mine. You are mine" (217). Here, Morrison returns to African, specifically, Yoruba and Igbo spiritual beliefs to draw upon the idea of the *abiku* or *ogbanje* to reenact the continuous return of the spirit child who persists in tormenting its mother, by returning again and again to claim her. As *abiku*, or the returned spirit of the dead child, Beloved carries with her the anger and knowledge of a traumatic past, which she, her mother, and other people cannot understand completely and cannot ignore or forget. In so doing, Morrison uses her *abiku* or *ogbanje* child to perform speech, saying those things, which were and are often unspoken.

The repetition of the language reinforces the repetition of return and of experience, as well as of the acts of horror. Here, the *abiku* may not necessarily be malevolent, but functions as the voice of trauma, a conduit for transmitting the past painful knowledge, to "pass on" information, to tell a story that is still inaccessible to the living or those who experienced the trauma. As Cathy Caruth claims, trauma "is always the story of a wound that cries out, that addresses us in the attempt to tell us of a reality or truth that is not otherwise available" (4). Caruth adds, "This truth, in its delayed appearance and its belated address, cannot be linked only to what is known, but also to what remains unknown in our very actions and our language" (4). Beloved as *abiku* or *ogbanje* and speaking voice(s) embodies both the wounded consciousness and scarred body of the African diasporic personhood.

According to many African cosmologies, including the Yoruba and Igbo cosmologies, which inform my interpretation of the *abiku* or *ogbanje*, the universe consists of three inseparable worlds: the perceptible, physical world of the living; the imperceptible spiritual world of the dead, spirits, and ancestors; and a third sphere—the world of the unborn, the future, which is generally unknowable, except by certain gifted individuals. The *abiku* or *ogbanje* straddles two worlds, inhabiting the world of spirits, but crossing temporal space to affect the world of the living. It is often believed that the *abiku* or *ogbanje* travels to the world of the living to share information, only to return to its locale of habitation (the world of the dead ancestors) before the age of two. As such, the *abiku* or *ogbanje* may not always be a threatening spirit or energy.

That Morrison's character Beloved is an *abiku* or *ogbanje* is evident by the nature of the memory she carries. Her consciousness represents the collective consciousness of the race, invoking the memory of the trauma of slavery. All are wounded in Beloved's consciousness—loved, lost, wounded. Therefore, it is no wonder that the community reads her as a threat, as a kind of evil that must be exorcized. In fact, La Vinia Delois Jennings suggests that "the fully grown, fleshed Beloved passes from a being akin to the Ibo Ogbanje or the Yoruba abiku, a spirit-child who reincarnates in human form to be with its mother, to dual manifestations of Dahomean/Haitian Erzulie, the loa of boundless emotion and ambivalent sexual morality; to the morrlay evil Kongo nodki kia dia, soul/psyche-eating witch" (62-63). She adds that Morrison's text "discursively draws a demarcation between the spirit of the crawling-already? girl and Beloved, the incarnated flesh-consuming ndoki whose hunger for Sethe's undivided attention and love is insatiable" (63). Whether or not Beloved is a witch is debatable. But, if read as witch, Beloved also threatens the survival of her siblings: Buglar and Howard, who flee to preserve themselves from her anger. She also threatens Paul D's manhood and survival by seducing him into a sexual liaison.

Still, I want to underscore an alternative reading of *Beloved* as a conduit, Morrison's attempt to recuperate a traumatic memory, to say that which has been covered or rendered "unspeakable" and unrepresentable. Besides, as a metaphor for the memory of a traumatic past, Beloved carries the significations of that past into the present. In the section quoted above, where Beloved interrogates her mother, it is the child-like Beloved whose consciousness seems to articulate the trauma of the Middle Passage or of slavery in general. She speaks the "traumatic experience" as an act of "bearing witness to some forgotten wound" (Caruth 5). In this act, therefore, Beloved helps Sethe and us, all those who read the text, to uncover, recover, and perhaps confront a buried painful past or memory. Such an act is not always negative, but sometimes, restorative, even healing.

Indeed, both Beloved and Sethe experience anguish, stemming from the anguish of bearing witness to an experience that cannot easily be represented or recaptured linguistically. Because language fails, the representation of these moments is marked by repetition and disorientation: Sethe is disoriented after her mother reveals her mark to her; Paul D is unable to speak about his treatment in the hands of School Teacher or in prison. Instead, he sings. Paul D tells Sethe how Halle shut down after witnessing his wife's molestation by School Teacher and his boys. In fact, Morrison presents the exchange between Paul D and Sethe in this section, like a call-n-response banter or a frenzied exchange between the two (68, 69).

A Laying of Hands

While *Beloved*'s function may be to restore memory, to reinvoke the past so that it may not be forgotten, Morrison's narrative seems to suggest the possibility of healing, through the gentle touch of another, as when Sethe places her hands on Paul D's knees to calm him after they share their experiences (68). Perhaps, it is only through the collective strength of the community. If the *abiku* returns to wound the body again with past traumatic scars, so as to force it to remember, Baby Suggs heals the body of those scars through a "laying of hands." In the woods of their resettled home in Ohio, Baby Suggs serves as an African shaman, a healer, who attempts to nurture the abused black (African) bodies and spirits back to health. According to Morrison, Baby Suggs accepted:

> no title of honor before her name, but allowing a small caress after it . . . became an unchurched preacher, one who visited pulpits and opened her great heart to those who could use it. In the winter and fall she carried it to AME's and Baptisits, Holinesses and Sanctifieds, the Church of the Redeemer and the Redeemed. Uncalled, unrobed, unanointed, she let her great heart beat in their presence. (87)

But Baby Suggs' work did not end at the churches; it is rather through the woodland healing of the community that Morrison would immortalize her. As if responding to a calling and to a place mapped out for her even before anyone could remember, Baby Suggs led her people through the woods to a place of healing, "the Clearing—a wide open place cut deep in the woods nobody know for what at the end of a path known only to deer and whoever cleared the land in the first place" (87). Like an ancestor, she watched and waited for her people. "In the heat of every Saturday afternoon, she sat in the clearing while the people waited among the trees" (87), Morrison writes. In this sacred space, Baby Suggs restored her people's humanity through the laying of hands. Here, she helped them to reclaim love, to love themselves and one another. Here, they claimed agency, which was denied them by slavery. Morrison's description is life-reinforcing: "After situating herself on a huge flat-sided rock, Baby Suggs bowed her head and prayed silently. The company watched her from the trees. They knew she was ready when she put her stick down. Then, she shouted, 'Let the children come!' and they ran from the trees toward her" (87). As healer, preacher, spiritual guide, Baby Suggs guided her people's recuperation from the trauma of slavery.

Like Baby Suggs, Pilate in *Song of Solomon* heals the wounded. Not only does she protect Milkman even before his birth, helping his mother (in labor pains during Mr. Smith's flight), but also, she attempts to nurture the broken hearted and sick Hagar, her granddaughter, back to health. Like Baby Suggs in the wilderness clearing, Pilate offers Hagar her personhood, reclaiming her body, even as Hagar insists that Milkman hates it. 'He loves silky hair' (314), she tells the ailing Hagar. Pilate's words are restorative as she reclaims Hagar's body, each body part at a time, in a lullaby-like chant: "'Penny-colored hair'... 'And lemon-colored skin.'... 'And gray-blue eyes.'... 'Hush. Hush. Hush, girl. Hush'" (316 – 317). Her act of spiritual recovery and protection culminates in the dirge that she performs besides Hagar's coffin. Placing three fingers "on the edge of the coffin," Morrison writes, Pilate "addressed her words to the woman bordered in gray satin who lay before her. Softly, privately, she sang to Hagar the very same reassurance she had promised her when she was a little girl" (319). Pilate's three-verse dirge, a performance of love and separation, is protective, asking *"Who's been bothering my sweet sugar lumpkin?"* and, then threatening, *"I'll find who's bothering my sweet sugar lumpkin"* (318). Her closing act at the funeral simultaneously claims and celebrates Hagar, ending with a proclamation: "And she was *loved!*" (319).

Again, Morrison deploys song as an aspect of language to convey narrative and to underscore character, particularly Pilate as the *griotte*, ancestor, healer, and blues singer. As in the opening event, where Pilate's singing guided Mr. Smith through transitional space (between the living and the ancestors), Pilate's singing at Hagar's funeral guides her granddaughter's spirit into the place of the dead ancestors. Later, in the novel, Milkman recognizes and reconnects lost pieces of his ancestral story. He finally comes to understand his past when he travels to the south and hears the song that Shalimar's children sing about the flying African. Thus, the song is restorative—a mechanism for healing identity. That recuperative feature is repeated towards the end of the novel as Pilate lies dying. In her final moment, she returns to song, asking Milkman "'Sing,'...'Sing a little something for me'" (337).

Closing

As a novelist, Toni Morrison also functions as a *griotte*, a raconteur, relaying and reconnecting the various tales about Africans from the old and the new world. The two novels examined in this essay underscore Morrison's artistic dexterity and effort to recover through her works the "'discredited knowledge' that Black people had" (Morrison 2288), the buried memories of Africa, of blackness, Sethe's lost mother tongue, the meaning of Shalimar's song, and the denied voices of the village or community. Indeed, Morrison's works form part of a larger performance of the memories of African survival and self-articulation in the new world.

Notes

1. Yoruba *abiku* or Igbo *ogbanje* is the restless spirit of a dead child who reincarnates several times to the same mother, often, to torment the mother. Generally, ritual offerings and prayers are made in order to hold the child in the world of the living.

2. This paper grows out of a long interest in the African presence in Toni Morrison's works, beginning with my reading of *The Bluest Eye*, then, *Song of Solomon* and *Beloved* in the mid-1980s. A series of conversations with several African Diaspora sisters, who shared a love for Morrison has sustained my interest over the years. In 2010, I presented an early version of this paper at "The Sixth Biennial Conference, "Toni Morrison and Circuits of the Imagination" in Paris, France. Two books examining some aspect of an African presence in Toni Morrison's works have appeared since my initial interest. See La Vinia Deloise Jennings' *Toni Morrison and the Idea*

of Africa (2008) and K. Zauditu-Selassie's *African Spiritual Traditions in the Novels of Toni Morrison* (2009).

3.   *Beloved* and *Song of Solomon* are set in the American Midwest. While *Beloved* is set somewhere near Cincinnati, Ohio, *Song of Solomon* begins in a city in Michigan that some have described as Detroit.

4.   While *Beloved* is set primarily in Ohio, Song *of Solomon* begins in Michigan and travels to the South as Milkman undertakes a quest to unravel the story of his ancestry. Although the performance of Africa spans the entire novel, the scope of this volume limits my analysis to those sections that are set in the Midwest.

5.   In the 1930s and 1940s, Lorenzo Turner conducted extensive research documenting Africanism in American speech, especially among the Gullah. See Turner *Africanisms in Gullah* (149), Holloway's "Introduction" in *Africanisms in American Culture* (1991). See the film *Daughters of the Dust* (1991), which explores the African presence in the Gullah culture of the Sea Islands. See also *The Language You Cry In* (1998), which traces, through language and song, the cultural connections between the Gullah off coastal Georgia and South Carolina and the Mende of Sierra Leone at http://newsreel.org.

Works Cited

Caruth, Cathy. *Unclaimed Experience: Trauma, Narrative, and History*. Baltimore and London: The Johns Hopkins UP, 1996.

Holloway, Joseph E. *Africanisms in American Culture*. Bloomington: Indiana U P, 1990, 1991: ix–xxi.

Jennings, La Vinia Delois. *Toni Morrison and the Idea of Africa*. Cambridge, Cambridge UP, 2008.

Morrison, Toni. *Beloved*. New York: Penguin, 1988.

_____. "Rootedness: The Ancestors as Foundation." The *Norton Anthology of African American Literature*. Eds. Henry Louis Gates, Jr. and Nellie Y. McKay. 2nd ed. New York: W. W. Norton, 2004: 2286 – 2290.

_____. *Song of Solomon*. New York, 1977.

Soyinka, Wole. *Idanre and Other Poems*. London: Eyre Methuen Ltd.,1967, 1969.

Zauditu-Selassie, K. *African Spiritual Traditions in the Novels of Toni Morrison*. Gainesville: U of Florida P., 2009.

It's Heaven: Sports Literature and Iowa's Pastoral Image _____

One of the most admired novels about baseball, W. P. Kinsella's 1982 book *Shoeless Joe*, is set in Iowa, a small state with no major-league sport franchises. Although this setting may seem odd, it was, of course, a deliberate choice. The novel began in 1980 as a short story, "Shoeless Joe Jackson Comes to Iowa", and, by his own admission, Kinsella, a Canadian native, first began writing about baseball as a resident of Iowa City (Horvath and Palmer 184), suggesting a conscious union of subject matter and place. Hugely popular in its own right, *Shoeless Joe* is known by millions of viewers through its 1989 film version, *Field of Dreams*, in which a lush cornfield appears to dramatic effect. So beloved was the film that it made a tourist destination out of Dyersville, Iowa, where it was shot. Kinsella's fable and the notion of a "Field of Dreams" have cemented in the popular imagination the utopian confluence of cornfields and baseball, so much so that any baseball fiction set in Iowa now likely presupposes a mythic view of the sport. This very particular setting, furthermore, is arguably a significant reason for the continuing popularity of both *Shoeless Joe* and *Field of Dreams* in that a story about the most pastoral of American sports takes place in America's most pastoral state.

As James R. Shortridge demonstrates, the Midwest has long been connected to the pastoral myth in the American imagination, a linking of region and mythology that "came to symbolize Arcadian idealism" (7). Midwestern pastoralism is embraced inside and outside the region. The debt that writers from the Midwest, for instance, owe to the Romantic, pastoral literary tradition is admirably explored by William Barillas. Furthermore, among Midwestern states, Iowa is perceived throughout the nation as the most endearingly rustic, the "heart" of the heartland, a place whose "rural image stays intact right up to the present time" (Shortridge 100). A state with a significant

124   Critical Insights

agricultural economy, even its largest city, Des Moines, epitomizes the "modern-day Middle-western 'capital'" through its "smaller size" than other cities in the region (Shortridge 104). Iowa's pastoral image is so widely accepted that it can tempt hard-data researchers into expressions of sentiment, as when the authors of the *Atlas of American Sport* succumb to rural idealization in their reference to "bucolic Shenandoah, Iowa" (Rooney 3).

Baseball also draws heavily from the pastoral tradition. In America, baseball is both idol and idyll. It is worshipped as "America's pastime," as a "game" played in "parks" by "the boys of summer." In big cities, these parks offer the respite of the country to weary urban dwellers. From the air, the most recognizable landscape in America is the baseball "diamond" with all of its suggestions of acquired value. More than any other American sport, baseball conjures in fans a desire for wholesomeness, a purity that requires vigilant protection from contaminants such as gambling and steroids. Baseball is America's pastoral fantasy, with ballplayers in place of shepherds. Given this vision, it is no wonder that Kinsella chose to set *Shoeless Joe* – and a second novel, *The Iowa Baseball Confederacy* (1986) – where he did.[1]

Naturally enough, as a novel ripe with magic realism and spiritual yearning, *Shoeless Joe* is enamored more with the idea of Iowa than with the actual place. The novel's narrator, Ray Kinsella, was born in Chicago and moved to Iowa to attend college. There, he marries a local young woman, Annie, and rents a farm. Farming for Ray represents an escape from the economic rat race, from having to sell insurance, and he tells us that he runs his farm "with pride and relief and joy" (10). In one of the novel's memorable lines, Ray insists that he loves Iowa: "I count the loves in my life: Annie, Karin, Iowa, Baseball. The great god Baseball" (6). After hearing a god-like voice, Ray builds a baseball field on his property, and the ghost of Shoeless Joe Jackson comes to play. In another memorable exchange, one that also appears in the film version, Shoeless Joe says to Ray "This must be heaven." To which Ray responds: "No. It's Iowa" (16).

Iowa is associated with love, baseball, freedom from the corporate world, faith. The state is part of Kinsella's evocative symbolism of rebirth and spiritual renewal, of second chances and second comings. Ray, the reader discovers, was born in April, which is of course when major league baseball seasons used to begin, a connection made clear when Ray says, "My birthstone is a diamond" (6). Iowa is also "a precious land" (5), as a series of gentle images makes clear:

> I knelt [in my garden], the soil cool on my knees...Suddenly I thrust my hands wrist-deep into the snuffy-black earth. The air was pure. All around me the clean smell of earth and water. Keeping my hands buried I stirred the earth with my fingers and I knew I loved Iowa as much as a man could love a piece of earth. (14)

On his farm, Ray plants corn – a member of the grass family; on his ball-field, he lovingly plants grass – Walt Whitman's powerful transcendental symbol.

Non-natural Iowa, however, disappoints narrator Ray Kinsella and, presumably, author W. P. Kinsella who has been praised for blending "real and fictional characters in ways that defy the mundane and day-to-day" (Anderson 9). For Kinsella the author, among the major American sports, baseball is best suited for the creation of "larger than life characters, for mythology" (Horvath and Palmer 188). And for all writers, Kinsella derides literary realism: "*Anyone* with basic skills can write documentary realism. Sport realism is boring; the good authors of sport literature realize that and rise above it, often way above it" (Horvath and Palmer 191). W. P. Kinsella is not interested, then, in baseball, as it is actually played, or in Iowa life, as it is truly lived, and despite insisting that he loves Iowa, Ray Kinsella thinks very little of the characters around him. Annie is an exception; a younger woman, almost always dressed sexily in plain work clothes, she supports Ray's wild actions with complete confidence. Other Iowa characters come in for less positive treatment. Annie's family are described as moralistic, "thickset peasants with red faces" (5). Her mother wears "silver-rimmed glasses flashing glints of disapproval at everything in sight" (23). Her brother is an avaricious "professor at the University of Iowa in nearby Iowa City. His area of expertise is the corn weevil" (24). In Des Moines, a city where "[g]rit crunches underfoot on the unswept sidewalks [and] [u]nshaven men with sunken eyes dog my steps," Ray buys a handgun to prepare for a kidnapping of J. D. Salinger (32). Even the retired farmer who plants Ray's corn, Chesty Seidlinger, cannot "truly understand" Ray and his baseball field. He, too, is censorious as he "penguins off toward his pickup truck, his back stiff with disapproval" (35). These portrayals convey a dislike for a state "where 50,000 people go to see the University of Iowa Hawkeyes football team while 500 regulars, including me, watch the baseball team perform" (6).

The novel's negative characterizations notwithstanding, real Iowans have embraced *Shoeless Joe* and *Field of Dreams*. The Web page for *The Field of Dreams Movie Site*© features an illustration of bushy corn and a deep green baseball diamond, with a photograph of the stately white farm house in the background. The movie's tag line, "If you build it, they will come" appears above a "Welcome" that reinforces Iowa's pastoral image: "Is this Heaven? No, it's Iowa. A place of fertile soil, traditional values and simple pleasure." A click on the link "Welcome to the Farm" yields a tribute to a cornfield that was turned into a movie set that is now carefully preserved as a shrine:

> A moment in time, a place in cinematic history, a mecca for anyone longing to be a part of something greater than themselves, inching toward a destiny that has no limits. What could be more inspiring? (*Field of Dreams* Movie Site)

Inspiring, unspoiled beauty was the aim of the movie makers who, in one telling, but largely unnoticed choice, planted and photographed a crop of field corn instead of seed corn even though the latter is more profitable and thus more commonly grown in northeastern Iowa.[2] Rows of seed corn alternate between tasseled and untasseled plants; field corn presents a unified and more picturesque wind-blown wave of tasseled tops.

In early 2013, the *Field of Dreams* Movie Site was purchased by an investment group that is building an adjacent complex of baseball and softball fields, All-Star Ballpark Heaven. Teams who register to play tournaments there are "guaranteed professional-grade fields," and "swag" is promised to every coach ("30 sec"). Despite this nearby commercialization, the Field of Dreams site remains deliberately basic. The corn does, in fact, grow right up to the outfield grass, and while the farm house cannot be entered, it is still immaculately white. Even the souvenir stand is kept simple: a glassed-in counter in a plain wooden shed, painted barn red.

The Movie Site's understated presentation reflects the personality of actual Iowans who seem to embrace a pastoral self-image and its corollary as the natural home of baseball. Iowans, even those who leave for urban excitements and national success, tend to idealize their home state. Well-regarded writer Susan Allen Toth, for example, recalls childhood drives through small Iowa towns in which she "learned to pay attention to monumental grain elevators, mellow brick schoolhouses, weathered houses with turrets and rambling porches, leafy avenues hushed by summer heat, and wildly colorful backyard gardens overflowing with hollyhock, zinnias, nasturtiums, petunias, and snapdragons" (14). Although she admits that most people, Iowans included, overlook the geographic variety and cultural complexity of the state, Toth insists that Iowa can "shimmer with possibilities, rather like the enigmatic cornfields in *Field of Dreams*" (15). In a real cornfield, Toth writes lyrically, a "row of corn might seem to move, or change, or murmur," permitting ghostly visions. For Toth, *Field of Dreams* is not merely a Hollywood fantasy but an expression of how Iowans genuinely feel about themselves and their state, even if they will not admit it: "Iowans don't usually consider themselves as romantics—which suggests they may not know as much about Iowans as they think" (15).

Iowa was also home to Hall-of-Famer and Cleveland Indians great Bob Feller, and the home-state museum devoted to him emphasizes his rural roots to celebrate both the state and baseball. Opened in June 1995 in Van Meter, The Bob Feller Museum presents its namesake as the quintessential success story. On the museum's Web site, a biographical essay, "Legends of the Ball," by Dennis Hoffman stresses Feller's wholesome Iowa origins by highlighting the historic barn that still "sits on the [Fellers'] old family farm" and the father-son relationship maintained through baseball, an enduring sentimental trope. Hoffman also yokes the virtues of hard work on the farm to pitching in the major leagues: "While other rural boys were working in the fields, Feller spent the summer vacation before his senior year of high school pitching for the Cleveland Indians" ("Legends").

Tellingly, Hoffman's second paragraph compares Bob Feller to "Roy Hobbs, Robert Redford's fictional character in *The Natural*" ("Legends"). The comparison is, of course, not to the character from the original novel *The Natural* (1952) by Bernard Malamud, a Roy Hobbs who in decided contrast to the 1984 film adaptation winds up disgraced. To maintain the innocence of baseball, Hoffman cannot point to the novel's portrayal of corruption and fall from grace. Instead, he wants Iowans to be proud that the famous son's formative years never left him. Hoffman concludes touchingly:

> Later, I asked Feller one last question: "If you could relive any one of the many great moments in your life, which one would it be?"
> Feller didn't hesitate.
> "Playing catch with my dad between the red barn and the house."
> ("Legends")

Complicating, while not completely abandoning, the romanticism of Iowa and baseball is writer Jerry Klinkowitz. Though not born in Iowa, Klinkowitz's connections to the state are firm and long-standing. His distinguished career as a scholar of American literature has occurred during a professorship at the University of Northern Iowa. The basis for his baseball books are his experiences as a member of the Board of Directors for the Waterloo Diamonds, a class-A representative for Major League teams until its move in 1994. The fiction in *Short Season and Other Stories* (1988) is, at times, lyrical about small-city baseball, even as it recognizes the realities of aging stadiums and sparse crowds typical of lower-level professional leagues in the 1980s. All of the stories portray characters connected to the fictional Mason City Royals, and in "Short Season," the narrator follows Carl Peterson, the Royals' manager, as he tours the outfield patrolling for "gopher holes" that might injure his players. Peterson and the groundskeeper are also concerned about the infield: "It's the original ground from 1946 when the park was built, and nearly half a century's weathering has turned it back into something not that far from virgin Iowa prairie" (Klinkowitz, *Short Season* 7-8). Here, even as Klinkowitz dramatizes the unglamorous stadium and the nearly thankless job of a Class A team manager, he evokes the pastoral; the sense of timelessness and the endurance of the land are connected to the sport of baseball as it is played in Iowa.

A passage in "Road Work" crystallizes the romance of baseball as rooted in rural landscape. As the team travels through northeastern Iowa, Peterson is struck by the state's beauty:

> The baseball seems so natural around here, part of the landscape and the culture, as if the diamonds emerged naturally from the ground beneath and might turn back to prairie grass any day now. So unlike his big-league days spent looking into apartment windows across Waveland and Sheffield avenues at Wrigley Field, or playing in a ball park afloat in the ocean of a concrete parking lot, Carl is enjoying this second career right here in God's country, like the beer labels say. (Klinkowitz, *Short Season* 147)

The evocative pastoralism of this description stems in part from the contrast between city and country life, the urban/rural split that appears in much of American culture as shorthand for the corruption that rural America supposedly redeems. Chicago is Klinkowitz's urban Other of choice, and "Sweet Home Chicago" describes pitcher Freddie Guagliardo's love of his home city. In contrast to the unhurried Iowa life found in other stories, Freddie's Chicago is an exciting place, full of colorful night life, bars that stay open after hours, and unpunished crime. The city's seedy thrills serve to accent Iowa's relative innocence.

Klinkowitz is not overly sentimental about minor-league baseball or life in Iowa, however. "Hot Dogs and the Sox" considers Buddy Knox, a third baseman from Dyersville. No small-town athlete making good, Buddy is dissipated by alcoholism, brought on by loneliness and boredom. When he was younger, Buddy went to White Sox games with his father. There he could buy beer for his dad because "[i]n Chicago nobody cared" (Klinkowitz, Short Season 112). While this line again suggests that big city and small-town values are at odds, Klinkowitz does not offer a simple portrait of rural virtue, for although Buddy is "the only Iowa kid on the club," he is part of a culture of small-town males who drink too much, drive too fast, and die young. The story ends with Buddy abruptly leaving the "Dugout Lounge" to drive to Chicago to "'see the Sox.'" Longing for a better life, Buddy seeks a redemption that the rest of the story disallows: "He loves baseball, and in Chicago baseball may once again love him" (Klinkowitz, *Short Season* 115).

In the novel *Basepaths* (1995), Klinkowitz's realism is even starker, less balanced by lyrical passages in praise of baseball's natural rhythms or redemptive possibilities. The protagonist is former major-league catcher Ken Boyenga who accepts a job to manage the Mason City Royals. The zany plot stages a series of events involving two reprobate ex-teammates of Boyenga; his wife, mother-in-law and sons; and a risibly unscrupulous board member for the Royals. While the story opens with Boyenga flying to Mason City and gazing fondly at the big city ball parks he passes over, it ends with him turning away from Sec Taylor Stadium in Des Moines as he flies to Kansas City to be fired from his managing job. The novel seems torn between narrating the hyperkinetic craziness surrounding baseball, in a *Ball Four* or *Bull Durham* mode, and its ending, which suggests that life in baseball takes a toll on men like Ken Boyenga who played in the major leagues but never as starters and who find few opportunities to continue their association with professional baseball.

Like *Short Season*, *Basepaths* resists an easy portrayal of baseball as the pastoral sport, and it does so by emphasizing constant change. In both books, Iowa is less a zone of stable peace and more a place that people pass through. Late in *Basepaths*, as Boyenga wakes in the house that his wife has rented in Mason City, "he thinks for a moment they're home" (183). Life in baseball has never allowed Boyenga and his family to have a permanent home, and Iowa does not give them that either. This emphasis on the temporary is foreshadowed early in the book when an airline agent tells Boyenga that Mason City "*is* a good place for young salespeople to start" (3). *Short Season* concludes with a dramatic no-hitter, but also with a sense of the fleeting. When the game ends, the fans linger; "the stands are still crowded with milling people anxious to love their Class A players while they're here. Next year, they know, a few of the weaker youngsters will be back. But the weakest will be out of baseball and the best sent up closer to the major leagues" (Klinkowitz, *Short Season* 186). The expectation that its talented offspring, including the adopted ones, will be nurtured and then sent away to the larger world is part of the Midwestern psyche.

More personally, Klinkowitz is affected by the loss depicted in *Owning a Piece of Minors* (1999), essays that detail his involvement with the management of the Waterloo Diamonds. When the team is sold and moved away in 1994, Klinkowitz, sounding like a populist farmer decrying big-money middlemen, blames a changing business model for ruining the small-town charm of minor league baseball:

> But with baseball's renewed popularity and the minors' fresh appeal, a new style of owner entered the game: someone with the bucks to capitalize an operation that as it broke even proved itself a most desirable toy.
> Folks like these were slicker than us. True, we'd acquired our franchise for nothing and had labored mightily to keep it essentially worthless, of value only to ourselves and the thousand or so fans who loved it on a daily basis. But these new people bought low and sold high as a way of life, as instinctive as breathing out and breathing in. (Klinkowitz, *Owning a Piece* 13)

He and the other members of the Board of Directors stand no chance against the sharpies of high finance, against "[f]ranchises with New York and Hollywood owners," (84) and against Major League Baseball's insistence on expensive improvements to the Waterloo stadium. Klinkowitz laments the figurative money machine in the garden.

Even though he most often seeks to write as truly as he can about baseball in Iowa, Klinkowitz cannot completely resist the romantic mode, at times suggesting the natural virtues of the game. The Des Moines I Cubs, the Chicago Cubs' AAA affiliate, and the other minor-league teams that still play in the state enjoy a significant following. Still, the I Cubs stadium used to be named Sec Taylor after a legendary sports editor for the *Des Moines Register*. Now it is called Principal Park after an insurance company. The *Register*, a newspaper with a storied history, used to be privately owned. Now the Gannet Corporation runs it, and since the paper's quality is subordinate to stockholder profits, in recent years, management has laid off dozens of editors and reporters. These are just two examples of corporate-creep into supposedly idyllic Iowa life and baseball. It is the same big-business-reach that Ray Kinsella tries to escape by becoming an Iowa farmer.

Despite this complexity, Iowans' pastoral self-image remains intact, as can be seen in the contrast between a film and a play that proffer, respectively, an outsider's and an insider's view of Iowa, using sports as the dramatic lens. *Sugar* (2008), made by two Brooklynites, is an unsentimental depiction of minor league baseball in Iowa. The film follows Miguel "Sugar" Santos, a 19-year-old pitcher from the Dominican Republic, who begins his baseball career in a camp owned by the Kansas City Knights. Young and confident, Santos boasts to his girlfriend, "Baby, there's no one better than me," and his fervent desire is to go to the United States, buy a Cadillac, and play in Yankee Stadium. Promoted to the Knights' Class A affiliate in Bridgetown, Iowa, Santos resides with an elderly couple. Helen and Earl Higgins board a player every year for their beloved Swing, and though they treat Santos with a measure of love, they cannot quite become his surrogate family, for he feels alienated in Iowa, where few people speak Spanish. When he begins to pitch badly, Santos re-considers his drive to become a big-league player and leaves the team for New York City. There, he finds people who know his language, and he reunites with Jorge Ramirez, another ex-Swing player. The film ends with Santos joining a number of other former minor leaguers from Latin America to play baseball for the sheer joy of it.

Sugar, as a number of critics have noted, does not follow the hackneyed losers-to-winners story arc of most sports movies. Nor does it adhere to the romanticism of baseball in Iowa. Neither magical nor uncaring, Iowa is simply and believably a strange locale for a young man from a much different culture. Eschewing the redemption-through-sports theme, the film provides a blunt examination of the difficulties immigrants face in Middle America. And even though the state is not devoid of Spanish-speaking people as the movie suggests, reflecting the outsider's mistaken notion that the Midwest lacks ethnic diversity, *Sugar* refuses the clichés of the American dream with a clear-eyed view of Iowa as a real place and of baseball as a manufactured allure. Significantly, the iconic cornfields of Iowa almost always appear through windows as Santos rides in cars and buses or sits in the Higgins's front room. Iowa's reputed pastoral possibilities are, for Miguel Santos and other itinerant ballplayers, sealed behind glass.

In contrast, *Six-on-Six: The Musical* affirms Iowans' favorable self-image. Written and directed by Robert John Ford, the musical was staged in Des Moines in 2009. A recording of the July 19th performance captures, despite the single-camera set up, the exuberance of Iowans poking fun at themselves while memorializing six-on-six high school girls' basketball, a game played in Iowa until the 1990s. In the six-on-six version of the game, teams were divided into two sets of three that played offense or defense exclusively. Neither set could cross the centerline, and players could dribble only twice before having to pass the ball. Nevertheless, in a 1978 article for *Sports Illustrated*, Iowa native Douglas Bauer noted the appeal of the game "in small Iowa farming towns" where it was "as deeply embedded in the psyche as the suspicion of skies and the certainty that a stranger is a Democrat" (16). Thirty-one years after Bauer's article, and roughly a decade after six-on-six was discontinued, Ford's musical celebrates in its first song a game last played—as the chorus croons—"in Iowa" in "another place in time." *Six-On-Six: The Musical* resurrects nostalgia for a sport seen as uniquely Iowan, and does so with modest Midwestern self-approval tinged with self-mockery.

Six-On-Six is essentially preservationist in that it dramatizes for Iowans their self-defining ethics. The story centers on the Edmund Eaglettes, their star player Jolynn who is poised to break the all-time scoring record, and newcomer Gloria whose mother sues to have six-on-six abolished in favor of five-on-five, which she sees as more favorable to college recruiters. The married lawyers Greg and Sarah represent opposing sides. And Sam, the organizer of the state tournament, learns to accept inevitable change. The play controls the psychic effect of change—in sports and in gender roles—by holding it within a comic and at times wistful sentiment. As Jolynn—both "America's" and Iowa's "sweetheart"—says, "Winning isn't everything, especially if you lose something in the process" (*Six-on-Six*). Change comes to Iowa, as it does everywhere of course, but Iowans can resist its erosion to core values.

Among those values is a pure motivation for high school athletics. While the adults fight in court over six-on-six as either a representation of tradition or a threat to gender equality, Jolynn responds with touching rue to media attention over the scoring record. "I just wanted to play basketball," she says, "to be the best I could be and to have fun doing it" (*Six-on-Six*) Too many people, she suggests, have forgotten the purity of sports: "Adults keep saying kids grow up too fast. [But] it's the adults who took away our childhoods" (*Six-on-Six*). Eventually, Sam and other adult characters agree, accepting five-on-five basketball because "it's what's right for the girls." Jolynn, "the girl next door," does not break the scoring record, but her team wins the tournament, and she insists that the "success of the team is what matters," a succinct expression of Iowa modesty and self-effacement.

This modesty notwithstanding, the implicit egotism of Iowans protecting innocence in sports might have come across as mawkish if the musical did not also mock this self-regard. The first song of Act

II, "A Little Bit of Heaven," for example, includes the lines "God was pleased when he made Iowa" a state "where pigs outnumber people by more than three to one" (*Six-on-Six*). The song is sung by participants in a pageant representing 48 of the nation's states, Virginia and West Virginia having been eliminated because they contain the word "virgin" and its suggestion of sex. The young woman who represents Iowa is dressed, of course, as an ear of corn, and the song crescendos in the joke, "Like Kevin Costner said. Is this Heaven? No, it's Iowa" (*Six-on-Six*). Played for laughs is Iowa's idyllic image, and the irony allows the actual Iowans in the audience to both accept and to stand humbly apart from that image. In *Six-On-Six*—produced by and presented to Iowans—Iowa is special. We know it, these residents say, but we also know that some of that specialness is a contrivance. Nevertheless, as Greg says while standing in Veteran's Memorial Auditorium, long the site of Iowa high school athletic tournaments, "This is a magical place. Listen to your heart" (*Six-on-Six*). These lines are delivered as Greg looks above the heads of the audience, perhaps through the fourth wall and out to the entire state of "I-o-way," as Sam pronounces it, where six-on-six has been "the pride and joy of all" (*Six-on-Six*). In keeping with the nature of comedy and with Iowans' desire for a cohesive sense of self, the show ends with the triumph of unity.

The pride Iowans take in their state and its sporting history is genuine and deserved. A 2006 edition of *Iowa Heritage Illustrated*, a publication of the State Historical Society, makes clear that Iowa embraced baseball before it became a professional sport and was long welcoming of African American and female ballplayers.[3] The issue also features black-and-white photographs of children enjoying baseball (7, 35) and of men playing the game on rough fields (24-25, 46, 47). Selected with care, these photos reinforce "Iowa's passion for the game" (Swaim 2) as rooted in rural innocence. For themselves and to others, Iowans use sports, most obviously baseball, to project and protect the self-conception that their optimism, cooperation, and unity are sustained by a pastoral heritage. Those who appreciate the baseball stories *Shoeless Joe* and *Field of Dreams* happily join in this distinctly Midwestern myth.

Notes

1. Film historians have also noted the connection between Iowa and the pastoral myth in popular culture. See Marty S. Knepper and John S. Lawrence.

2. I am grateful to Iowa native Paula Lovell for this observation.

3. John Liepa, for instance, discusses a noteworthy contest between teams from Marshalltown and Fort Dodge held in 1867. That was two years before the professional members of the famed Cincinnati Red Stockings went undefeated in 1869 and "'revived [national] interest in the sport'" (Liepa 16). See articles by Ralph J. Christian and Ginalie Swaim on Iowans' acceptance of African Americans and women, respectively, in baseball.

Works Cited

Anderson, Andrew. "A Field of Questions: W. P. Kinsella Comes to Ithaca." *Baseball/Literature/Culture: Essays, 2002-2003*. Ed. Peter Carino. Jefferson, NC: McFarland, 2004. 9-18.

Barillas, William. *The Midwestern Pastoral: Place and Landscape in Literature of the American Heartland*. Athens: Ohio UP, 2006.

Bauer, Douglas. "Girls Win, Boys Lose." *Sports Illustrated*, March 6, 1978, 34-40. Rpt. in *Grass Roots & Schoolyards: A High School Basketball Anthology*. Ed. Nelson Campbell. Lexington, MA: The Stephen Greene Press, 1988. 15-21.

Christian, Ralph J. "Bud Fowler: The First African American Professional Baseball Player and the 1885 Keokuks." *Iowa Heritage Illustrated* (spring 2006) 87.1: 28-32.

Field of Dreams Movie Site. Iowa Memories, LLC. 2013. Web. 5 Sep 2013. <http://www.fodmoviesite.com/>.

Hoffman, Dennis. "Legends of the Ball." Van Meter Memories, Inc. 2012. Web. 5 Sep 2013. <http://www.bobfellermuseum.org/halloffamer_bobFeller/bob_feller_biography.asp>.

Horvath, Brook K. and William J. Palmer. "Three On: An Interview with David Carkeet, Mark Harris, and W. P. Kinsella." *Modern Fiction Studies* 33.1 (Spring 1987): 183-94. *Iowa Heritage Illustrated*. "Collector's Issue! Baseball in Iowa." Spring 2006. Vol. 87. No. 1.

Kinsella, W. P. *The Iowa Baseball Confederacy*. Boston: Houghton Mifflin, 1986.

_____. *Shoeless Joe*. 1982. New York: Ballantine, 1987.

_____. *Shoeless Joe Jackson Comes to Iowa: Stories*. Ottawa: Oberon P, 1980.

Klinkowitz, Jerry. *Basepaths*. Baltimore: Johns Hopkins UP, 1995.

_____. *Owning a Piece of the Minors*. Carbondale and Edwardsville: Southern Illinois UP, 1999.

_____. *Short Season and Other Stories*. Baltimore: Johns Hopkins UP, 1988.

Knepper, Marty S. and John S. Lawrence. "World War II and Iowa: Hollywood's Pastoral Myth for the Nation." *Representing the Rural: Space, Place, and Identity in Films about the Land*. Eds. Catherine Fowler and Gillian Helfield. Detroit: Wayne State UP, 2006. 323-339.

Liepa, John. "The Cincinnati Red Stockings and Cal McVey, Iowa's First Professional Baseball Player." *Iowa Heritage Illustrated* (Spring 2006) 87.1: 12-17.

Rooney, John F., Richard Pillsbury, and Jeff McMichael. *Atlas of American Sport*. New York: Macmillan, 1992.

Six-On-Six: The Musical. Dir. Robert John Ford. Perf. Megan Walz, Alexis Van Vleet, Sandy Henry, Ed McAtee, and Greg Millar. Right Brain Productions. 2009. DVD.

Sugar. Dir. Anna Boden and Ryan Fleck. Perf. Algenis Perez Soto and Rayniel Rufino. 2008. Sony Pictures Classics. 2009. DVD.

Swaim, Ginalie. "Iowa's Passion for the Game." *Iowa Heritage Illustrated* (Spring 2006) 87. 1:2.

_____. "Iowa Women in Baseball." *Iowa Heritage Illustrated* (Spring 2006) 87.1: 8-9. "30 sec All Star Ballpark Heaven." *All-Star Ballpark Heaven*. Go the Distance, LLC. 2013. Web. 5 Sep 2013. <http://allstarballparkheaven.com/>.

Toth, Susan Allen. "Iowa." *The American Midwest: An Interpretive Encyclopedia*. Eds. Richard Sisson, Christian Zacher, and Andrew Clayton. Bloomington: Indiana UP, 2007. 12-16.

Big Shoulders, Cat Feet: The Midwestern Dimensions of Carl Sandburg and *Chicago Poems*

Phillip A. Greasley

Carl Sandburg's life and writings reflect his consummate Midwesternness. He is most renowned as a poet but was also a socially engaged platform speaker, journalist, biographer, novelist, children's writer, and collector of American slang, folklore, stories, and songs. Discussion of Sandburg's most important volume, *Chicago Poems*, and other representative writings will demonstrate the Midwestern roots, values, and connections underlying his life and literature. To understand Sandburg and *Chicago Poems*, it is necessary first to understand the national and Midwestern contexts, including the major political, economic, and social situations and movements that had shaped the region's values and defined its character—and thereby Sandburg's.

Within a year of the 1783 Treaty of Paris, which formalized America's independence from Britain, the Congress of the Confederation of the nascent United States began to pass legislation setting the groundwork for governing and developing the new and uniquely American territory west of the Appalachian Mountains. The resulting ordinances drew on Enlightenment ideas, particularly belief in progress, education, and equality, as emphasized by David D. Anderson in "The Origins and Development of the Literature of the Midwest" in *The Dictionary of Midwestern Literature, Volume One* (10-12). The foresight and impact of these ordinances cannot be overstated; for example, in a nation that permitted slave-holding through the early 1860s, the Northwest Ordinance recognized the innate dignity of all human beings and prohibited slavery in the Midwest from the outset.

As discussed by Philip Greasley, in his Introduction to *The Dictionary of Midwestern Literature, Volume One*, the Midwest consists of the states that emerged from the original Northwest Territory, the territory west of the Appalachians, north and west of the Ohio River, and east of the Mississippi River, as set forth in the

Ordinances of 1784, 1785, and 1787. The areas initially involved include today's Ohio, Indiana, Illinois, Michigan, Wisconsin, and Minnesota east of the Mississippi. The region subsequently added the Midwestern states carved from territory annexed through the Louisiana Purchase of 1803: western Minnesota, Iowa, Missouri, Kansas, Nebraska, North and South Dakota (2). The Ordinances of 1784, 1785, and 1787 provided the basis upon which land could be surveyed and sold, inhabitants in these and subsequently acquired American territories could govern themselves, and territories could move toward statehood on an equal basis with the original thirteen states.

The Midwest was a magnet for settlers. It offered some of the world's most fertile soil. Its climate, river systems, and Great Lakes made water available for consumption, agriculture, and industry, along with accessible routes into and through the region. Abundant resources, including prime farm land, timber, fish and game, and minerals, enriched the region.

During the late 1700s and the early 1800s, Americans crossed the Appalachian Mountains seeking opportunity. Immigrants also streamed in from countries where land was owned, social classes fixed, and life tenuous. The Midwest, America's first "West," offered land and prospects for economic and social advancement. Furthermore, government support for education in these territories assisted the region's settlers in achieving their potential.

Chicago, at the southwestern edge of the Great Lakes route into the heart of the rising nation, was on the route for many westward-moving Americans and immigrants. As railroads developed, linking American farms and population centers in the second half of the nineteenth century, they also fostered Chicago because, farther north, the lake made land travel into and out of the interior impossible. Later, Chicago's location in the east-central Midwest also made it ideal for receiving, processing, and trans-shipping Midwestern crops, livestock, goods, and resources.

Laboring people from across the world flocked to the Midwest, retaining their traditions but also building new lives. What they found exceeded their dreams while simultaneously exacting a great price. Cheap, fertile land was abundant, but homesteading was dangerous, back-breaking, uncertain work, as seen in *O Pioneers!* (1913) by Willa Cather and *Giants in the Earth* (Norwegian 1924-25, English 1927) by Ole E. Rølvaag. Making it worse, newcomers to rural areas or to the region's rising industrial cities were easy prey. The unsophisticated, weak, newly arrived Americans, and immigrants were often victimized by land speculators, as witnessed in Hamlin Garland's *Main-Travelled Roads* (1891); by the predatory mentality of the corrupt, unregulated urban-industrial centers, seen in Theodore Dreiser's *Sister Carrie* (1900); and by the unscrupulous manipulation of laborers and citizens portrayed by Upton Sinclair in *The Jungle* (1906).

Class differentiation existed in the Midwest, but it was less pronounced than on the long-settled East Coast and elsewhere in the world. Most coming to the Midwest were poor laborers, not the educated, sophisticated, wealthy, or powerful elite who had less need to relocate. These new settlers, particularly the immigrants, regularly sought security by settling in communities with relatives and others who shared their origins and languages. Beyond the difficulties of daily life, farmers faced the established power and influence of the East, its banks, and its railroads. In the cities, predators included political machines, whose "ward heelers," low-level political operatives, made available grueling, low-paying jobs that, in collusion with corporations and government, kept laborers permanently poor, insecure, and beholden to the machines.

Working conditions and wages were abysmal. The absence of a social safety net and laws governing working conditions, setting minimum wages, and mandating sustainable work days and weeks worsened the situation. Where labor laws existed, they protected corporate interests, not workers. Those protesting wages or working conditions were regularly labeled anarchists or socialists, blacklisted, and beaten by corporate goon squads, local police, and even the National Guard. Hard times intensified urban labor distress. Labor actions frequently culminated in bloody confrontations, as exemplified by Chicago's Battle of Halsted Viaduct in 1877, the

Haymarket Massacre in 1886, and the south-suburban-Chicago Pullman Strike of 1894.

In rural areas, conditions were equally bad. John D. Hicks explains in his 1961 book *Populist Revolt: A History of the Farmers' Alliance and the People's Party* that Midwestern farmers' organizations opposed banks holding farm mortgages, railroads setting monopolistically high and discriminatory rates for shipping grain, and grain elevators depressing prices paid to farmers (63, 67. 75). Farm mechanization and overproduction added to farmers' problems (57). As a result, farm prices declined steadily from 1870 through 1897 (55). Faced with rising debt, Midwestern farmers attempted to reduce the absolute value of that debt by reversing the dollar's significant post-Civil War appreciation (88). They sought to inflate the U.S. currency through the unlimited coinage of silver. The People's or Populist Party scored some third-party victories in this fight, but ultimately, their agrarian initiatives were preempted by the existing political parties.

The rural debt crisis during the late 1800s and early 1900s led to an exodus from farms, small-town America, and trouble spots around the world and a subsequent influx of migrants to the Midwest's industrial cities. City life appeared exciting and allowed escape from farm isolation and drudgery. Cities were technologically advanced and offered jobs and the possibility of advancement, yet their dangers were extreme. Urban centers, with their large, vulnerable, often immigrant populations, practiced unchecked capitalism. Pay was low, work was difficult and dangerous, and laborers worked long hours in unsafe, unhealthy conditions. Child labor was routine. Corporations colluded with government. Community food, air, and water were often tainted. Literary works like Dreiser's *Sister Carrie* and Sinclair's *The Jungle* portray the excitement of turn-of-the-twentieth-century Midwestern industrial cities as well as the dog-eat-dog mentality operating there.

Social justice initiatives and political movements attempted to respond to urban abuses. Germany contributed enlightened concepts of social justice along with many displaced people seeking refuge in Chicago and the upper-Midwest following Germany's mid-nineteenth-century revolutions. *Twenty Years at Hull House with Autobiographical Notes*, published in1910, recounts the 1889 founding, by Jane Addams and Ellen Gates Starr, of Hull House, America's first settlement house (66). It worked to alleviate the economic, educational, and social travail of Chicago's poorest, most disadvantaged populations and offered assistance, health information, and educational and social opportunities for adults and children. Hull House also researched urban problems and advocated corrective governmental action.

Anarchism was another potential avenue for redress. Both the United States Constitution and Christianity enshrine individual freedom and responsibility while rejecting the claims of numbers and power to right. Thomas Jefferson, Henry David Thoreau, and Jane Addams stood among the many Americans strongly committed to individual rights and control over their lives. Terrible conditions and the extreme power imbalance between the powerful (government, corporations, and the wealthy) and the powerless (employees and citizens) near the turn of the century kept Midwestern cities on the verge of explosion. In her 1970 book *Native American Anarchism: a Study of Left-Wing American Individualism*, Eunice Minette Schuster explains that anarchism is premised upon belief in the individual's natural right and moral responsibility to control over him or herself (8), "his own tools, his mind, his body, and the products of his labor" (10). As a social system, it relies on voluntary cooperation (7) and "protection of the weak" "to restrain the ruthlessness of the...fittest" (10). It demands individual liberty and can also "demand that society destroy all authority" (8). Midwestern anarchism produced random acts of violence and sabotage, but ultimately, it was never able to create any viable system.

Socialism was another avenue for addressing these inequities. In *Carl Sandburg: A Biography* of 1992, Penelope Niven indicates that American socialism took many forms, most unrelated to and unaware of the communist revolution (79). Midwestern socialists in particular sought governmental action, not revolution, to address a wide range of workplace and societal abuses and to improve public well-being.

The late 1800s and early 1900s also witnessed strong Progressive efforts to deal with Midwestern problems. In his 1963 book *The Progressive Movement 1900-1915*, Richard Hofstadter explains that, approaching the twentieth century, Americans increasingly realized the human and environmental cost of America's economic advance. People were being exploited by railroads and:

> ...the high cost of credit, . . . [and] an unjust burden of taxation. . . .the cities . . . were . . . industrial wastelands—centers of vice and poverty, ugly, full of crowded slums . . . . Big business choked free competition and concentrated political power . . . business competitors and industrial workers alike had been exploited. . . . Moreover, business . . . had debased politics: working with powerful bosses . . . it had won favors and privileges in return for subsidies to corrupt machines. Domination . . . by political bosses . . . was now seen to be a threat to democracy itself. (2)

The Progressive movement sought to redress the many evils attending American industrialization and "to work out a strategy for orderly social reform" (3). Progressives like Wisconsin's Robert La Follette, Chicago's Jane Addams, and many others worked to protect the weak; make food, working, and community conditions safer; provide workers with a living wage; and reduce economic disparities.

Carl Sandburg's life, values, and writings reflect the ferment of his American and Midwestern contexts. He was born in Galesburg, Illinois, a railroad town where, as elsewhere in the Midwest, immigrants were numerous and tied to low-wage jobs. "Swedes comprised a sixth of . . . [Galesburg's] population," (Niven 4). Sandburg himself was the son of working-class Swedish immigrants who struggled to maintain their tenuous working-class foothold and their aspirations to lower-middle-class standing. Throughout his life, Sandburg's father, August, was employed as a blacksmith's helper for the railroad, working ten-hour days, sixty-hour weeks (2). Prior to her marriage, his mother was a hotel maid (3). August Sandburg's physically demanding job, and his fixation on work and critically-needed income must have influenced Carl's own lifelong commitment to work. He consistently took on multiple concurrent jobs. His family's struggle ignited his passion for social justice and provided the theme for his writings.

Sandburg spoke Swedish before English and, like most immigrants, sought to become part of the anglicized American mainstream, even morphing his Swedish first name, Carl, to Charles (Niven 4); decades later, he reclaimed his immigrant heritage, reverting to Carl at age thirty-two (160).

Sandburg's years as a Wisconsin labor organizer, his position as secretary to Emil Seidel, Milwaukee's socialist mayor, and his journalistic and literary writings all focused on the Midwest. While he was, at best, an urban writer, he also recognized, embraced, and celebrated the region's rural heritage and values. Thus, for example, his writings depict Chicago, the Midwest's leading city, in his 1916 collection *Chicago Poems*, the rural Midwest in his 1918 *Cornhuskers*; and Midwestern industrial life in his 1920 *Smoke and Steel* (1920). Sandburg's poems center not on physical urban or rural settings, but on their spiritual counterparts and antecedents, the strength, courage, and vitality of the laborers who built the skyscrapers, plowed the land, and made the Midwest vital. His 1927 *American Songbag* collects America's best-loved folksongs as reflections and embodiments of American character. His lifelong fascination with Midwestern and American slang also bespeaks exploration of democratic society as captured in its speech. In 1936, when the United States was mired in the Great Depression, Sandburg sought to uplift Americans' spirits. His Whitmanically expansive volume, *The People, Yes*, celebrates laborers and democracy, using the speech, stories, and traditions that embody and affirm the nation's character.

Sandburg's multi-volume biography of Lincoln, *Abraham Lincoln: The Prairie Years* (1926) and *Abraham Lincoln: The War Years* (1939), exemplifies the author's life-long focus on the working class, the Midwest, and democratic values. Abraham Lincoln, more than anyone else, epitomizes the Midwest, the American Dream, and America's democratic potential. His life reflects the dream of a better tomorrow that brought millions of poor, landless people to the American interior. Beginning on the frontier at the lowest social levels, Lincoln rose, through his own effort, to achieve the presidency of the United States at the nation's moment of greatest crisis. His trajectory from frontier log cabin to the White House achieved mythic levels exceeding even those of the fictional Horatio Alger. Himself an immigrant to Illinois, by way of Kentucky and Indiana, Lincoln understood the importance of land, opportunity, and hard work. Raised in a largely one-class frontier settlement, democratic principles came naturally, and Lincoln understood the Midwest's colossal significance. As President in his December 1, 1862 Second Annual Message to Congress, he discussed the region at length, referring to the Midwest as "the great interior region" and adding: "The other parts [of the nation] are but marginal borders to it." Lincoln's death added to his democratic myth, making him a martyr to the cause of the Union and democracy, emancipating its enslaved people, and preparing to "bind up the nation's wounds" as he had promised in his Second Inaugural Address. Sandburg saw the Midwestern laboring class as epitomizing American democracy and Lincoln's values as standing at the core of democratic America.

Sandburg's writings celebrate the strength, dignity, and courage of working men and women who go forth every morning, confronting impossible situations, carrying unbearable loads, living under unspeakable conditions. His writings passionately attack the abuses Sandburg witnessed through his family's life, as a hobo on the road, and via his journalistic experience in Chicago and Wisconsin. His writings transmute these experiences into passionate affirmations of democratic men and women and equally passionate indictments of the system responsible for the deplorable conditions so many were forced to endure.

As a writer and labor organizer, Sandburg subscribed to conservative, constructive socialism. Like the Wisconsin Social-Democratic Party, with which he was affiliated, he sought:

> reformed government; . . . elimination of corrupted power, . . . prohibition of child labor; protection of rights of women in the labor force; the right of literate women to vote; tax reform, including a

graduated income tax; urban renewal; free medical care and school textbooks; public works projects to improve the environment and provide work for the unemployed; state farm insurance; pensions; workmen's compensation; municipal ownership of utilities; higher wages and shorter hours for working people; better working conditions for everyone (Niven 137).

Though certainly not the norm in his day, these hardly constitute a radical agenda today. Most are now embodied in American law and practice.

In *Chicago Poems* Sandburg portrays "common" laboring people that previous poetry had typically ignored or presented negatively. This volume, however, like all of Sandburg's writings, focuses squarely on and celebrates them. It portrays Chicago as the creation of its many laborers. The primary focus in *Chicago Poems* is on a series of individual worker-hero portraits, each affirming the courage and spirit of laborers in poems like "The Shovel Man," "a dago [ditch digger] working for a dollar six bits a day / And a dark-eyed woman in the old country dreams of him for one of the world's ready men with a pair of fresh lips and a kiss better than all the wild grapes that ever grew in Tuscany" (*Chicago Poems*, 1916 edition, 16). The "Jew fish crier" "dangles herring before prospective customers evincing a joy identical with that of Pavlowa dancing" ("Fish Crier" 18). "Onion Days" celebrates the strength and pride of the pregnant Mrs. Pietro Giovannitti, whose husband died in a work-related tunnel explosion, but she continues, strong and proud, picking onions ten hours a day at progressively decreasing wages. The poem asserts, "Mrs. Pietro Giovannitti is far from desperate about life; her joy is in a child she knows will arrive to her in three months" (28). "Dynamiter" portrays a man wanted as "an enemy of the nation," who "laughed and told stories of his wife and children and the cause of labor and the working-class. / It was laughter of an unshakable man knowing life to be a rich and red-blooded thing" (44). Rather than viewing him as a criminal, Sandburg lauds him as "a lover of life, a lover of children, a lover of all free, reckless laughter everywhere—lover of red hearts and red blood the world over" (44). In sum, Sandburg's city is the creation of its myriad proud workers, all identified by their work. If Chicago is the "Hog Butcher . . ./ Tool Maker, Stacker of Wheat, Player with Railroads, and the Nation's Freight Handler," ("Chicago" 3) it is the creation of his proletarian masses, "Shoveling, / Wrecking, / Planning, / Building, breaking, rebuilding" (4). Sandburg even personifies the city as just such a laborer:

> Under the smoke, dust all over his mouth, laughing with white teeth,
> Under the terrible burden of destiny laughing as a young man laughs,
> Laughing even as an ignorant fighter laughs who has never lost a battle,
> Bragging and laughing that under his wrist is the pulse, and under his ribs the heart of the people,
> Laughing!
> . . . proud to be Hog Butcher, Tool Maker, Stacker of Wheat, Player with Railroads and Freight Handler to the Nation (4).

Sandburg's poetry adopts the techniques of advancing literary realism in telling the stories of individual laborers, democratic men and women. Rather than allow powerful, prestigious East Coast centers to define his city and his region condescendingly, these poems assert and personify the city's strength, spirit, and dignity from inside the American heartland. They make the most of Sandburg's immigrant experience and his journalistic background, which gave him an eye to the problems of the people and an ear for their speech.

Sandburg's writings follow Whitman in celebrating democracy and using common speech, free verse, and repetitive oral structures. In advancing Whitman's worldview and style through several decades of American democratic struggle, Sandburg's poetry, while still celebratory, recognizes more fully the immediacy of opposition and the possibility of defeat. His writing is less flamboyant, more restrained and terse; his vocabulary simpler. Having come to poetry via working-class life, oratory, and Midwestern journalism (Niven), Sandburg consciously adopted the language of the streets. He rejected the inflated diction and hackneyed romantic rehash of previous poetry, lending his poetry added strength and immediacy as it confronts pressing social problems. Sandburg's writings complement the vocabulary of realistic, contemporary speech with the oratorical technique of repetitively lengthening the rhetorical period to build expansive moods, then ramming home his points with short, staccato statements. The tone of *Chicago Poems* is further modulated by Sandburg's alternating sections of direct, forceful, socially engaged oral poetic calls for action with almost wordless imagist poems. The latter achieve moments of transcendence amid natural beauty away from or in contrast to the city, as with "Fog" (71) and his "Nocturne in a Deserted Brickyard." Under moonlight, the potential for beauty of even that degraded urban-industrial brickyard catches the poet unaware.

> Stuff of the moon
> Runs on the lapping sand
> Out to the longest shadows.
> Under the curving willows,
> And round the creep of the wave line,
> Fluxions of yellow and dusk on the waters
> Make a wide dreaming pansy of an old pond in the night. (130)

The volume expands Sandburg's democratic affirmation with a message to the workers of America and the world. The "War Poems (1914-1915)" section responds to Europe's ongoing World War I, which the United States had not yet entered. It addresses the workers of the world, affirming their strength and dignity, recoils at the horror of war, and calls on them, as in "And They Obey," to refuse the demands of governments and aristocrats that laborers bear the burden of war and pay with their lives (93).

Sandburg's participation in the Midwest's largest and most important literary movement, the Chicago Renaissance, also underscores his Midwestern experience and values. Chicago's literary renaissance existed in three phases from the late 1880s through the early 1950s. Bernard Duffey, in his *The Chicago Renaissance in American Letters* of 1954, describes the Renaissance's first genteel phase and its second phase, the "Liberation" (125). *The Black Chicago Renaissance* of 2012, by Darlene Clark Hine and John McCluskey Jr., describes the third phase of the city's literary renaissance.

The first phase of the renaissance was associated in time and impulse with Chicago's 1893 World's Fair, the Columbian Exhibition, which attempted to gain national and international recognition for Chicago as a cultural center. Rather than celebrating contemporary architectural advances already evident in Chicago, the fair's planners adopted Greek revival architecture and Renaissance motifs associated with traditional Eastern and European culture. Similarly, Bernard Duffey's volume reports that while first generation Chicago Renaissance writers addressed Midwestern issues, they fostered "the upward movement" (31) and aspired to traditional cultural, civic, and literary norms and East Coast recognition. The second generation of the Chicago Renaissance, Duffey's "Liberation," did not accommodate or seek to be defined by external audiences, distant cultural centers, or the literature of the past. Like other adherents of liberation, Sandburg sought recognition for and from his region. He rejected East Coast cultural and literary hegemony and its less-than-subtle dismissal of the Midwest as an unsophisticated, unliterary cultural backwater unworthy of notice. *Chicago Poems* and Sandburg's other works adopt post-colonial values and approaches in asserting Midwestern life and literature against the prevailing literary norms.

Sandburg was a central participant and a leading light of the Renaissance's second phase. While the "Liberation" included writers in all genres, it was most significant for its poetry and its rejections of expected poetic forms, subjects, and diction. At best, "Liberation" poetry rejected elite subject matter, elevated poetic diction, and starry-eyed romanticism. It substituted poetry that rode the tide of advancing literary realism and reflected contemporary Midwestern experience. Along with Sandburg's *Chicago Poems*, Edgar Lee Masters' *Spoon River Anthology* (1915) and Nicholas Vachel Lindsay's *General William Booth Enters into Heaven* (1913) exemplify the "Liberation's" thematic and stylistic shifts.

Sandburg strongly advocated literary and cultural liberation. His Midwestern working-class loyalties and literary usages arose from and spoke to the democratic masses. He retained a high romantic view of human beings, but rejected romantic assumptions that good would always triumph. Rhyme, syllabic verse, and elevated diction had no place in his writing. Rather than conform to older literary values, he adopted and fostered poetry reflecting the contemporary speech and democratic worldview of Chicago and the Midwest's laboring populations.

Stylistically, Sandburg wrote using terse, common language. Thus, for example, "Chicago," the lead poem of *Chicago Poems* opens with the decisively anti-poetic words "Hog Butcher" (3). With these words, Sandburg sent a shot across the bow of prevailing literary norms and opened the door to new expectations for poetry. In doing so, Midwestern "Liberation" poets, like Sandburg, Masters, and Lindsay and literary magazines, like *Poetry: A Magazine of Verse* and *The Little Review* shook American poetry loose from nineteenth-century poetic norms and opened the door to further reform. For a time during its literary renaissance, Chicago became America's literary capital. Another Midwestern city, St. Louis, with its guiding literary force, William Marion Reedy, and his publication, *Reedy's Mirror*, had earlier pointed the way to Chicago's radical poetic reform, and many "Liberation" writers heard and heeded his message (Niven 112).

Sandburg, like Edgar Lee Masters, benefitted from Reedy's tutelage, encouragement, and advocacy of literary realism, as embodied in the then-new translation of *Epigrams from the Greek Anthology* (Niven, 245-47). Reedy influenced his pupils, both in terms of language use and in the recourse to structures featuring individual "portrait poems" (246). Theodore Dreiser was another early Midwesterner who captured the energy and naturalistic amorality of turn-of-the-twentieth-century urban-industrial Chicago and did so using realistic language. Dreiser, too, encouraged and tutored Sandburg and was the first to propose publication of the collection that became *Chicago Poems* (268).

Public support, personal encouragement, opportunities for interaction with like-minded writers, avenues for publication, and funding were critical to Sandburg and other Chicago Renaissance writers. Harriet Monroe's groundbreaking *Poetry: A Magazine of Verse*, founded and located in Chicago, with ties to that city's industrial, civic, and literary leaders; connections to established poets, editors, and critics in the East and Europe; and willingness to advocate for new poets and poetry, provided the necessary literary gathering point and support. *Poetry's* award in 1914 to Carl Sandburg of the $200 first annual Levinson Prize for Poetry (Niven 254) provided the public recognition Sandburg badly needed, the money to allow him to continue experimenting, and the encouragement to do so. Moreover, after the first failed attempt to publish the volume, Alice Corbin Henderson of *Poetry* and Louis Untermeyer made the connections resulting in *Chicago Poems'* publication by Henry Holt and Company. Later, when the conservative literary journal, *The Dial*, attacked that volume and the "'hog butcher' school of poetry" (*The Dial*, quoted in Niven 243), Monroe defended him editorially in *Poetry's* May 1916 issue with "The Enemies We Have Made." There she said:

> It is possible that we have ventured "rashly" in "discovering" Mr. Sandburg and the others, but—whom and what has *The Dial* discovered? We have taken chances, made room for the young and new, tried to break the chains which enslave Chicago to New York, America to Europe, and the present to the past. What chances has *The Dial* ever taken? What has it ever printed but echoes? (*Poetry*, quoted in Niven 243).

Chicago Poems embodies the Midwestern literary and democratic values so evident throughout Carl Sandburg's life. It focuses on "common" Americans and the unvarnished realities of their tenuous lives in the nation's hog-butchering, industrial interior. Despite the immensely difficult situations faced by laborers, their strong, proud, courageous lives shine through, producing compelling, inspiring poetry marked by poignant images, unassuming heroism, and uncommon beauty amid destructive naturalistic surroundings. Sandburg and *Chicago Poems* attest to and affirm the strength and character of the Midwest and its people, which is the epitome of America and democracy.

Works Cited

Addams, Jane. *Twenty Years at Hull-House with Autobiographical Notes.* New York: Macmillan Company, 1910.

Anderson, David D. "The Origins and Development of the Literature of the Midwest." *Dictionary of Midwestern Literature.* Vol. 1. Bloomington: Indiana UP, 2001. 9–24.

Cather, Willa. *O Pioneers!* New York: Houghton Mifflin Co., 1913.

Congress of the Confederation. "Northwest Ordinance of 1784." - *Wikisource, the Free Online Library.* n.p., n.d. Web. 20 Sept. 2013.

Congress of the Confederation. "Land Ordinance of 1785." *Wikisource, the Free Online Library.* n.p., n.d. Web. 20 Sept. 2013.

Congress of the Confederation. "Northwest Ordinance (July 13, 1787)." *Wikisource, the Free Online Library.* n.p., n.d. Web. 20 Sept. 2013.

Dreiser, Theodore. *Sister Carrie.* New York: Doubleday, Page & Company, 1900.

Duffey, Bernard I. *The Chicago Renaissance in American Letters: A Critical History.* East Lansing: Michigan State College Press, 1954.

Garland, Hamlin. *Main-Travelled Roads.* New York: Harper & Brothers, 1891.

Greasley, Philip A., ed. *Dictionary of Midwestern Literature. Vol. 1: The Authors.* Bloomington: Indiana UP. 2001.

Hicks, John Donald. *The Populist Revolt: A History of the Farmers' Alliance and the People's Party.* Lincoln: U of Nebraska P, 1961.

Hine, Darlene Clark and John McCluskey Jr. *The Black Chicago Renaissance.* Urbana: U of Illinois P, 2012.

Hofstadter, Richard. *The Progressive Movement 1900-1915.* Englewood Cliffs: Prentice Hall, 1963.

Lincoln, Abraham. "Abraham Lincoln's Second State of the Union Address." *Wikisource, the Free Online Library.* n.p., n.d. Web. 20 Sept. 2013.

_____. "Abraham Lincoln: Second Inaugural Address." *Wikisource, the Free Online Library.* n.p., n.d. Web. 20 Sept. 2013.

Lindsay, (Nicholas) Vachel. *The Congo: And Other Poems.* New York: MacMillan Company, 1914.

Masters, Edgar Lee. *Spoon River Anthology.* New York: MacMillan Company, 1915.

Niven, Penelope. *Carl Sandburg: A Biography*. New York: Charles Scribner's Sons, 1991.

Rølvaag, Ole E. *Giants in the Earth*. New York: Harper, 1927.

Sandburg, Carl. *Abraham Lincoln: The Prairie Years*. New York: Harcourt, Brace & Company, 1926.

_____. *Abraham Lincoln: The War Years*. New York: Harcourt, Brace & Company, 1939.

_____. *American Songbag*. New York: Harcourt, Brace & Company, 1927.

_____. *Chicago Poems*. New York: Henry Holt and Company, 1916.

_____. *Cornhuskers*. New York: Henry Holt and Company, 1918.

_____. *Smoke and Steel*. New York: Harcourt, Brace and Howe, 1920.

_____. *The People, Yes*. New York: Harcourt, Brace & Company, 1936.

Schuster, Eustice Minette. *Native American Anarchism: A Study of Left-Wing American Individualism*. New York: Da Capo Press, 1970.

Sinclair, Upton. *The Jungle*. New York: Doubleday, Page & Company, 1906.

Humor Me, I'm from the Midwest: Mike Perry and the Trope of Poking Fun at Ourselves _____

Christian Knoeller

In "The Origins and Development of the Literature of the Midwest," David Anderson, founder of the Society for the Study of Midwestern Literature, explores how the interpretation of shared historical experience has given rise to a distinctive cultural and literary tradition. "Midwestern writers," he notes, "fuse time and place and people" to reveal "the meaning of human experience as it is manifested in that place" (9). And this regional experience is rooted in historical change: the indigenous cultures and their oral traditions gave way to waves of explorers, missionaries, travelers, pioneers, and settlers, while the landscape was altered by cutting forests, draining wetlands, and plowing up prairies. As a writer depicting the particulars of place and the character of his community, Michael Perry is heir to the region's history and literary traditions. His rendering of contemporary Midwestern experience is predicated on a powerful founding narrative still vivid in the region's living cultural memory: the self-sufficiency of settlers on the edge of civilization that once would have been glorified as the frontier. As Anderson concludes, "As the Midwest constructed an identity, a reality, and an enduring myth out of the elements of its complex origins and development, so it constructed a literature that at once explains and interprets that development" (12).

Yet another regional sensibility also animates Perry's narrative and underlies its wit: a self consciousness rooted in the presumably unsophisticated character of hamlets, such as New Auburn, Wisconsin, which Perry calls home. There, eking out a living under adverse circumstances often demands ingenuity. Faced with life-threatening winter weather, for instance, one must be able to depend on neighbors. The shared hardships of residents in such isolated communities undoubtedly give rise to bonds of interdependence and friendship. Perry's role as volunteer fire fighter

---

and paramedic represent an extension—albeit an institutionalized one—of the altruism characteristic of sparsely populated provinces of the Upper Midwest.

Perry's rural humor is admittedly well-plowed ground. Garrison Keillor, for example, has long charmed radio audiences with rambling monologues featuring the folks of fictional Lake Wobegone in Minnesota's fabled North Woods: their foibles and cares, idiosyncrasies and misadventures. His homespun mix has struck a chord of nostalgia with listeners nationwide who have made *Prairie Home Companion* a veritable institution on public radio. The popularity of his signature storytelling has spawned a merchandizing empire replete with publications and even a feature film. In fact, he possesses such celebrity status that Keillor penned the screenplay and cast himself as the lead, while landing Robert Altman as director. His radio variety-show format incorporates live musicians and old-time radio theater skits. Reminiscent of the big top circus circuits, the program relies on travel to enhance local interest. Each program features resident guests pitched to local sensibilities—another slice of Americana. In neighboring Wisconsin, several radio shows have successfully emulated Keillor's program, gaining geographical reach as contestants phone in from around the country. Imitators emanating from the North Woods include Michael Feldman's "Whad'ya Know?" produced by Public Radio International and based in Madison, Wisconsin, as well as the Big Top Chautauqua of Bayfield, Wisconsin, a non-profit tent theater that is adjacent to the storied Apostle Islands and overlooks Lake Superior. Both are traveling shows that allude to the same nineteenth-century agrarian traditions for entertainment that *Prairie Home Companion* has popularized, including homegrown acoustic music.

For nearly four decades, Keillor has attracted a remarkably faithful audience on national radio, establishing him as, arguably, the most popular American humorist of our time, certainly on radio. And radio itself is a throwback to an earlier era and evokes sentimental yearnings for life in a presumably simpler world. It is akin to the impulse underlying back-to-the-land movements associated with 1960s counterculture. If satellite dishes have become a feature of rural landscapes throughout the country, they are still liable to be flanked by cordwood, cattle gates, garden plots, and, just as often, the rusting hulk of a pickup truck or obsolete tractor. This is Michael Perry's world. Above all, his writing can be viewed as an extension of long-standing regional traditions, including barnyard humor—and the trope of poking fun at ourselves.

Perry burst onto the national literary scene in 2002 with *Population: 485*, a loosely-knit collection of personal essays depicting the idiosyncrasies of small-town life in the rural Midwest from the unlikely vantage point of a volunteer firefighter and emergency medical technician (hence the sly subtitle "Meeting your Neighbors One Siren at a Time"). Since then, three more volumes have rapidly followed from HarperCollins: *Off Main Street* (2005); *Truck: A Love Story* (2006); and *Coop* (2009).

Introducing a 2011 interview upon publication of Perry's fourth book of essays, Megan Zabel traces the trajectory of his oeuvre to date:

> In his first book, the heavily lauded *Population: 485: Meeting Your Neighbors one Siren at a Time*, Michael Perry wrote about moving back to his hometown of New Auburn, Wisconsin, after years away and getting reacquainted with the community as a member of the volunteer firefighting department.... [in] his new memoir, *Coop: A Year of Poultry, Pigs and Parenting...* Perry has traded in his house in the village of New Auburn for 37 overgrown acres in the country with his wife and daughter, with a new baby en route. Perry takes on fowl, firewood, and pigs while reflecting on his unorthodox childhood–being raised in an obscure fundamentalist faith by dairy-farmer parents who took in dozens of foster children–for clues as to how to proceed as a farmer, as a husband, and a father. (Zabel n.p.)

This upbringing–coupled with more recent experiences experimenting with a semi-subsistence lifestyle–provide fodder for spinning humorous anecdotes as well as extemporaneous philosophizing. Asked in an interview whether he ever worried about running out of material, he replied that to the contrary: in fact, he worries about running out of *time* (Zulkey n.p.).

Wary of hackneyed stereotypes of regional characters—or any essentialized impression of Midwestern "identity"—this chapter explores a recurrent trope in Perry's work: self-effacing anecdotes and asides that provide humor at his own expense. While occasionally making fun of others, he more often bears the brunt of his own jokes. It remains an open question whether the trope of poking fun at oneself relies on conventional rural stereotypes, specifically, the longstanding pantheon of "country bumpkins," "local yokels," and "hayseeds." Walter Blair and Hamlin Hill describe the "traditional homespun bumpkin" underlying popular culture icons such as Hollywood's Beverly Hillbillies: "stereotypes championing homely sagacity in the face of egghead logic" (489).

Perry seems able to avoid such stereotypes because the joke is so often on him. He portrays himself as whimsically inept at doing many different things, whether as parent or handyman, husband or hunter, auto mechanic or author. In fact, such claims of futility have become an important part of his charm as a writer. Perry clearly follows in the tradition of Midwestern humor by relentlessly depicting himself in such self-effacing ways, what Blair and Hill refer to as the comic stance of *undue inferiority*.

Perry attributes his penchant for humor to being brought up on a farm in northern Wisconsin and considers his sensibilities to be characteristic of the region where he grew up. In the preface to a book of regional history, Perry provides a brief sketch of regional character as hard working and heartfelt but occasionally mischievous as well:

> *Farm Life* tells the story of Chippewa Valley farming clearly, honestly, and best of all, with heart. I make that claim from just one humble point of authority: I was raised a farm boy in the Chippewa Valley... I grew up on that manner of rough-hewn practical joke. It was homespun humor, and it made the endless chores go better." (Smoot 5)

This description matches Perry's persona as author: growing up on a farm, which provides just the right "street cred" and barnyard swagger. He is amused at his "reputation in literary circles as some sort of backwoods, blue-collar, rough boy" (Brown n.p.). This cultivated public persona, however deliberately constructed, arguably comes with the territory as a resident of the sparsely populated North Woods. His hometown of New Auburn, he confides, "was born as a lumber camp" (Brown n.p.). The author bio in *Off Main Street* capitalizes on this image: "raised on a small farm in northwestern Wisconsin, where he remains a resident today.... While his writing reflects a wide range of experience, he is proud to say that he can still run a pitchfork and milk a cow in the dark" (*Off Main*, front matter n.p.).

Growing up on a farm has undoubtedly contributed to Perry's lingering agrarian ambitions. By the time his family settled on 37 acres outside New Auburn, they had accumulated a haphazard menagerie: seventy chickens, four pigs, three sheep, and one goat, not to mention a pet guinea pig. "We don't buy meat because for two years now, all the meat in the freezer came from our pigs or chickens or off the back 40 during deer-hunting season" (Zabel n.p.). Perry acknowledges that this experiment in self-sufficiency has literary antecedents in the work of authors, such as Wendell Berry, Barbara Kingsolver, and Michael Pollan, who have each explored the virtues of ecologically friendly diets and lifestyles. However, Perry is quick to distance himself from such high-minded writers. By contrast, his own work depicts "what the experience really turns into when regular people do it, and do it kind of half-successfully" (Zabel n.p.). Underscoring his rough-and-ready image, he confides that his own reading tastes are considerably more lowbrow, and he claims that he "prepared for the writing life by reading every Louis L'Amour cowboy book he could get his hands on–most of them twice" ("Bio" n.p.).

Perry takes pains to explain that his homestead is a hobby or "backyard" farm, compared to the neighbors who toil to eke out a living from their crops and dairy herds and whom he describes with admiration: "Out of respect to the dedicated farmers of my childhood and the many dawn-to-dusk farm families of my contemporary acquaintance, I must rush to point out that I make a living as a writer and performer while raising a few animals on the side" (Ladd n.p.).

He is admittedly an amateur who dabbles in animals; if his pigs were to die it might spoil the weekend, he explains, but could bankrupt his neighbors. In this regard, he again assumes the stance of "undue inferiority" posited by John Gerber as a common convention among comic narrators (Blair 323).

Perry's writing is decidedly regional: the title of his successful first book, *Population 485*, refers to his own hometown of New Auburn. "I've always been from 'Nobbern,'" he says, "even when I've lived elsewhere," such as Wyoming where he worked as a cowboy to pay his way through nursing school (Reading n.p.). In this sense, his work follows in the tradition of nineteenth-century local colorists. Claude Simpson, writing in the 1960s in *The Local Colorists*, characterized the lure of the local for American writers of that period:

> the psychological need to interpret local character, local geography, local flora and fauna, local idiom and folkway, seem to underlie this impulse that kept a generation of essayists and storytellers busy. Their method was to excite by emphasizing the exotic and picturesque... also 'showing things as they are.'" (qtd. in Blair 270)

As Walter Blair and Hamlin Hill explain in *America's Humor*, realist writers bucked the tide of modernization and urbanization that threatened to homogenize distinctive regional dialects and culture: "One aim of the local colorists," they report, "in those rapidly changing times was to preserve some of these memories" (270).

While Perry is rarely one to sentimentalize bygone times, he laments the disappearance of family farms in his region as *way of life*:

> Getting to know and work with your neighbors.... something that was integral part of my farming childhood, and yet evaporated over time and automation.... It kills me to see farm after farm succumb. I grew up on a dairy farm surrounded by dairy farms touching dairy farms county to county, and right now you can drive three miles before you come to the first dairy farm and it'll be at least that far before you come to the next. And yet, I know farmers who worked

themselves to a skeleton for decades and had nothing to show for it but that land. (Buffalo np)

Here, Perry echoes a familiar narrative lamenting the decline of traditional agrarian lifestyles since the nineteenth century. Though Perry is less prone than his local colorist predecessors to succumb to nostalgia, his essays are set in the agricultural time-capsule of the Upper Midwest, specifically an isolated hamlet in Northern Wisconsin, where fierce winters conspire to keep the population of communities such as New Auburn below five hundred.

In *Population: 485*, Perry relates an incident that reveals his innate love-hate relationship with being a local celebrity. A booster at the bank in his hometown invites Perry to appear in the local Jamboree Day parade—not pulling a float with a tractor, as he might have hoped, but rather "On a float," she tells him. "We'll put a sign on there that says Writer" (108). He is mortified at the prospect, imagining neighbors looking on: "these loggers, these butchers, these farmers, nurses carpenters, gas station cashiers, concrete trowelers, and truckers," which is to say self-respecting, blue-collar folk. He pictures himself on the float, a local author "decked out maybe with some spangles and crepe-paper steamers... like a dairy princess" (108). While others might have welcomed the exposure, Perry bristles at the indignity. He deflects any delusions of grandeur saying only that "With all due respect to the lady who wanted to put me on a float, I have a pretty good sense of the scope of my renown.... I am a tiny fish in a puddle of a pond. In short, I am not float-worthy" (115). He reports just how neighbors actually look upon his paltry lifestyle: "They also look at my house, with its peeling paint, rusted screen, and a used Chevy in the weedy drive (last week while I was mowing the driveway a wheel fell off my mower) and figure Mr. Successful Writer better get it together and sell some movie rights" (Zulkey n.p.). In short, "I am surrounded by people who know me too well to be impressed with me," he says (Reading n.p.).

When he speaks to community writing groups, he claims to have learned to write by "a childhood spent slinging manure.... Standing inside a manure spreader chipping frozen cow manure off the beater bars when it's ten below, that builds character" (110). Speaking to local farmers attending a luncheon sponsored by a seed corn salesman, Perry describes how he "led off [his] reading with the thing about learning to write by cleaning calf pens" (125). He reports having "used the same illustration to explain [himself] to butchers, truckers, and turkey pluckers. Believe me, they get it" he says (110). Yet, this barnyard analogy is a double-edged sword; he often feels like an imposter in both worlds: "I am a dilettante in either camp," he laments. "I own a rusty old pickup truck, but it's not running right now, and I don't know how to fix it.... I have read great works of literature, but recall only the grossest details. I can no more diagram a sentence than rewire an alternator" (110-11). In *Truck*, he describes the same beloved vehicle as rusted out: "unpainted, punched with dents... I've had it for just short of twenty years. Last time I got it running, maybe six years ago, the gas tank sprung a leak and all the fuel ran out" (7).

A similar sense of inadequacy and self-consciousness arises when meeting with editors in Manhattan, while on the road doing book tours. His description follows in the comic tradition Blair and Hill chronicle in nineteenth-century literature by incorporating "crude outsiders from the mountains, sticks, or canebrakes [who] appeared in more civilized settlements... wandered into towns and cities, gawking and mystified... baffled by urban ways... comic collision lay in contrasting social levels" (159-60). Perry's account of life in the "Big Apple" follows suit:

> Before I depart New York my editor takes me to lunch at the Monkey Bar. I become uncomfortable with the stares of men in the four-figure suits, to say nothing of their companions: women apparently obtained on lease from some photo shoot intended to advertise a perfume the scent of which I can never quite place, although I suspect it is bottled in a slim decanter of frosted glass to which is affixed an embossed platinum label reading *Utterly Unattainable Homeboy.*" (*Truck* 143)

Perry, it seems, could happily live without all the pomp and circumstance associated with commercial publishing. "Exclude issues of culinary excellence, and there is no question I am more comfortable attending the smelt feed at the Legion Hall than I am choosing from six forks on the five-star mezzanine" (124). The rural Midwesterner in him recoils at the pretense of the urban sophisticate.

Perry's forays into the world of technology only underscore his naiveté. "It is my understanding that the original purpose of Craigslist was to help people in San Francisco locate apartments," he writes. Even if a person living in the country were savvy enough to bargain hunt on-line, after all, consider the sophistication of the merchandise: "I am tickled to think it would end up causing two knuckleheads in Wisconsin to fight over used barbed wire and secondhand pickle buckets" (200), not to mention plastic pig-watering barrels and carp hunting gear (Ladd n.p.). Still, he avoids the hyperbole of a Hollywood Hillbilly: "When you come from rural stock, there is this tendency to overplay the rube. To swipe your toe in the dirt and reckon, well, shoot-fire, I don't know nothin' 'bout birthin' no babies. Or shake your head in wonderment at the fripperies of city life" (120). Instead, Perry parodies conventional stereotypes of rural folk as ruffians, presumably crude and uncouth, whose dialect would undoubtedly be stigmatized.

In *Coop: A Year of Poultry, Pigs, and Parenting*, Perry describes the trials and tribulations of exploring self-sufficiency. He recognizes the temptation to romanticize this lifestyle: "Pausing ax in hand to gaze off across the territory, I picture myself as some austere pioneering backwoodsman on the order of Abe Lincoln—albeit dumber, stubbier, and unlikely to alter the course of human events, unless you count snoozing at the stoplight" (17). In short order, the fabled Daniel Boone is reduced to Thurber's Walter Mitty. In *Truck*, he underscores the widening gap between a rugged frontier past and the vacuum-packed present: "We lean to our shovels with stoic determination, secretly delighted that in the age of heated seats and convenience-store cappuccino we can still pretend to be pioneers as we strike out for milk and eggs up the block at the Gas-and-Go" (32).

If the mythical Midwesterner is a practical mechanic, the archetypal tinkerer, perhaps Perry's greatest nemesis on the farm is assuming the role of handyman. "If necessity is the mother of invention," he confides, "I am its ham-fisted stepchild" (159). Indeed, this refrain becomes a veritable motif in *Coop*. "As a wannabe handyman," he tells us:

> I am haunted by high hopes, false starts, and even worse finishes. Evidence surrounds me: the engine heater I bought and left beneath the truck seat until the packaging fell away; the bathroom faucet I bought after purchasing my New Auburn house twelve years ago and never installed (it's still there, under the sink. (44)

In *Truck*, he reports, "The truck is on my to-do list. I have a busted screen door on that to-do list. It's been flapping in the breeze since the Clinton administration" (8). Admittedly, any homeowner can recite a litany of unfinished chores. "I feel young but pressed for time," he confides. "I am beginning to get a sense of all I will leave undone in this life" (8). In the end, Perry persuades us that he is indeed a consummate knave of all trades and assuredly master of none.

To illustrate, Perry attempts to cobble together a lean-to for his pigs:

> Nothing says redneck like a blue tarp roof, and I swore I wouldn't go that way. As usual, I overdreamed and underbudgeted, and wound up banging together a bunch of castoff two-by-fours, several chunks of warped particleboard and—due to hit the road for a stretch with no time for shingling—finished it off with," you guessed it, "a nice blue tarp. (211)

Or consider his luck actually managing livestock:

> I have had my heart set on owning pigs for a while now, but as with so many of my projects, reality has taken a backseat to cogitation. A lovely thing, to sit back and ponder what One Shall Accomplish without having to actually lace one's boots. To price sausage makers prior to carrying a single bag of feed. Farmers though we are, my family is short on pig experience. Dad didn't care for the smell of them, so we never raised any. (183)

This admission follows the brief account of wrestling a pig, and being bit on the behind by a dog *at the same time*—which, he points out, amounted to "two firsts in one day."

One might expect that writing itself might be a point of pride. Not so, Perry contends: "In public, I am prone to saying freelance writing is a slightly less reliable way of making a living than farming" (55), which is to say dicey at best, given the precarious financial straits faced by recent generations of farm families:

> "How many times as a farm kid did I hear guys in overalls at the feed mill tell the joke about the farmer who won several million dollars in the lottery. 'What are you going to do with all the money?' the reporter asked him 'Well,' the farmer drawled 'I reckon I'll just keep on farming 'til it's all gone." (Buffalo n.p.)

Asked to describe how he writes, Perry explains that his "writing process is unpretty and more like grunting than singing" (*What* np).

Nonetheless, Perry is chagrinned to catch himself passing down barnyard proverbs to his daughter: "firewood warms you twice—once when you split and stack it, and once when you burn it. I predict by the time Amy is nine, 'Firewood warms you twice' will make her list of Top Five Phrases Most Likely to Make Me Roll My Eyes at the Old Guy" (135). Even a child, he seems to say, can spot such countrified clichés a mile away. And lest he ever get a swollen head, his daughter has a knack for cutting his reputation down to size:

> Not so long ago I stepped through the front door to find Amy in the middle of the kitchen unrolling a flag-sized poster of me. It was from a book tour stop somewhere back along the line. My visage was full-color and big as a cheese platter. Amy held the poster unfurled before her, and I admit I savored the moment right up until she turned and laid it faceup on the bottom of the guinea pig cage. (161)

When it comes to auto mechanics, that perennial bastion of male prowess, Perry admits to being completely out of his element, introducing *Truck: A Love Story* with an "Author's Note" that expresses trepidation over whether serious gearheads will deem his amateur efforts wanting: "For those of them brave enough to read this book, I suspect they will feel as if they are watching a walrus attempting to play the piano" (xii). "My capacity for mechanical minutiae doesn't go much past lug nuts," he confides, "Embarrassing, for a guy to have such affection for an old truck yet know so little about it" (7). Hunting, that other exemplar of raw machismo, reveals equally whimsical shortcomings. While in a tree stand waiting for deer, "I once watched a partridge feeding for half an hour until he was directly beneath me, at which point, because I do love fresh partridge, I tried to hit him with my thermos but missed wide right, and when the sound of his wings faded I immediately missed his company" (*Truck* 228).

On the domestic front, Perry reports an aversion to the culinary arts: "When I cook, I tend to wing it. Baking requires follow-through and exactitude, to which I respond, Hey! Wanna go ride bike" (23). As for his physical appearance, Perry portrays himself in the way his readers have come to expect—squat, balding, and ill-clad—albeit good naturedly:

> I wish I had thick beautiful hair the same way I wish I was six-foot-two with abs. I'm not, and so it goes. I'm okay with that... I'm of the leather sandals persuasion tonight, having left my usual steel-toed boots in the motel. Baggy shorts, no socks, a heavy shapeless sweater in case it gets cool. Fashion is hopeless with me. Don't have the body for it, for one thing. The runways of Paris and Milan are rarely devoted to the short and stocky among us. (93, 128)

In the case of gardening, troubles commence as the annual barrage of fliers from mail-order nurseries begins to arrive:

> Seed catalogs are responsible for more unfulfilled fantasies than Enron and *Playboy* combined...the annual seed catalog review adds up to a perennial tradition of willful delusion... I am in essence a minor god, with plans for my few square feet of the earth. I shall sow, and I shall reap. I am a catalyst in the cycle of life. I am also

distracted by all the pretty pictures….Never shop for groceries on an empty stomach, they say. Corollary riff: Never order seeds when the world is frozen stiff and leafless. (30-1)

Melodrama aside, Perry the gardener falls victim to his own imagination.

Still, he perseveres, keeping methodical records from year to year to learn from his mistakes. "Today I reviewed my gardening notes, which is a hoot...there are some undated comments that provide certain sad clues:

Thyme—dead-ish.
Leeks... didn't do well, I think leeks go to seed on yr 2...
Shallots. Three years running now, and I have yet to harvest one.
Pickling cuke. A particularly poignant entry. I made two batches of refrigerator pickles. The first batch sprouted moss. The second batch turned fizzy" (237).

Taking pity on him, Perry's brother John drops off box after box of his own homegrown produce. He credits his rural kin with culinary common sense: "When my NASCAR-loving brother-in-law, who's about as organic as a naugahyde seat cover, told me he was raising his own pigs and chickens because he wanted to know where his kid's food came from, I figured 'Well, now we're getting somewhere'" (Buffalo n.p.). To retaliate, Perry resorts to an elaborate practical joke, delivering a "deeply withered parsnip and a carrot the size of a crayon" to his brother with the following solicitation:

We understand the temptation to simply load up on pig dung and grow the biggest dang vegetables you can. Good for you. We here at Deliciously Sensitive Farms, however, specialize in custom-grown, esthetically pleasing vegetable miniatures... Send no money now. But please consider the following memberships in our exclusive, earth-centered, utterly Mother-Friendly, community-based sharing circles...
Stunted Pumpkin of the Month Club...
Federation of Anemic Beets. (238-9)

Meanwhile, rabbits incessantly pilfer the garden produce. His property, he laments, has turned into a veritable "rodent preserve." His attempts to pass pathetically dwarfed crops off as culinary delicacies to his green-thumbed brother only underscores the author's unrepentant ineptitude.

Having convincingly portrayed himself as utterly inept at doing virtually anything he tries his hand at—be it parent or handyman, husband or hunter, auto mechanic or author—what debacle could possibly come next? In constructing the character of his narrator in this way, Perry deftly follows in the venerable "native" tradition in rural American humor that Hill depicts as "a backwoodsman facing a hostile frontier, or a contemporary, this character faces an *exterior* reality with gusto and exuberance. Even as the 'inspired idiot' of the school of literary comedians, laughing at himself rather than the world around him" (171). Perry's writing consistently reflects this time-honored tradition of self-effacing Midwestern humor—above all, the trope of poking fun at ourselves.

Works Cited

Anderson, David D. "The Origins and Development of the Literature of the Midwest" in *Dictionary of Midwestern Literature, Volume One, The Authors*. Ed. Phillip A Greasley. Bloomington: U of Indiana P, 2001. 9-24.

Blair, Walter and Hamlin Hill. *America's Humor from Poor Richard to Doonsebury*. New York: Oxford UP, 1978.

Brown, Rebecca. "Interview with Michael Perry, Author of *Population 485: Meeting Your Neighbors One Siren at a Time*." *RebeccaReads.com*. RebeccaReads, 16 July 2006. Web. 9 June 2001. <http://www.rebeccasreadsarchives.com/interviews/authors/081504_perry_intervw.html>.

Hill, Hamlin. "Modern American Humor: The Janus Laugh." *College English* 25: 3 (December 1, 1963): 170-176.

"Interview: Visiting Author Michael Perry." *Buffalo Rising*. Buffalo Rising Media, 8 June 2010. Web. 9 June 2011. <http://www.buffalorising.com/2010/06/ Ladd, Mary. "interview-visiting-author-michael-perry.html>.

The Poop Interviews: '*Coop*' author Michael Perry." *The Poop: The Chronicle Baby Blog*. 30 Apr. 2009. Web. 9 June 2011. <http://blog.sfgate.com/parenting/2009/04/30/the-poop-interviews-coop-author-michael-perry/>.

Perry, Michael. *Population 485: Meeting Your Neighbors One Siren at a Time.* New York: HarperCollins, 2002.

_____. Foreword. *Farm Life: A Century of Change for Farm Families and their Neighbors.* By Frank Smoot. Eau Claire, WI: Chippewa Valley Museum Press, 2004.

_____. *Off Main Street: Barnstormers, Prophets & Gatemouth's Gator.* New York: HarperCollins/ Perennial, 2005.

_____. *Truck: A Love Story.* New York: HarperCollins, 2006.

_____. *Coop: A Year of Poultry, Pigs, and Parenting.* New York: HarperCollins, 2009.

_____. "Biography." Sneezingcow.com.Michael Perry, n.d. Web. 9 June 2011. <http://sneezingcow.com/biography/>.

_____. "What is your Writing Process Like?" *Sneezingcow.com.* Michael Perry, 15 Jan. 2009. Web. 9 June 2011. <http://sneezingcow.com/2009/01/15/what-is-your-writing-process-like/>.

Reading Group Guides. "A Conversation with Michael Perry." *ReadingGroupGuides.com.* The Book Report, Inc., n.d. Web. 7 Nov. 2011. <http://www.readinggroupguides.com/guides3/population_4852.asp>.

Zabel, Megan. "Chickens are the New Black: An Interview with Michael Perry." *Powells.com.* 7 April 2009. Web. 9 June 2011. <http://www.powells.com/blog/interviews/chickens-are-the-new-black-an-interview-with-michael-perry-by-meganz/>

Zulkey, Claire. "The Michael Perry Interview." *Zulkey.com.* 14 Oct. 2005 Web. 9 June 2011. <http://www.zulkey.com/diary_archive_101405.html>.

"Figures of Transmotion": Bison Hunt Narratives as *Mise en Abyme* in the Native Literatures of the American Midwest

Matthew Low

The final chapter of Cormac McCarthy's novel *Blood Meridian* (1985) shifts the narrative away from the desert locales of Mexico, Arizona, and southern California, where most of the novel has been set, closing instead on the short-grass prairies of northern Texas. On the one hand, this move takes the unnamed protagonist away from the scenes of cross-cultural ultra-violence (Americans, Mexicans, and Native Americans all taking their turn slaughtering one another) that comprise the majority of the novel's first 300 or so pages. On the other hand, despite the fact that the protagonist has been physically removed from these border wars and aged a couple of decades, McCarthy makes it clear that not much has changed. Yet, rather than depicting further human-to-human atrocities, attention is shifted briefly to the mass slaughter of bison that took place on the prairies and plains of the American Midwest in the mid-to-late nineteenth century.[1] The introduction of the "old buffalo hunter," with whom the novel's protagonist has a brief interaction, ensures that *Blood Meridian* keeps its focus on the death, destruction, and violence that characterized the settlement of the trans-Mississippi West, so vividly recalled when the hunter describes:

> the buffalo and the stands he made against them, laid up in a sag on some rise with the dead animals scattered over the grounds and the herd beginning to mill and the rifle barrel so hot the wiping patches sizzled in the bore and the animals by the thousands and tens of thousands and the hides begged out over actual square miles of ground and the teams of skinners spelling one another around the clock and the shooting and shooting weeks and months till the bore shot slick and the stock shot loose at the tang and their shoulders were yellow and blue to the elbow and the tandem wagons groaned away over the prairie twenty and twenty-two ox teams and the flint

hides by the ton and hundred ton and the meat rotting on the ground and the air whining with flies and the buzzards and ravens and the night a horror of snarling and feeding with the wolves half crazed and wallowing in the carrion. (330)

The placement of this nightmarish scene at the outset of the novel's closing chapter—in the moments right before the protagonist meets again the otherworldly Judge Holden and most likely meets his end—is neither exclamation point to the horrific violence that precedes it nor anti-climax, but rather a mirroring of the narrative as a whole. In other words, the old buffalo hunter, who is so beleaguered by the extermination he has witnessed and participated in that he openly wonders "if there's other worlds like this... Or if this is the only one," plays back for the protagonist—and thus the reader as well—a micro-narrative of the death, destruction, and violence that he has lived through himself, just with a slight shift in geography and actants (330).[2]

As a narrative technique, the sort of intratextual mirroring employed by McCarthy in this example is generally designated by the term *mise en abyme* (literally "placed into abyss"), which has multifaceted usages in the worlds of art, literary, and cultural criticism. As a visual concept, *mise en abyme* is most commonly identified as the coat of arms that features a smaller replica shield placed within a larger, more or less identical, shield. Within the field of literary—and more specifically, narrative—studies, the concept is defined in its simplest sense by Martin McQuillan as, "A replica of a text or narrative embedded within that text or narrative" (322). Werner Wolf adds a little more complexity to the idea of *mise en abyme* by classifying the technique as "a discrete lower-level element or structure [that] 'mirrors' an analogous element or structure on the framing higher level" (65). By invoking the idea of 'levels,' Wolf is calling attention to the multiple layers of diegesis (also commonly referred to as "worlds" or "storyworlds") that might comprise a given text or narrative. A common example of *mise en abyme* that calls attention to a narrative's diegetic levels is the "play within a play" that occurs in Act III of *Hamlet*, wherein

Hamlet, Claudius, and others (occupying a higher level of diegesis) watch a troupe of actors reenact (at a lower level of diegesis) the suspected murder of Hamlet's father by Claudius. In this instance, the mirroring that takes place here is not simply for effect, but has direct impact on the outcome of the play to follow. This is not a requirement of *mise en abyme*—in fact, such is likely not the case in the McCarthy example demonstrated above—but it does show that there are more than aesthetics at stake in this narrative technique, including even ideology and ethics, as will be clearly demonstrated in other examples to follow.

Perhaps the definitive study of *mise en abyme* as a multifaceted and complex phenomenon is Lucien Dällenbach's *The Mirror in the Text* (1977). Dällenbach identifies two "properties" that are essential in literary examples of *mise en abyme*, namely "the reflexive character of the utterance" and "its intra- or metadiegetic quality" (53). The emphasis placed on reflexivity is done in part to distinguish from what some might label redundancy—as in an unnecessary repetition of the same image, trope, or idea in a given narrative—with Dällenbach arguing that through *mise en abyme* "redundance is diminished; the narrative becomes informing and open—and above all it accepts, after having imposed its own form on its 'analogue,' that the latter, in turn superimposes its own form on the narrative" (57). The example from *Blood Meridian* exemplifies this characteristic, as the story told by the old buffalo hunter of the slaughter he participated in should not be read as redundant (what some might call, in this case, anti-climax, coming as it does so close to the novel's completion); instead, the image of slaughtered bison is "superimposed" upon the preceding images of massacred human beings to reinforce the theme that the practice of Euro-American settlement of the trans-Mississippi West was a supremely violent, and senseless, enterprise for both humankind and the natural world. This scene, in the final chapter of *Blood Meridian*, is also useful for illustrating Dällenbach's second criteria for *mise en abyme*, that it be either "intra- or metadiegetic" in relation to the primary narrative of which it is a part. Distinguished from "metanarratives" that disrupt the "narrational control" of a given narrative, Dällenbach instead has in mind "utterances [that] neither change the narrational agency nor suspend diegetic continuity: totally dependent on the primary narrative, they follow its course and are arranged within its universe" (51). Such a description perfectly addresses the scene with the old buffalo hunter in McCarthy's text: the novel has moved away from its primary narrative—the story of the protagonist and his encounters with Judge Holden—but will return to it before the novel comes to a close; the old buffalo hunter's account of the destruction of the bison constitutes an "indirectly reported narrative"; and it remains a part of the "universe" (what a narrative theorist might call "storyworld"), within which the rest of the novel exists (51). Following the theorization of Dällenbach and others, who address *mise en abyme* as a unique and impactful narrative phenomenon employed in not a few prominent works of literature, what might appear to be a minor scene in *Blood Meridian* instead is notable because "it brings out the meaning and form of the work" (Dällenbach 8).

That McCarthy includes this account by the old buffalo hunter in his quintessential anti-Western is fitting, moreover, because scenes of hunting and killing bison are a central component of the corpus of texts *Blood Meridian* subtextually responds to and comments upon: namely, nineteenth-century journals, travelogues, and memoirs written by the explorers, tourists, and adventurers who were among the first Euro-Americans to venture out upon the prairies and plains of the trans-Mississippi West. Accounts of joining native hunting parties, organizing large bands of trigger-happy soldiers, or even venturing out alone to track, hunt, kill, and clean the American Midwest's keystone mammalian species comprise significant chunks of prose in the journals of the Lewis and Clark expedition, the travelogues of "learned" tourists like George Catlin and Washington Irving, and the memoirs of soldier-adventures like George Armstrong Custer and Buffalo Bill Cody. And like the scene in McCarthy's more recent novel, a case can be made that such accounts are reflexive of the larger narrative of which they are a part, an instance of *mise en abyme* that not only captures the "meaning and form" of the primary narrative, but the distinctive ideology of this corpus of texts as well.

The coincident rise in the nineteenth century of American literacy rates and settlement of the land acquired in the Louisiana Purchase—land subsequently explored and chronicled by the Corps of Discovery, whose publications were among the first to fall into this emerging genre of American letters—made narratives written by those with first-hand experience of frontier life extremely popular and marketable. It is no surprise, then, that as the nineteenth century progressed, more and more of such works were commissioned—often by the nascent American government itself—written, and published; without being overly reductive, it is possible to see within many of these works a recognizable formula emerging that commonly included: celebration of the bravery of American soldiers and settlers venturing into these unknown locales; condescending encounters with "friendly" indigenous communities, along with a simultaneous trepidation, even revulsion, upon entering "hostile" native lands; and a general disdain for the barrenness of a region that would be labeled "The Great American Desert." Yet, more than just adhering to a proven set of plot points, the similarities found among theses nonfiction narratives of exploration, expedition, and tourism can be linked to the larger project of converting (one might even say colonizing) this region into land suitable for American settlement, enterprise, and commerce.

For instance, addressing the "dense body of American writing" that emerged at this time, Post-colonial critic Edward Said has observed an "extraordinarily obsessive concern... with United States westward expansion, along with the wholesale colonization and destruction of Native American life... an imperial motif emerges to rival the European one" (63). Therefore, narratives written during this time in American history, like other texts documenting the implementation of colonial and imperial practices, ought to be read as "a vision of a moment" and account for the inherent methodology for they reveal the eradication of the unknown, the unfamiliar, and the undesirable (Said 67).

With this sort of reading in mind, the frequently documented intradiegetic narratives of hunting bison that recur throughout Euro-American nonfiction travel writing from this period take on added importance. For, to return to the previous discussion of *mise en abyme*, these micro-narratives of hunting bison frequently mirror the primary narratives, within which they are included, and in doing so, highlight some of the most negative and damaging components of Euro-American imperialism: the celebration of senseless violence, the eradication of indigenous life, and the perpetuation of policies and practices meant to further devalue and degrade whatever stands in the way of "progress".

One author in particular, Washington Irving, is instructive in this regard because his firsthand account of traveling to this region in *A Tour on the Prairies* (1835)—the first of three so-called "western narratives" that he published in the mid-1830s—embodies the "obsessive concern" with the trans-Mississippi West, and especially the need to textualize one's experiences. Irving was already a well-traveled literary celebrity when he set out on his "tour" in 1832, and he acknowledges, in a brief introduction to the text, that the reader likely has expectations for the writing he will produce as a result of his travels, expectations that he downplays in the introduction, but duly fulfills in the pages that follow. Moreover, Irving had close ties to many of the American statist concerns of this time and place, as he met both William Clark and an imprisoned Black Hawk before beginning his official "tour," which happened to be part of a Jacksonian exploratory expedition that would eventually lead to relocation of Creeks and Cherokees to this land west of the Arkansas River, a relocation known as the Trail of Tears.

Perhaps most importantly, Irving's work came at an important juncture in American westward expansion, as it followed, by a couple of decades, the journals of explorers like those of the Corps of Discovery or Zebulon Pike. However, Irving's travel writing predated the large-scale movements of exploration, settlement, and publication yet to come, which is one reason why Donna Hagensick is able to claim that Irving's work during this period can be "deemed largely responsible for subsequent western migrations" (185).

As *A Tour on the Prairies* progresses, Irving makes known, on numerous occasions, his desire to participate in a bison hunt. So, in Chapter XXIV, about two-thirds of the way through the book, when he is finally able to do so, the account is given its own chapter and treated with notable enthusiasm, as he makes clear that otherwise, the "novelty of the expedition was wearing off" (109). As word of bison spotted in the area puts his trigger-happy companions in a minor frenzy, satiated only momentarily on an ill-fated flock of turkeys, the pursuit of four bison eventually gets underway and results in the cornering of one, so "that the inexperienced hunters might have a chance" at taking a shot or two (110). At first, the bison is peppered with rifle balls that "glanced his mountain of flesh without proving mortal," before giving way to Irving's dramatic narration of the coup de grâce:

[The bison] made a slow and grand retreat into the shallow river, turning upon his assailants whenever they pressed upon him; and when in the water took his stand as if prepared to sustain a siege. A rifle ball, however, more fatally lodged, sent a tremor through his frame. He turned and attempted to wade across the stream but after tottering a few paces, slowly fell upon his side and expired. It was the fall of the hero, and we felt somewhat ashamed of the butchery that had affected it; but, after the first shot or two, we had reconciled it to our feelings by the old plea of putting the poor animal out of his misery. (111)

A second bison hunt is recounted in Chapter XXIX that is even more descriptive and involved, but the outcome is the same, with Irving resolving to put his "victim" out of its misery, though this time, the bison's tongue is carved out and given to Irving as a "trophy" (137). Similar scenes appear in Irving's two other "western narratives," *Astoria* (1836) and *The Adventures of Captain Bonneville* (1837)—though in these instances, he is narrating hunts undertaken by others—as well as in the travelogues of his contemporaries George Catlin and Francis Parkman, then perpetuated (even amplified) by later visitors to this region, as exemplified by the writings of Custer and Cody. In each instance, the concept of *mise en abyme* illuminates the capacity of such intradiegetic hunt scenes to reflect back upon *raison d'être* of these nineteenth-century Euro-American travel narratives themselves, as well as the imperializing impulse

Said identifies pervading Western culture as a whole. In other words, these micro-narratives of the hunt for bison mirror ideologies of removal, violence, and domination that ultimately define the textual production of Irving and his contemporaries.

As an extension of his critique of Western colonial ideology in *Culture and Imperialism* (1993), Said also offers an alternative way of reading and interpreting colonial and postcolonial narratives, which he terms "contrapuntal reading," which he goes on to define as "[taking] account of both processes, that of imperialism and that of resistance to it, which can be done by extending our reading of the texts to include what was once forcibly excluded" (286). With such a reading practice in mind, this study will now shift its focus on narratives representative of perspectives, beliefs, and ways of life "excluded" by Euro-American print statism. In doing so, the concept of *mise en abyme* and its application to scenes of hunting bison will remain consistent, with the purpose of demonstrating that such accounts need not be read solely as reflexive of policies and practices destructive to the indigenous life of the American Midwest. Instead, building on the work of Anishinaabe scholar Gerald Vizenor, the appearance of bison in the native literatures of the American Midwest will be read as "figures of transmotion, not dominance" (*Fugitive Poses* 136). In a seminal work on Native American cultural sovereignty, *Fugitive Poses* (1998), Vizenor defines "transmotion" at one point as "a reciprocal use of nature," and later in the same text as "an original natural union in the stories of emergence and migration that relate humans to an environment and to the spiritual and political significance of animals and other creations... transmotion is natural reason, and native creation with other creatures" (15, 183). Whereas the bison hunt narratives of Euro-American authors function as *mise en abyme* within larger narratives, expressing "dominance over nature," the native authors discussed in what follows employ bison and bison hunts as instances of *mise en abyme* within larger narratives expressing "an ethical presence of nature, native stories, and natural reason" (183).

Born the same year as the Battle of Little Bighorn (1876), Yankton Sioux writer Zitkala-Ša wrote prolifically at the turn of the twentieth century, at once chronicling her own experiences as a child during turbulent times for the Sioux in both poetry and prose, but also compiling collections of stories from Sioux oral tradition. One such story, "When the Buffalo Herd Went West" (undated; first published 2001), fits into a series of stories about the Sioux trickster Iktomi. As such, it lacks concrete geography or chronology, set instead in a mythical time and place, and has an obvious didacticism as its purpose. It is, above all else, a story about scarcity, of what might happen if the Sioux were to lose their primary food source— the bison—but also about the dangers of life on the prairie, as early in the story, it is revealed that the protagonist's husband has been "crippled by accident in a buffalo chase" (13). Eventually, the wife encounters a "man of empty words" who is in possession of a "magic bladder" that can produce a bison and a white pony with which to hunt and kill it. After they come into possession of the magic bladder themselves, the man and woman appear to have resolved the threat of scarcity looming over them throughout the whole story:

> They took it carefully down from the pole, carried it out of doors, and unloosed the neck of the bladder. Immediately a wild buffalo ran out, bellowing and pawing upon the earth, and a white pony followed closely behind.
> They tied the bladder and the man caught the pony, mounted it without saddle or bridle, and chased and killed the buffalo! Thus they had meat and skins in plenty. (17-18)

Tellingly, the first thought of the man and woman upon receiving such a bounty—of which they are careful not to abuse, as they "tied the bladder" as soon as a single bison and pony are set loose—is of "sharing their game with their people," rather than keeping it to themselves (18). However, because this is a cautionary tale, the trickster Iktomi eventually comes in possession of the "sacred bag" and clumsily allows it to fall "wide open," setting loose a "herd so great it was impossible to number them," which then proceeds to trample Iktomi and the woman in its stampede to the west (18-19). Most likely written sometime in the early twentieth century, already a couple of decades removed from the near destruction of the great bison herds that roamed the American Midwest, the presence of bison in this narrative is a reminder of the fragility of the resources upon which the human characters rely, the dangers of treating these resources greedily, and the consequences of living so carelessly as to lose the bison forever. Unlike the bison hunt narratives that are comprised of chase, capture, and coup de grâce, in Zitkala-Ša's narrative the roles are reversed, as it is the careless human characters who are overtaken by an animal "roaring with a voice of thunder" (19).

The theme of scarcity also pervades Luther Standing Bear's short narrative "Standing Bear's Horse" (1934), about a hunting expedition on which a man, presumably the author's father, reaches a point of near desperation for lack of finding food. The opening of the story relates that "the enemies of the Sioux had been troubling them, taking their ponies and running off the buffalo" (32). Though these "enemies" are never named, given the time period, in which Standing Bear lived—born eight years prior to the Battle of Little Bighorn—it is easy to envision encroaching Euro-American settlers as a possible culprit. After setting out to drive their enemies off, the Sioux war party returns to find their land scorched by a prairie fire and all of the animals gone, including the bison upon which they rely for food. Days pass with no sign of relief, and eventually Standing Bear resolves to kill his beloved horse the next day if the scarcity persists. He then leaves the party "to go away alone and pray to the Great Mystery—pray for food that his companions and pony might be spared" (35). Standing Bear's prayers are not in vain, as shortly thereafter, a bison appears and a brief narrative of the hunt ensues: "the miracle had happened. There below him in a little patch of green by a seeping spring stood a lone buffalo... Standing Bear wasted not a shot. The first one weakened his game. The second one—and his prayer was answered" (35).

Though of sparse detail, the essential elements of Standing Bear's hunt are nonetheless clearly conveyed in this account. Its succinctness is especially striking when compared with those bison hunt narratives featured in the work of Irving and his contemporaries; here, two shots are fired and the outcome is implied, not belabored, whereas Euro-American corollaries frequently revel in the labor of narrativizing these scenes, before celebrating the animal's demise. To this point, Standing Bear's account does not end with celebration, however warranted it might be for bringing an end to the near-starvation of this band of Sioux warriors, ending instead with commemoration: "In later years Standing Bear the First showed Standing Bear the Second the exact spot where the Great Mystery had placed the buffalo" (36). As the story comes to a close, it leaves no question as to the origin of the bison that saved Standing Bear and his companions, further removing it from nineteenth-century analogues that vilify and even monsterize the bison that are being hunted and killed.[3]

These narratives of bison and bison hunts in the writing of Zitkala-Ša and Luther Standing Bear clearly attribute something otherworldlyor downright spiritual to these animals, upon which Sioux culture so heavily relied for its material, cultural, and metaphysical needs. In this way, the animals of these narratives can be described, to return to Vizenor, as "figures of transmotion." Extrapolating on Vizenor's use of that term, John Gamber asserts that the concept of transmotion "illustrates crossings of temporal, species, ethereal, and mental boundaries," as is certainly true of the bison that appear in "When the Buffalo Herd Went West" and "Standing Bear's Horse" (222). Moreover, as *mise en abyme*, the brief accounts of actual hunts in these narratives convey a great deal about this close connection to the bison—those partaking in the hunts do not do so for the "sport" of killing as many as they can, nor does the narration revel in the inherent violence of the hunt sequence, and above all else, gratitude is expressed when the hunt is finished—and therefore, by extension, can be read as embodying what Vizenor terms "survivance." A term that is intentionally difficult to pin down, partially in the spirit of Jacques Derrida's *différance*, Vizenor has been employing his coinage "survivance" for over two decades, quite often in the context of Native American literature, as a way to articulate "an active resistance and repudiation of dominance, obtrusive themes of tragedy, nihilism, and victimry" ("Aesthetics of Survivance" 11).

The narratives composed by Zitkala-Ša and Luther Standing Bear are expressions of survivance in themselves; as *mise en abyme*, their intradiegetic bison hunt narratives are thus reflexive of the narrative as a whole in the sense that, "The creation of animals and birds in literature reveals a practice of survivance" ("Aesthetics of Survivance" 12). The bison in these stories are not "put out of their miseries"; instead, their appearance is a sign of hope and the perpetuation of indigenous culture and society in the American Midwest, if not in actuality than through their existence in the narratives of which they play a crucial role.[4]

The appearance of bison as an indicator of communal health and cultural perpetuation has continued on in more contemporary native literature as well. With this in mind, Blackfeet writer James Welch's 1986 novel *Fools Crow*, published just one year after McCarthy's *Blood Meridian*, offers a fitting work with which to close this study, as it ties together images, ideas, and themes explored in the narratives discussed above. Like the narratives of Zitkala-Ša and Luther Standing Bear, Welch's novel also depicts an indigenous society being challenged by the pressures of Euro-American incursion on its traditional home grounds, which of course includes the systemic removal of the bison that serve as a primary means of subsistence for the Blackfeet. Like *Blood Meridian*, Welch's novel sets out to challenge traditional accounts of the settlement of the West, particularly the manner in which Native American communities were forcibly removed from their lands. Itself a historical novel, fictionalizing real-life Blackfeet, like Owl Child and Mountain Chief, *Fools Crow* is primarily set in the late 1860s in Montana and culminates with the Marias Massacre in January of 1870. Coupled with the spread of smallpox throughout the Blackfeet community and the destruction of their primary food source, by the novel's close Welch's protagonist, Fools Crow, has lived through enough violence and death that one might expect the sort of weariness expressed by McCarthy's old buffalo hunter as he wonders "if there's other worlds like this... Or if this is the only one" (330).[5] However, just as Vizenor's concept of survivance emphasizes an "active presence" of indigenous life and culture throughout North America, so too does Welch invest a much higher degree of agency in the lives of his native characters as they negotiate the threats posed by Euro-American settlement.

One way that such agency is granted, as in "Standing Bear's Horse," is through prayer. Late in the novel, as the Blackfeet look to a future of uncertainty after the Marias Massacre and the devastation smallpox has wrought upon their society, Welch recounts how the people "prayed for long summer grass, bushes thick with berries, all things that grow in the ground-of-many-gifts. They prayed that the blackhorns would be thick all around them and nourish them as they had nourished the before-people" (388-389). It would be wrong to interpret this prayer for the return of the bison (blackhorns) as an act undertaken by those pushed to the brink of a collapsing society, struggling for any chance of survival; instead, this scene is best read as an articulation of survivance, particularly as Karl Krober envisions its capacity "to subordinate *survival*'s implications of escape from catastrophe and marginal preservation; *survivance* subtly reduces the power of the destroyer... its connotations [are] not toward loss but renewal and continuity into the future rather than memorializing the past" (26, his emphasis). It is significant, therefore, that the closing scene of the novel suggests that the prayers of the Blackfeet have been answered. In a paragraph typographically removed from the rest of the novel, as well as removed from the primary narrative of Fools Crow and the remaining Blackfeet, Welch ends by depicting a world in which the bison are thriving:

> Far from the fires of the camps, out on the rain-dark prairies, in the swales and washes, on the rolling hills, the rivers of great animals moved. Their backs were dark with rain and the rain gathered and trickled down their shaggy heads. Some grazed, some slept. Some had begun to molt. Their dark horns glistened in the rain as they stood guard over the sleeping calves. The blackhorns had returned and, all around, it was as it should be. (390-391)

On the one hand, this is a perfect example of what Vizenor has in mind in his development of the term survivance, as its wording is clearly meant to convey not so much return—which would imply that the bison had been successfully conquered or dominated—but continuity, or in Vizenor's wording, "an active presence" (*Fugitive Poses* 15). On the other hand, returning to the primary narrative technique at stake in this study, this passage is also emblematic of *mise en abyme*, as its relationship to the primary narrative is one of metadiegesis (which Dällenbach notes "involve[s] a suspension of the diegesis," such as occur in "dreams"), and it is a powerful reflection back upon the form, meaning, and ethics of the novel as a whole (51). Even as the novel works toward these closing lines, an aura of uncertainty hovers around the whole text, with the fate of Fools Crow and the Blackfeet seemingly in doubt from almost the first line. Reading this closing scene with the bison as *mise en abyme* ultimately reveals that, in fact, the outcome never was in doubt, that the Blackfeet could not be subjected to Euro-American dominance, and that the prairie ecosystem, on which they lived, would continue to thrive as vibrantly as its keystone animal species.

Notes

1. Though most of the narratives considered in this study use the word "buffalo" to refer to the animal in question, outside of direct quotations, the word "bison" will be used, as it more accurately describes the species of American bison (*Bison bison*) addressed in each narrative. For a useful background on this species and how it was hunted to near extinction in the nineteenth century, three useful works to consult are: Andrew C. Isenberg's *The Destruction of the Bison: An Environmental History, 1750-1920* (2001), Dale F. Lott's *American Bison: A Natural History* (2003), and Michael Punke's *Last Stand: George Bird Grinnell, the Battle to Save the Buffalo, and the Birth of the New West* (2007).

2. The term "actants," as used in narrative theory, is attributed to the Structuralist Algirdas Greimas. Shlomith Rimmon-Kenan offers a helpful paraphrase and analysis of Greimas work in *Narrative Fiction* (2002), noting that they can be thought of as "the subordination of characters" that tend to be "invested with specific qualities in different narratives" (34-35). The six actants are sender, object, receiver, helper, subject, opponent, the last of which is probably most relevant to McCarthy's description of the slaughter of the bison.

3. Irving's contemporary George Catlin, for instance, describes a wounded and dying bison as a "grim-visaged monster," going on to challenge, "I defy

the world to produce another animal that can look so frightful as the large buffalo bull, when wounded as he was, turned round for battle, and swelling with rage" (27). Accompanying this description in Catlin's text is a painting he has done of the wounded bison that does indeed enhance its monstrosity.

4.   The quoted lines here are taken from a section of *Fugitive Poses* in which Vizenor describes his own tragicomic attempt to hunt and kill a squirrel. The full passage reads: "The Boy Scouts of America and the Izaak Walton League taught me and other hunters of my generation the monomercies of the coup de grâce. We learned as hunters and later as authors never to let a wounded animal suffer. Wounded animals were put out of their miseries; at heart, our miseries of the animal other in literature" (130).

5.   The insinuation that there might be "other worlds" is particularly relevant to Part Four of *Fools Crow*, the end of which takes place in the mythical realm of Feather Woman, and includes a vision — which feels quite prophetic at the time in which it takes place — Fools Crow has about the catastrophic end of the Blackfeet. A major component of this vision, in addition to the loss of his family and traditional home grounds, is the final disappearance of the bison:

> Fools Crow began to look for those places which the blackhorn herds favored this time of the year. He searched around the Sweet Grass Hills, the Yellow River, the Shield-floated-away River, Snake Butte and Round Butte. But he did not find the blackhorns. He looked along the breaks of the north of the Big River, and he looked to the country of the Hard Gooseneck and the White Grass Butte, the Meat Strings. But there were no blackhorns… It was as if the earth had swallowed up the animals. Where once there were rivers of dark blackhorns, now there were none. To see such a vast, empty prairie made Fools Crow uneasy. Perhaps the magic of the yellow skin had chosen to hide the blackhorns from him. (356)

6.   It is telling that Welch does not choose to end the novel here, or even with this sentiment of defeat and "victimry" (to use another Vizenor word); had the novel closed with Part Four, it would be little different from the end of *Blood Meridian*, or even the nineteenth-century travel narratives to which it is responding. Instead, Welch closes with a scene of the bison's presence, not absence, making its *mise en abyme* one of survivance, not dominance.

Works Cited

Catlin, George. *Letters and Notes on the Manners, Customs, and Conditions of the North American Indians* (1841). Vol. 1. New York: Dover Publications, Inc., 1973.

Dällenbach, Lucien. *The Mirror in the Text.* Trans. Jeremy Whiteley with Emma Hughes. Chicago: The U of Chicago P, 1989.

Gamber, John. "Tactical Mobility as Survivance: *Bone Game* and *Dark River* by Louis Owens." *Survivance: Narratives of Native Presence*. Ed. Gerald Vizenor. Lincoln: U of Nebraska P, 2008. 221-246.

Hagensick, Donna. "Irving: A Littérateur in Politics," *Critical Essays on Washington Irving*. Ed. Ralph M. Aderman. Boston: G.K. Hall & Co., 1990. 178-190.

Irving, Washington. *A Tour on the Prairies* (1835). *Three Western Narratives*. Ed. James P. Ronda. New York: Modern Library, 2004.1-162.

Isenberg, Andrew C. *The Destruction of the Bison: An Environmental History, 1750-1920*. Cambridge: Cambridge UP, 2001.

Kroeber, Karl. "Why It's a Good Thing Gerald Vizenor Is Not a Indian." *Survivance: Narratives of Native Presence*. Ed. Gerald Vizenor. Lincoln: U of Nebraska P, 2008. 25-38.

Lott, Dale F. *American Bison: A Natural History*. Berkley, CA: U of California P, 2003.

McCarthy, Cormac. *Blood Meridian: Or the Evening Redness in the West* New York: Vintage, 1985.

"*Mise en abyme*." *The Narrative Reader*. Ed. Martin McQuillan. London: Routledge, 2000. Print.

Punke, Michael. *Last Stand: George Bird Grinnell, the Battle to Save the Buffalo, and the Birth of the New West*. Lincoln, NE: U of Nebraska P, 2007.

Rimmon-Keenan, Shlomith. *Narrative Fiction: Contemporary Poetics*. 2nd ed. London: Routledge, 2002.

Said, Edward. *Culture and Imperialism*. London: Chatto and Windus, 1993.

Standing Bear, Luther. "Standing Bear's Horse" (1934). *Stories of the Sioux*, Ed. Frances Washburn, 32-36. Lincoln, NE: U of Nebraska P, 2006.

Vizenor, Gerald. *Fugitive Poses: Native American Indian Scenes of Absence and Presence*. Lincoln, NE: U of Nebraska P, 1998.

_____. "Aesthetics of Survivance: Literary Theory and Practice." *Survivance: Narratives of Native Presence*. Ed. Gerald Vizenor. Lincoln: U of Nebraska P, 2008. 1-24.

Welch, James. *Fools Crow*. New York: Penguin, 1987.

Wolf, Werner. "*Mise en cadre*—A Neglected Counterpart to *Mise en abyme*." *Postclassical Narratology: Approaches and Analyses*. Eds. Jan Alber and Monika Fludernik. Columbus: The Ohio State UP, 2010. 58-82.

Zitkala-Ša. "When the Buffalo Herd Went West." *Dreams and Thunder: Stories, Poems, and the Sun Dance Opera*. Ed. P. Jane Hafen. Lincoln: U of Nebraska P, 2001. 13-20.

In the Heart of the Land: Midwestern Plays and Playwrights _____

David Radavich

The Midwest is not well known as a culture and is often thought of as the "not place"—"fly-over country" —not worth seeing between the dynamic coasts and not the storied South, with its conflicted Civil War history. "America's breadbasket" is often derided for being boring and sometimes admired as reliable and predictable, delineated mostly by flat landscape and fertile soil. But in fact, the heartland has proven surprisingly dramatic from its origins as an American region. Seeing is not always believing. Under its seemingly placid exterior, the Midwest teems with unresolved tensions of self, community, and destiny showcased clearly in its theatrical masterworks.

Ohio-born William Dean Howells (1837-1920), the "Dean of American letters" in the second half of the nineteenth century, wrote over thirty plays, though his primary success came as novelist, essayist, and editor. A number of his early plays, like *Out of the Question* (1877) and *A Counterfeit Presentment* (1877) feature a striking Midwesterner, a "natural gentleman," invariably an engineer or practical-minded problem-solver, who ends up rescuing the more traditionally cultivated Northeasterners around him. Missourian Mark Twain (1835-1910) stands as one of the icons of American literature, yet few remember that he wrote some eleven dramatic pieces, at least two of them worthy of production.

Howells teamed up with Twain on several occasions, most notably perhaps in their delightful comedy, *Colonel Sellers as a Scientist* (1887). This theatrical romp enacts the exploits of a flamboyant scientist/inventor from the Midwest, who arrives with his family in Washington, D.C. with aims to revolutionize American society and culture. For one thing, the Colonel proposes moving the national capital from Washington to Saint Louis: "Saint Louis is the political centre of the country, and will soon outstrip Chicago as the moral and religious centre" (236). This comedy offers the first full-throated assertion of Midwestern confidence and significance. The central character of Twain's later *Is He Dead?* (1898) is another delightful romp, this time in the cultural mecca of art, Paris, where a character named Chicago concocts an elaborate scheme to defraud art connoisseurs by arranging the fake death of a living artist, complete with a state funeral on the Champs Élysées.

The plays of Twain and Howells are among the earliest on record from the Midwest, apart perhaps from Native American pieces and immigrant drama only now being discovered. The enactments of Midwesterners in these early plays set the tone for drama of the region for decades to come, continuing to our day. And the centrality of Howells and Twain to our national literature signals that Midwestern drama has likewise occupied a central place in American theatre, with many of our most celebrated playwrights enacting and demonstrating Midwestern themes and connections.

Drama from the heartland stands out from that written elsewhere in the country in a number of respects. As in plays written in almost any culture, many are set in the home. But the Midwestern home differs noticeably from homes depicted in the American Northeast, South, and West. It is not tormented by the zealous religiosity of the Puritanism of the Northeast nor the racial legacy of slavery and the Civil War in the South. Unlike the transient abodes of the West— tepees, camps, motels, apartments—the Midwestern home is situated temporally in the present, well rooted in its environment, solid and reliable, if sometimes confining.

In Midwestern plays, time is not historical or linear but cyclical, tied to the seasons of growing—planting, fertilizing, weeding, harvesting. The Midwest is not a region subject to the seasonal influx of tourism or the long winters or summers of more extreme climes. Time in the heartland offers a comfortable reliability, though not without periodic meteorological hardships, especially droughts and tornadoes. Midwestern plays also focus, to a noticeable extent, on physical work and the daily rhythms of life—cooking, cleaning, getting ready for work, going to bed. Middle American culture, as enacted on stage, finds meaning in the chores of living as they reveal personalities, goals, relationships, and ideologies.

Dramatic characters in Midwestern plays likewise distinguish themselves from those of other regions. These characters are not fast-talking, like New Yorkers, or colorful story-tellers, like Southerners, but laconic. They struggle coming to words. In fact, language often becomes a drama in itself, the creative tension involved in facing, naming, and expressing one's deepest goals and self. Midwestern characters are often practical in orientation, capable of managing in the world of objects and everyday realities. They are perceived as honest, reliable, and relatively simple—what you see is what you get—though their personalities often radiate a depth and mystery not capable of being expressed in words.

Midwestern language thereby often seems quiet and forthright. Speech tends to be unadorned—rhetorical flourishes are regarded with suspicion, sometimes even disgust—though a kind of poetry is achieved through imagery and rhythmic repetition. In an astonishing number of Midwestern plays, however, dramatic situations that begin in the comforting sameness of ordinary life spin suddenly out of control into more transcendental territory—like the tornado in the iconic *Wizard of Oz* that renders everything suddenly in vibrant color—with language that becomes choric, ghostly, or surreal (or all three at once). Such abrupt shifts in language signal that the Midwest is much deeper and wilder than it seems, a place of unpredictable surprises.

The issues that Midwestern plays deal with most frequently tend to be iconic: defining the self, deciding whether to go or stay, standing up against injustice, facing personal or social demons. These concerns may result from the Midwest's enduring association with the land. Soil and water and air are essential not only for survival in "America's breadbasket" but also for prosperity and well-being, since food crops, lifestock, and related natural resources undergird every aspect of life. Poisoning the "well" of one's natural environment leads to lethal consequences for entire communities, as a number of Midwestern works attest. Underneath the commonly assumed undramatic demeanor of Midwestern culture, life-and-death dramas are being enacted on a daily basis, both in real life and on stage.

Following the early examples of Twain and Howells, Midwestern drama surged in the twentieth century, taking center stage nationally. Frank Baum's *The Wonderful Wizard of Oz*, first published in 1900, sets out all of the above-mentioned themes and became an immediate and enduring hit, especially after the 1939 film adaptation starring Judy Garland as the wide-eyed, sensible Dorothy. William Vaughn Moody (1869-1910) has been unfairly forgotten as a significant poet and playwright who died at a tragically early age. His *The Faith Healer* (1909) is the first major full-length play set in the Midwest and features a full cast of Midwestern characters. Like Baum's *Wizard of Oz*, it showcases all the iconic Midwestern elements: home rooted in its environment, daily patterns of work, laconic language spinning into choric transcendence, self and family confronting big questions.

The first third of the twentieth century witnessed the astonishing rise of female playwrights from the Midwest, all of whom won national awards and recognition, ushering in a theatrical feminism never seen before. Zona Gale's *Miss Lulu Bett* (1921) became the first play by a woman, and the third overall, to win the Pulitzer Prize for Drama. Zoë Akins (1886-1958) became famous for her "society plays" and won a Pulitzer Prize in 1935 for her dramatization of Edith Wharton's novel, *The Old Maid*. Rachel Crothers (1878-1958) triumphed on Broadway from 1906 to 1937 during a career unmatched for sustained excellence and richness of invention. Midwesterners at first appeared only obliquely in her plays, but as she became more self-assured and successful, she set scenes in places like Dubuque, Iowa. Crothers received the National Achievement Award from Eleanor Roosevelt in the White House in 1938. Her work merits much more attention and performance.

Susan Glaspell (1876-1948) became a leading figure of the famous Provincetown Players, second only to Eugene O'Neill in influence. The taut realism and insistent feminism of *Trifles* (1916), a one-act play, have led to frequent performances and its being regularly anthologized. *The Inheritors* (1921) is a fascinating history play set in the Midwest, while *The Outside* (1917) and *The Verge* (1921) push expressionism in exciting avant-garde directions unseen before in American theatre. Although *The Outside* and *The Verge* take place in her adopted New England, Glaspell was defiantly Midwestern, becoming the first playwright to actively celebrate her home region. She went on to win the Pulitzer Prize for *Alison's House* in 1931.

The success of these female playwrights underscores the duel elements of Midwestern culture, emphasizing equal rights and the fight for social justice. The 1920s also saw the first flowering of African-American drama from the Midwest, which, in strength and vitality, is second to none. The first major figure was Langston Hughes, iconic figure in the Harlem Renaissance, who was born in Joplin, Missouri and raised in Lawrence, Kansas and other cities in the Midwest. Although he is viewed primarily as a poet, and an enduring one, he nonetheless wrote many plays, including a series in conjunction with Gilpin Players at Karamu House in Cleveland, Ohio. Lorraine Hansberry (1903-1965) emerged as a major figure several decades later, scoring a big hit with the iconic *A Raisin in the Sun* in 1959. She was the first black woman to have a play on Broadway. Her later work explores fascinating new racial territory, but her career was cut tragically short by her death at a relative young age. Charles Gordone (1925-1995) became the first African-American to receive the Pulitzer Prize for *No Place for Somebody* in 1970, a striking portrait of urban life in the period.

A commanding figure of the 1930s was the cosmopolitan Thornton Wilder (1897-1975), one of America's premier novelists and playwrights, the only author to win Pulitzer Prizes in both drama and fiction. Born and raised in his early years in Wisconsin, Wilder traveled the world and was highly educated and widely connected. His formative theatrical years were spent at the University of Chicago, where he wrote many of his path-breaking one-acts like *The Long Christmas Dinner* and *Pullman Car Hiawatha*, both of 1930. He went on to write the iconic *Our Town* (1938), a play set in New Hampshire, but exhibiting many Midwestern elements. *Our Town* is the most frequently performed of all American plays. *The Front Page* of 1928 by Ben Hecht (1894-1964) and Charles

MacArthur (1895-1956) was likewise very successful, serving as the prototype for countless "newspaper dramas" in subsequent films and television series.

Another great American playwright, who arose in the late 1930s and triumphed for the next two decades, was Tennessee Williams, who lived for over twenty years in the Midwest, mostly in Saint Louis. He wrote some twenty-five plays set in this city, which he always labeled Midwestern, in contrast to the famous southern plays of his theatrical maturity. His signature Midwestern play is *The Glass Menagerie* of 1945, which features an autobiographically-based main character, who longs to escape the confines of the Midwest. Later, southern plays like *A Streetcar Named Desire* and *A Cat on a Hot Tin Roof* nonetheless embody many characters and elements from his time in the Midwest. The late tragicomedy, *A Lovely Sunday for Creve Coeur* of 1979, once again set in Saint Louis, rewrites the ending of *The Glass Menagerie*; this time, the central character does not escape the Midwest, but decides to confront reality and remain.

Arthur Miller is not a Midwestern playwright *per se*, but he attended the University of Michigan, and two major plays are set in the heartland. *The Man Who Had All the Luck* of 1944 fuses Jewish and Midwestern notions of karma. *All My Sons* of 1974 continues the karmic structure with commentary on family and the legacy of World War II. *Death of a Salesman* of 1949 is set back in the Northeast following the author's return, but the Midwest makes clandestine appearances through elements from Miller's time living in Michigan. His formative years in the Midwest established a sound theatrical foundation for his subsequent career.

Perhaps the most successful American playwright of the 1950s was William Inge (1913-1973) of Independence, Kansas, who enjoyed an astonishing run of four hits on Broadway, all made into successful films: *Come Back, Little Sheba* of 1950, *Picnic* of 1953, *Bus Stop* of 1955, and *The Dark at the Top of the Stairs* of 1957. He also wrote the screenplay for the Oscar-winning *Splendor in the Grass* of 1961. Inge's dramatization of Midwestern themes resonated well during the post-war era of fellow-Kansan Eisenhower, since it was a period marked by rapidly shifting family relations and burgeoning awareness of sexual politics.

In the 1960s and '70s, Midwestern playwrights continued their prominence in American theatre. Four male dramatists documented the troubled state of masculinity in a period of radically altered gender norms. David Rabe (b. 1940) electrified the theatrical world with his searing Vietnam trilogy, *The Basic Training of Pavlo Hummel* of 1971, *Sticks and Bones* also of 1971, and *Streamers* of 1976, which became the signature dramatic treatment of that conflict. *Basic Training* traces the introduction of a wide-eyed Midwesterner into the complex realities of modern war. *Sticks and Bones*, by contrast, is set in the conventional Midwestern home, detailing the fractures of a representative "all-American" family riven by the son's experience in Vietnam. *Streamers*, set in an army barracks, delves more deeply into the cauldron of sexuality and race in the midst of profound social change. Rabe's later masterpiece, *Hurlyburly* of 1984, further documents masculine decadence and confusion during this period.

Lanford Wilson (1937-2011) created his own masterful trilogy during the late 1970s and 1980s, but set it in his native central Missouri. *Fifth of July* of 1978 revolutionized Broadway with its depictions of a settled gay male couple, one a disabled Vietnam veteran, as the central protagonists. This Chekhovian play has become a classic of the decade. *Tally's Folly* of 1982, a charming, bittersweet play, won the 1982 Pulitzer Prize. *Tally and Son* of 1985 offers a more comprehensive perspective on local and national history and family legacy over generations. An earlier play, *The Mound-Builders* of 1975, is set in southern Illinois and focuses on anthropology and Native American culture.

Sam Shepard (b. 1943) has achieved fame as both a talented actor in major films and as author of dozens of plays, many of them iconic and enduring. He was born and raised in Illinois but moved to California with his family in his later youth. Several early plays deal with his Midwestern experience, most notably *Buried Child* of 1978, which delineates a dysfunctional family whose secrets are intimately tied to the land. Shepard went on to achieve fame with his startling and path-breaking western plays, among them *Fool for Love* of 1979 and *True West* of 1980, featuring marginal characters in explosive, transient situations. But the celebrated actor and playwright returned to live in the Midwest over a decade ago and has resumed writing plays set in the heartland. Among these is the striking *God of Hell* of 2004, which envisions a Wisconsin farm contaminated by nuclear radiation. Strikingly, the lead female character of this play stands up against injustice and male insanity, a departure from Shepard's earlier male-centered plays.

David Mamet (b. 1947) has achieved success as both playwright and screenwriter of such award-winning films as *House of Cards* and *Homicide*. His taut, repetitive, incantatory Midwestern dialogue has influenced a number of writers and entered the national lexicon. Many of his plays are set in or near his native Chicago. *Sexual Diversity in Chicago* of 1976 established Mamet as a fresh new voice, but *American Buffalo* of 1977 has become canonized as a major American play, featuring three wounded male con-men/ drifters who wrestle for supremacy in a two-bit pawn shop. Mamet focuses almost exclusively on male characters who are wounded, conflicted, fearful, and competitive, often over or through sex. *Glengarry Glen Ross* of 1983, which won the Pulitzer Prize, focuses on predators and victims in the world of real estate. *Speed-the-Plow* of 1989 moves to the shark-infested culture of Hollywood and includes an important female character. But Mamet is at his best enacting the dislocations of declining patriarchy and the effects on men struggling to find and maintain their place.

These four prize-winning male dramatists provide perhaps a "book end" to the notable female playwrights half a century earlier, but a couple women emerged in this period with a substantially different perspective. One is Marsha Norman, a child of Louisville, Kentucky, a border city with a mixed southern-Midwestern heritage. Norman's plays exhibit and even enact this dual-region tension. *Third and Oak: The Laundromat* of 1978 includes overt Midwestern elements, as one of the main characters hails from Columbus, Ohio. But it is in Norman's *'night, Mother* of 1981, which won the 1983

Pulitzer Prize, that the battle between Midwest and South takes center stage. There, Midwestern practical, blunt truth-telling collides head-on with the creative, evasive, story-telling of the gregarious South. On a number of occasions, Norman has commented on the writers she admires, many of them Midwestern. *'night, Mother* links her to another great bi-regional writer in formerly abolitionist northern Kentucky, Wendell Berry.

For the most part, Midwestern drama has rooted itself in everyday realism, somewhat heightened and at critical moments spinning into transcendental space. But an undercurrent of the fantastical has always flowed not far below the surface, dating back to the Twain-Howells collaboration, *Colonel Sellers as a Scientist*. Midwestern playwrights have, over the decades, explored imaginary terrain like the glittering Emerald City and Kingdom of Oz. In the 1920s, Rachel Crothers set a play called *Venus* on the planet of the same name, where genders can be chemically nullified or reversed. Tennessee Williams' expressionistic 1941 play set in Saint Louis, *Stairs to the Roof*, features characters named simply Mr. P., D., Q., and T. and ends with the main young couple flying off into outer space with fireworks and a banner declaring, "THE MILLENNIUM" (98-99). Experimental Midwestern plays in this mode almost always include an implicit argument for social justice, reversing the forms of oppression found in the present here on realistic earth.

Fitting clearly into this experimental tradition are the early plays of Adrienne Kennedy like *Funnyhouse of a Negro* of 1964, which shocked audiences with its audacious mixture of race and history and won the Obie Award. This phantasmagoric play focuses on a mixed-race female who assumes a variety of masks appropriated across time and space, including Queen Victoria and the Duchess of Habsburg, and who interacts with characters as diverse as Jesus and Patrice Lumumba, assassinated first president of the Congo. *The Owl Answers* of 1965 continues in the same vein, but Kennedy has subsequently adopted a radically realistic perspective in plays like *The Ohio State Murders* of 1992, which takes understatement to a powerful dramatic (Midwestern) extreme, as the central character narrates a series of horrific events in her native Ohio with a deliberately uninflected argument for social justice.

A more widely performed African-American playwright is August Wilson (1945-2005), whose ten-play epic cycle documents black life over every decade of the twentieth century in his native Pittsburgh. The action of his plays is solidly rooted in the nitty-gritty realities of marginal urban life, but Wilson incorporates many elements of African and Caribbean culture, including slave songs, gospel music, and voodoo ritual, transcending the present. Many works like *Fences* of 1985 and *The Piano Lesson* of 1990, both of which won the Pulitzer Prize, enact the legacy of the Great Migration of blacks from the South to northern cities and rural areas in order to find work, own property, and achieve dignity. The struggle for African-American freedom forms a powerful thread in all his work, but not without great costs and considerable psychological damage. Wilson barely completed his immense cycle of plays before his untimely death in 2005.

The twentieth century proved to be a period in which many Midwestern plays and playwrights triumphed. That pattern has continued into the present century, with authors like Chicago-born David Auburn (b. 1969) and Tracy Letts (b. 1965) continuing to produce notable work. Auburn's *Proof* of 2001 won the Pulitzer Prize with its depiction of a young, gifted female mathematician and her troubled relationship with her father. Letts' *August: Osage County* of 2007, set in his native northeastern Oklahoma, won the Pulitzer Prize in 2008. It is a family drama largely realistic in orientation, with a southern element of ancestry contextualizing the current action set in a Midwestern-style home. Letts moved to Chicago at the age of twenty and has been an active member of the Steppenwolf Theatre Company for many years.

Midwestern drama has enjoyed success for almost a century and a half, winning awards and becoming established as part of the American theatrical canon. This has occurred even as many Americans are not clear about just what the Midwest is or even where it is. One of the interesting questions is why Midwestern drama has resonated so consistently and so well with American audiences. Eugene O'Neill, for instance, is an undeniably great American dramatist, among the top two or three of our theatrical masters. Yet, his often stern, demanding northeastern sensibility can be challenging to audiences. Midwestern plays and musicals, on the other hand, seem approachable and unpretentious, "everyday" and "all-American."

Drama from the Midwest is rooted, as noted before, in realism, which has been the default literary style of American culture as a whole for some time. Playwrights from the heartland have grown up with and absorbed that orientation, using it to their advantage. The iconic shift to other-worldly realms that occurs midway through many Midwestern plays offers both dramatists and audiences an opportunity to explore the strange implications and transformations of the familiar. Midwestern language is typically rather simple and uninflected, at least on the laconic surface, though it can rise to poetry through repetition and skillful use of rhythm. Speakers of this dialect are easier to understand than many Southerners or Northerners, and their conversation refers less frequently to events of regional historical significance. These qualities of realism and commonly understood language have made Midwestern plays ideal for film or television, media national in distribution.

The history of the Midwest is largely one that involved the transition from an agricultural economy to small towns and burgeoning cities. The region has become prosperous through abundant natural resources and through manufacturing, though the latter has conspicuously moved overseas in recent decades, resulting in the "Rust Belt." Compared to the South or Northeast, the Midwest is less scarred by history, though the treatment of Native Americans and other minorities was often horrific. Many of the central dramas of the South—Civil War, Confederacy, Reconstruction, Jim Crow—are not as widely shared in the rest of the country. The long, rich history of the Northeast and spectacular financial excesses of Wall Street are less directly experienced elsewhere in the U.S. The fundamental dramas of the Midwest, by contrast—coming to language, defining the self, fighting against social injustice, claiming one's place— resonate almost everywhere.

One could argue that the relative invisibility of the Midwest has contributed to its success. One Southerner was overheard asking, "Does the Midwest even have a culture?" Until fairly recently, virtually all Midwestern playwrights felt driven to leave their region in order to find success and fortune, first on Broadway and then later, in Hollywood. Authors like Rachel Crothers did not "come out" as Midwesterners until relatively late in their careers, when their success was already assured. In today's more diversified theatrical world, many more dramatists are choosing to stay and work out of Chicago, Detroit, or Kansas City. August Wilson spent much of his fabled career in Minneapolis/Saint Paul.

For outsiders, the Midwest is a largely unknown and unmarked place onto whose back screen their own dreams and struggles can easily be projected. Over the course of the past century, Midwesterners on stage and screen have become the boy or girl "next door," not terribly unlike themselves—or at least a self they can imagine. The Midwest has often been mythologized in plays and films as a small-town, nostalgic utopia of community connectedness and familiar patterns of time and season. This notion is certainly outdated and has always been compromised, as numerous authors from Middle America have demonstrated. But the central dramas of the Midwest are human ones, fundamental to our basic existence and survival. For decades, playwrights from the heartland have been asking if we will destroy ourselves, whether we can find a home, whether we can achieve justice and wholeness as individuals and communities. These questions will likely obsess us for years to come, making theatre from the Midwest enduringly approachable and relevant.

Works Cited

Howells, William Dean and Mark Twain. "Colonel Sellers as a Scientist." *The Complete Plays of William Dean Howells*. Ed. Walter J. Meserve. New York: New York UP, 1960.

Williams, Tennessee. *Stairs to the Roof.* New York: New Directions, 2000.

A Discovered Land: Willa Cather's Pioneers

John Rohrkemper

Perhaps the most important fact about Willa Cather and her relationship to the Midwest is that she was not from there. She is not a native Midwesterner. This is ironic since, to many, she is the quintessential Midwestern writer. Many readers, including many who never have seen native prairie grass, are introduced to the geography and life of the prairies through her novels. Many of those readers find it a starkly, exotic place, and I have no doubt that many will always think of Cather and *O Pioneers!* or *My Antonia* when they hear or read of the Midwest.

And yet, Cather is a native Virginian, from Winchester in the northern part of the state, the Shenandoah Valley on the edge of the Appalachians, fifty miles northwest of the District of Columbia, near where Virginia, West Virginia, and Maryland meet. The rugged terrain and its citizenry that had been long-settled and drew its ancestry largely from the British Isles was far different from the prairie landscape and mixture of French Canadian and northern, central, and eastern European immigrants she would chronicle in her great Midwestern novels and stories. And that's precisely the point. Cather's forebears were Welsh and Scots-Irish Presbyterians. Jasper Cather was the first of his family to come to America, settling in Western Pennsylvania in the eighteenth century, and serving in the Continental Army during the American Revolution. After the war, he bought Virginia land and the family remained on or near the family homestead on Flint Ridge in Frederick County, near Back Creek Valley (Woodress 13). The Cathers were to remain for nearly a century and became a prominent family in the area. Their time as Virginians was not without controversy, though. Willa's great grandfather, James, was anti-slavery, but also was a fervid states' rights advocate and sided with the Confederacy during the Civil War, but his son and Willa's grandfather, William, was a Union man and his neighbors never entirely overcame their resentment of this allegiance.

Despite these lingering resentments, Willa was born on December 7, 1873 to a prosperous family of some local significance. Cather's biographer, James Woodress describes the environment, into which she was born:

> Back Creek Valley in Frederick County, Virginia, at the end of 1873 was...thinly settled.... The farms in that part of the Shenandoah Valley, which lies some fifty miles west-northwest of the national capital, were mostly hilly, and their thin, rocky soil was not well suited to agriculture.... No family had owned more than a few slaves before the war and many settlers...worked their slatey acres with their own sweat.... Much of the land was still wild forest." (12)

It was, in most ways, an idyllic childhood, stable and secure. Most of the residents, including Cather's family, were comfortable in their homogeneity. The African American population was smaller than in other parts of Virginia, since the rocky farmland and relatively small family farms had never been particularly conducive to the kind of industrial farming that had exploited slave labor. Cather's neighbors mostly traced their ancestry to the British Isles and were uniformly Protestant. In her girlhood, Cather had been enchanted by the romance of the Confederacy's failed cause, but in later life, she resisted attempts to be characterized as a Southern or Virginia writer. Like Mark Twain, as she became more deeply committed to a realist aesthetic, she became increasingly disenchanted with what she perceived as a destructive Southern sentimentality. Woodress notes that Cather later developed an "adult distaste for the polite conventions and ritual blather of genteel southern society":

> Cather always had ambivalent feeling about her southern background. When she visited Virginia in 1913 [the year her first great Midwestern novel, *O Pioneers!* was published] she was eager to get away from the romantic southern attitude she found in both sexes. (28)

Despite her later ambivalence about her birthplace, during those early formative years of Cather's life, Virginia was home.

By the time Willa and her family moved to Nebraska, her Uncle George and Aunt Franc had lived there for ten years and her Cather grandparents had lived there for nearly as long. In 1880, Willa's father went to Nebraska to visit his parents, bother, and sister-in-law and, less than three years later, sold the family's Virginia homestead and followed the other Cathers west. Cather's family arrived in Red Cloud, Nebraska in April of 1883. Willa was not quite nine-and-a-half years old. The contrast was dramatic between the stark, open, nearly treeless Midwestern prairie and forested Virginia, with its limited horizon shaped and confined by surrounding mountains. Woodress claims that the "the jolting ride" west "made an indelible impression on young Willa":

> She had come to Nebraska, she wrote later, from "an old and Conservative society, from the Valley of Virginia, where the original land grants made in the reigns of George II and George III had been going down from father to son ever since, where life was ordered and settled." Now she was in a brand-new country lost in a sea of grass devoid of human habitation. The familiar mountains that she had seen every day back home had been obliterated. (35-36)

Cather's first thoughts were desolate upon arriving in this new land: "'I felt a good deal as if we had come to the end of everything—it was a kind of erasure of personality." (Woodress 36) But after the first shock of relocation wore off, Cather began to find the value in her new home. As biographer Sharon O'Brien has noted: "The wrenching move from a sheltered, fertile landscape to a barren land was, Cather later thought, the greatest trauma of her childhood. But the dislocation also stimulated creativity and self-renewal" (73). And O'Brien further notes that:

> As her friend and fellow novelist Dorothy Canfield rightly observes, "an imaginative and emotional response to the great shift from Virginia to Nebraska" was at the heart of Cather's fiction. Not her rootedness in Nebraska, but her transplanting from one radically different landscape and community to another at a formative, impressionable age powerfully affected her writing. *(59)*

And so the Midwest was a *new* world to her, not *the* world, as we tend to think of our first homes, the places into which we are born. At an age when a precocious girl was old enough to have established a sense of what the world looked like, of the way its inhabitants looked, talked, and behaved, she was uprooted and had to confront an alien landscape, hear strange new tongues, and learn new customs. Young Willa Cather was obviously taken with this new world, absorbed it, and as an adult—and largely after she had removed herself from the place and come back East—she was to write about it with the vividness of someone who saw the Midwest as a place of difference rather than familiarity, who understood what made the Midwest distinctive if not unique. She understood that the Midwest was not *every*where, but a very specific *some*where.

In his biography, *Willa Cather: A Literary Life,* James Woodress discusses Cather's most formative period:

> She…believed that most of the basic material a writer works with is acquired before the age of fifteen. That's the important period [she told an interviewer]. Those years determine whether a writer's work will be poor and thin or rich and fine. On another occasion she narrowed this time span to the period between the ages of eight and fifteen, thus excluding from her scheme the years she had lived in Virginia. (40)

But Woodress misses an important point here. Cather, in this latter occasion, indicates that she believes a writer's most important period begins at eight, one year—about a year-and-a-half actually—*before* she, herself, made the most eventful move of her life. What matters for Cather's artistic career, and for the meaning of the Midwest to her and to that career, is that decisive year or so in Virginia when her thoughts about the world could be formulated so that they then could be turned upside down with her move to Nebraska. What she was to learn, but only later was able to articulate through her fiction, is the confrontation of the "I" and the "not I", that is, the nexus of fiction, which allows the fiction writer to escape her solipsism and imagine other lives, other worlds. And as a nine-and-a-half-year-old—a liminal age between childhood and adolescence—she also had to adapt emotionally to her new surroundings, had to rethink the meaning of her life and her selfhood, even as she moved halfway across a continent.

The power of those Midwestern works—and I think of some of the early stories like "Peter" and "On the Divide," but particularly the great early novels, especially *O Pioneers!* and *My Antonia*—is the exuberance of the novelist as discoverer—as pioneer, if you will—who says "look at what I've found; you thought the world looked one way, but let me show you an endlessly vital *other* way to look at things." And Cather discovered that if, for her, the Midwest could be *another* world, then there might be more *other* worlds as well. Years later, in the preface to her first novel, she wrote:

> One of the few really helpful words I ever heard from an older writer I had from Sarah Orne Jewett when she said to me: "Of course, one day you will write about your own country. In the meantime, get all you can. One must know the world *so well* before one can know the parish." (*Alexander's Bridge* 942)

Cather was nearly forty before she wrote about her "own country," her "parish," and by then, she had travelled widely and gotten to know much of the world. But, even in a smaller way, her coming to consciousness in Virginia, and then the later revelation of Nebraska, had given her a glimpse of a larger world, and made this new Midwestern world such a momentous discovery for her.

The first reality that the newly-arrived Midwesterners had to deal with was the land itself, the largely treeless prairie with its sweltering insect-infested summers and frigid winters. Her first Midwestern novel, the 1913 *O Pioneers!*, immediately immerses us in that harsh environment:

> One January day, thirty years ago, the little town of Hanover, anchored on a windy Nebraska tableland, was trying not to be blown away. A mist of fine snowflakes was curling and eddying about the cluster of low drab buildings huddled on the gray prairie, under a gray sky. The dwelling-houses were set about haphazard on the tough prairie sod;

some of them looked as if they had been moved in overnight, and others as if they were straying off by themselves, headed straight for the open plain. (3)

While Cather stresses the harshness of the climate and the impermanence of human endeavors to establish a prairie foothold, she also emphasizes, in this first chapter, the different ways that its new settlers cope with such hardship. The novel's protagonist, Alexandra Bergson, and her childhood and later adult friend, Carl Linstrum, face the same winter prairie but react to it quite differently. Alexandra's eyes "seemed to be looking…into the future" while Carl's eyes "already seemed to be looking into the past." Carl will eventually leave the Divide and return East, but Alexandra will stay and confront the future and the great fact of:

the land itself, which seemed to overwhelm the little beginnings of human society that struggled with its solemn wastes. It was from facing this vast hardness that the boy's mouth became so bitter; because he felt that men were too weak to make any mark here, that the land wanted to be left alone, to preserve its own fierce strength, its peculiar, savage kind of beauty, it uninterrupted mournfulness. (8)

So it is this "discovery" of the Midwest that characterizes Cather's sense of the place, and her greatest works about the Midwest most often examine the lives of European immigrants who also discover this new world. Cather was mindful that not everyone was cut out to be a discoverer, a pioneer. In fact, in *O Pioneers!* she declared "a pioneer should have imagination, should be able to enjoy the idea of things more than the things themselves" (25).

In her prairie novels and stories, but also in her later writing about the Southwest, Cather tended to emphasize the importance of one's imagination in creating a habitable landscape. Jamie Hudzik has aptly observed that Cather imagines three different types of characters embodying different relationships to this alien landscape. The first type she characterizes as *resistant*. A resistant character views the land as a burden, even an enemy that must be resisted and conquered. The second kind of character is *adaptive* and is able to "adjust to the harshness of the land and see its underlying worth," and can find whatever value might exist, even in an apparently hostile environment. The third type Hudzik identifies as the *transcendent* character, one who can become "one with the land" through the power of imagination, can "unite the natural and spiritual worlds," and can mythologize the land and thus make it more accessible to others (3-4).

In *O Pioneers!,* all three types exist in Alexandra Bergson's immediate family. Her father, John Bergson, sees the land as a foe, personifies it as an untamable enemy. And, perhaps for this reason, it makes him old by the time he's in his forties, and, we are told, it ultimately kills him:

> In eleven long years John Bergson had made but little impression on the wild land he had come to tame. It was still a wild thing that had its ugly moods.... Mischance hung over it. Its Genius was unfriendly to man.... This land was an enigma. It was like a horse that no one knows how to harness, that runs wild and kicks things to pieces. (11-12)

So, while John Bergson's resistance proves fatal, his wife, Alexandra's mother, is a more successful immigrant, one who finds accommodation with her new world:

> Alexandra often said that if her mother were cast upon a desert island, she would thank God for her deliverance, make a garden, and find something to preserve....She made a yellow jam of the insipid ground-cherries that grew on the prairie, flavoring it with lemon peel; and she had made a sticky dark conserve of garden tomatoes. She had experimented even with the rank buffalo-pea, and she could not see a fine bronze cluster of them without shaking her head and murmuring "What a pity." When there was nothing more to preserve, she began to pickle. (15-16)

Of course, Mrs. Bergson not only puts preserves and conserves on the pantry shelf, but also preserves as much of a way of life as has been possible to maintain from the old country; she conserves the family's cultural resources as "she had worthily striven to maintain some sense of household order amid conditions that made order very difficult" (15). Cather further asserts Mrs. Bergson's adaptability when she notes that "she had never quite forgiven John Bergson for bringing her to the end of the earth; but now that she was here, she wanted to…reconstruct her old life in as far as that was possible" (16).

Alexandra is a transcendent character. Her dying father recognizes this quality in her and leaves her as the chief steward of the family's farm property. Near the end of "The Wild Land," the first section of the novel, we see that John Bergson, despite his own failure to imagine the land adequately, has made the right choice in selecting Alexandra as his successor. She looks radiant as she rides across the Divide one day, shortly after her father's death and experiences an intense, mystical connection with the land:

> For the first time, perhaps, since that land emerged from the waters of the geologic ages, a human face was set toward it with love and yearning. It seemed beautiful to her, rich and strong and glorious. Her eyes drank in the breadth of it, until her tears blinded her. Then the Genius of the Divide, the great free spirit which breathes across it, must have bent lower than it ever bent to a human will before. The history of every country begins in the heart of a man or woman. (33)

And then later that evening, Alexandra has another transcendent experience as she finds comfort and unity with the vast grandeur of the nighttime sky and also with the smallest life beneath her feet:

> Alexandra drew her shawl closer about her and stood leaning against the frame of the mill, looking at the stars which glimmered so keenly through the frosty autumn air. She always loved to watch them, to think of their vastness and distance, and of their ordered march. It fortified her to reflect upon the great operations of nature, and when she thought of the law that lay behind them, she felt a sense of personal security. That night she had a new consciousness of the country, felt almost a new relation to it…. She had never known before how much the country meant to her. The chirping of the insects down in the long

grass had been like the sweetest music. She felt as if her heart were hiding down there, somewhere, with the quail and plover and all the wild things that crooned or buzzed in the sun. Under the long shaggy ridges, she felt the future stirring. (36)

Significantly, this passage brings to an end the section entitled "The Wild Land". This is immediately followed by a section that is set sixteen years later and called "Neighboring Fields". The wild land that had bedeviled John Bergson has been tamed by what Sharon O'Brien calls "love and yearning" for the land by "a conqueror who wins by yielding" (429). Another way to say this is that the land is made habitable through the power of the transcendent imagination, a deep awareness of her connectedness to and oneness with the land that Alexandra shows, while standing beneath that starry sky and amid the small wild things of the earth. This imaginative reconciling of herself to this "wild land" allows Alexandra to find her place in this strange and often daunting new world and to transform a perilous world into a nurturing one. And it was a similar gift that marked Cather's relationship to her new world, that allowed her to formulate a new consciousness of the land, and to create in her fiction an imaginative vision of the prairie that still shapes our sense of the Midwest.

If the first challenge for the immigrant is to find a livable relationship with the land, the other challenge is to find a place among its human society. It might be noted that Cather blithely ignores the fact of Nebraska's many centuries of native habitation when she imagines it as a virtually empty, open space and imagines that, in Alexandra, "for the first time, perhaps, since that land emerged from the waters of the geologic ages, a human face was set toward it with love and yearning" (71). For the sake of her pioneering tale it apparently was important that her immigrants were truly pioneers opening up a new land. But, if she ignored Native Americans, O'Brien describes how she was dazzled by the diversity of the peoples she found in Nebraska in the late nineteenth century:

Within a short ride [of her new Nebraska home] were neighbors Cather had not encountered in Virginia: the immigrants from Scandinavia, Bohemia, France, and Russia attracted to Nebraska in the 1870s and 1880s by promises of cheap land and fertile soil. Coming from the homogeneous Anglo-Saxon culture of white settlers in the Shenandoah Valley—where the sharpest divisions were between Baptists and Presbyterians, supporters of secession and Union sympathizers—she was excited by the discovery of difference. (71)

Cather celebrated that diversity in her great early novels, *O Pioneers!* and *My Antonia*, in which her heroines are Scandinavian and Bohemian, respectively, but in many other works as well. When her creative vision began to look beyond the Midwest, she continued to identify locales and moments in time, in which a rich mixture of cultures produced a vibrant new culture, such as in the 1927 *Death Comes for the Archbishop,* set in the Southwest and chronicling the fertile mingling of French, Spanish, and Indian cultures. In Cather's Nebraska, ethnic traditions remain prominent and ethnic predispositions trump any easy melting pot ideal.

In some ways, Cather seems to reflect the prevailing ideas about race that dominated late nineteenth and early twentieth century thinking when there was a widespread interest in presumed racial differences among the immigrants. In his study of the European the immigrant experience in his *Whiteness of a Different Color: European Immigrants and the Alchemy of Race,* Matthew Frye Jacobson examines nineteenth- and early twentieth-century conceptions of race, in which immigrants were thought not only to be of different socially constructed ethnicities, but of biologically different races. Hence, people defined as Hebrews, Celts, Mediterraneans, Iberics, and Teutons were thought to be of distinctly different racial groups. These supposedly inherent and seemingly immutable differences were often used to exclude immigrants from being fully accepted as Americans. Jacobson contrasts these racially-obsessed assumptions with what contemporary scholars in many disciplines have shown us: that "races are invented categories—designations coined for the sake of grouping and separating peoples along lines of presumed differences," and not biological mandates. (4) Race is invented by humans and not by nature.

Cather did not seek to exclude immigrants from full access to the promise of America, but we might sense a dated attitude about racial difference when Cather discusses the young men of the Divide:

> The French and Bohemian boys were spirited and jolly, liked variety, and were as much predisposed to favor anything new as the Scandinavian boys were to reject it. The Norwegian and Swedish lads were much more self-centered, apt to be egotistical and jealous....The French boys liked a bit of swagger, and they were always delighted to hear about anything new: new clothes, new games, new songs, new dances. (110)

And perhaps the best example of the spirited boys, and the most vibrant individual in the novel is Amédée Chevalier, a new father who is enraptured by his son and plans to have twenty children to populate the Divide. Amédée's death, from peritonitis resulting from a ruptured appendix, sets in motion events that will bring the novel to a tragic conclusion, but in their optimism and bonhomie, Amédée and his wife Angélique cannot even imagine a tragic ending. They have become American dreamers, confident like so many Americans in literature and life, that the future only offers opportunities and more opportunities. When Angélique tells Emil, Alexandra's brother, that her husband has gone off to work his fields even though he has been ill, we are told:

> Angélique did not speak with much anxiety, not because she was indifferent, but because she felt so secure in her good fortune. Only good things could happen to a rich, energetic, handsome young man like Amédée with a new baby in the cradle and a new header in the field. (124)

Despite their often-unfounded optimism, Cather clearly appreciated and celebrated the vibrant spirit of French immigrants like Amédée and Angélique, and the native intelligence she often associated with Bohemian immigrants. But it is important to note that her immigrants are celebrated for their difference, for their distinctiveness and not for their adherence to the melting pot myth that was beginning to become prevalent to explain the supposed ease with which immigrants wanted to and could shed their ethnic background and merge into a homogeneous Americanness. Cather had experienced enough of that homogeneity in her first home, Virginia. One of the important things she learned as a result of her coming to this new land was the value of diversity.

Thus, Cather's view of the immigrant experience was quite different from that of one of the age's most significant historians, Frederick Jackson Turner, who, in his 1893 essay, "The Frontier in American History," argued that the value of the frontier in part was that it quickly erased European customs and ideologies and thus made the transition from European to American relatively seamless. Guy Reynolds, after noting that Turner read but disliked Cather's fiction, concludes that:

> Despite his interest in the culturally varied West it is clear that Turner's America was a nativist Utopia filled with immigrants of English and north European descent. Although Turner was anything but a racist, there is no doubt that he was happiest envisioning an America made up of migrants from a relatively confined and traditional stock of origins. (66)

Cather reflected on the significance of those diverse European immigrants on her and on her adopted state in an article she wrote for the September 5, 1923 issue of *The Nation* magazine," Nebraska at the End of the First Cycle." Cather stresses the diversity of the state by noting that, in the 1910 census, there were three times as many foreign-born as native Nebraskans living in the state (334). And she *celebrates* the diversity as well: "Colonies of European people, Slavonic Germanic, Scandinavian, Latin, spread across our bronze prairies like daubs of color on a painter's palette. They brought with them something that this neutral new world needed even more than the immigrants needed land" (335). Cather further compares these new arrivals favorably with the native-born Americans who:

> were seldom open-minded enough to understand the Europeans, or to profit by their older traditions. Our settlers from New England, cautious and convinced of their own superiority, kept themselves insulated as much as possible from foreign influences. The incomers from the South—from Missouri, Kentucky, the two Virginias—were provincial and utterly without curiosity. (335)

Cather further suggests that she was not content to view such difference from afar, but claims that, as a girl and young woman, she would spend her Sundays alternately attending services with a Norwegian or Danish or Swedish congregation, going to church with German Lutherans, or hearing sermons in French or Czech at nearby Catholic parishes (334).

Moreover, Cather argues that the lasting legacy of the immigrants for the state and the country may be their cosmopolitanism. She says that whenever she contemplates the ethnic cemeteries of her home state, she can't help thinking that:

> Something went into the ground with those pioneers that will one day come out again. Something that will come out not only in sturdy traits of character, but in elasticity of mind, in an honest attitude toward the realities of life, in certain qualities of feeling and imagination.... It is in the great cosmopolitan country known as the Middle West that we may see the hard molds of American provincialism broken up; that we may hope to find young talent that will challenge the pale proprieties, the insincere, conventional optimism of our art and thought. (388)

Guy Reynolds has suggested that the celebration of ethnic diversity that Cather evidences in the 1913 *O Pioneers!* and, we might add, in this 1923 essay, had much to do with the increasing xenophobia of America in the years in which Cather was writing. That narrow provincialism culminated in the Johnson-Reed Act of 1924, a highly restrictive immigration law that effectively ended eighty years of robust immigration. That period of immigration had forever changed America and eventually led us to re-imagine ourselves as "a nation of immigrants." But, if most Americans were turning more anti-immigrant in the decade or so leading up to the act, Cather clearly offered a counter-thesis. Reynolds argues that in *O Pioneers!* Cather's refutation "of nativism, of narrow or xenophobic provincialism is pertinent to the context in which Cather wrote... Cather is setting up fictionalized communities of relevance to an America that was becoming ever more marked by racial diversity" and ethnic animosities (57-58).

At the age of nine-and-a-half Willa Cather discovered a new land and the varied peoples who came to inhabit it. That revelation forever marked her life—and her art. She never lost a keen eye for and a deep appreciation of the land wherever she found it—whether the rocky Atlantic coastal shore of Maine, or the arid beauty of the American Southwest, or any number of places where she cast her gaze. She also came to value the diversity of the people who came to America searching for a better life and left America the better for doing so. She celebrated the stark landscape and the hearty people she had come to know and love in her youth, even when it was unpopular to do so. She taught us all, even those of us native to the Midwest, how to look at and understand the meaning of her discovered land.

Works Cited

Cather, Willa. "Nebraska at the End of the First Cycle." *The Nation* 5 Sept. 1923. Reprinted in *O Pioneers!* Ed. Sharon O'Brien. New York: W. W. Norton & Co., 2008. 331-338. Norton Critical Editions Series.

_____. *O Pioneers!* New York: Vintage, 1992.

_____. Preface to *Alexander's Bridge. Cather: Stories, Poems, and Other Writings*. Ed. Sharon O'Brien. New York: The Library of America, 1992. 941-943.

Hudzik, Jamie. *A Consciousness of the Land: Cather, Landscape, and Transcendence*. Unpublished Honors Thesis, Elizabethtown College, 2005.

Jacobson, Matthew Frye. *Whiteness of a Different Color: European Immigrants and the Alchemy of Race*. Cambridge: Harvard UP, 1998.

O'Brien, Sharon. *Willa Cather: The Emerging Voice*. New York and Oxford: Oxford UP, 1987.

Reynolds, Guy. *Willa Cather in Context: Progress, Race, Empire*. New York: St. Martin's Press, 1996.

Woodress, James. *Willa Cather: A Literary Life*. Lincoln: U of Nebraska P, 1987.

Critical Insights

Chicago and Peter DeVries' *Map of Desire* _____

Guy Szuberla

For many readers and most critics, Peter DeVries' characters will forever roam a fictional suburban and exurban world, a lush and well-upholstered land a commuter's ride away from New York City. In this standard view of his fiction, his comic heroes busy themselves sopping up martinis, romping in the new sexual freedoms, and searching for the great good place to live. Their home address— whether in Avalon, Merrymount, or Decency, Connecticut—floats somewhere to the east and south of John Cheever's Shady Hill, not far from Updike's Saltbox and Eastwick, Massachusetts. His novels, once they are assigned to these locations, can be read as a kind of enlarged and recast *New Yorker* cartoon: the plots turn in a kaleidoscopic whirl of endless cocktail hours; his characters speak in faddish clichés and modish jargon, what DeVries liked to call "brittle dialogue." As his protagonists pursue suburban sexual adventures, they prove themselves to be at once stylish and feckless. Some thirty years ago, the *Avenel Companion to English & American Literature* crowned DeVries "the comic laureate of suburbia" (72). Jeffrey Frank, in a 2004 *New Yorker* essay, spoke of him with greater precision as "an observer of spoiled middle-class white America, a place populated by comfortable yet perpetually ill-at-ease-heroes." Frank added, with no particular emphasis, that this "territory" represents the "agonies and pleasures of suburban life in the twentieth century" (46-7).

It may come as a surprise to some to learn that Peter DeVries was born in Chicago, 27 February 1910, the second child and first son of Joost and Henrietta Eldersveld DeVries, immigrants from the Netherlands. He grew up in Englewood, on Chicago's south side, in the vicinity of 67th and Halsted. There, among the German and Irish packinghouse workers, families of Dutch descent had settled in the late nineteenth century (Pacyga, 496-97). The young Peter DeVries was educated in the neighborhood parochial schools, at Engelwood

Christian School and Christian High School; he went on to enroll at Calvin College in Grand Rapids, Michigan, graduating with a B.A. in English in 1931. His parents, and no doubt the teachers who drilled him in the rigors of theological dogma and dispute, expected him to become a minister in the Dutch Reformed Church. He did not.

DeVries left Chicago in 1944. For several years, he had served as editor of *Poetry* magazine. He had written and published two novels—*But Who Wakes the Bugler* of 1940 and *The Handsome Heart* of 1943—and was about to complete a third, *Angels Can't Do Better* of 1944. All three of them are, more or less, autobiographical; all three, set in Chicago and on flat, firm Midwestern ground. Through James Thurber's intervention, DeVries was offered a half-time editor's job at *The New Yorker*. On the strength of the offer, he moved to Greenwich Village in New York and, in 1948, to Westport, Connecticut, where he lived until his death in 1993. Twice a week for many years, he commuted to New York to select cartoons, edit them, and rewrite captions for *The New Yorker*. He became, in short, a rooted and tax-paying citizen of the East-coast exurbia, perfectly positioned to be the comic chronicler of suburban angst and exurban envy.

But that's only half his story and far too compressed and simple a formula. DeVries himself, from time to time, suggested another vantage point on his fiction. When questions in interviews turned to his childhood and to his Chicago past, his answers seldom varied from one autobiographical explanation:

> I was born in Chicago in 1910 into a Dutch immigrant community, which still preserved its old-world ways. My origins would have been little different had my parents never come to America at all, but remained in Holland. I still feel somewhat like a foreigner, and not only for ethnic reasons. Our insularity was twofold, being a matter of religion as well as nationality. In addition to being immigrants, and not able to mix well with the Chicago Americans around us, we were Dutch Reformed Calvinists who weren't supposed to mix. . . .We were the elect, and the elect are barred from everything, you know, except heaven. (Newquist 146)

Later, in this same 1963 interview, he wonders out loud if a "case" might not be made that his fiction, given its recurrent "fascination with the sophisticated and 'worldly' world," was a "vicarious escape from this . . . painful immigrant childhood, with its sense of exclusion and inferiority" (147).

Such a case can be made. Not every DeVries novel maps a "vicarious escape" from immigrant origins and Chicago's South Side. And yet, from *Angels Can't Do Better* of 1944 through *The Blood of the Lamb* of 1962, *The Vale of Laughter* of 1967, *Forever Panting* of 1973, *Into Your Tent I'll Creep* of 1971, and on to *The Glory of the Hummingbird* of 1974, *Slouching Toward Kalamazoo* of 1983 and *The Prick of Noon* of 1985, DeVries' characters, in recurring scenes and story-lines, have brooded over their origins, have tried, generally with comic futility, to disguise and deny them. "I came from . . . Backbone, Arkansas," Eddie Teeters (a.k.a., Monty Carlo) says in *The Prick of Noon* , "and I vowed never to come from there again. Never, ever" (6). Don Wanderhope, the main character of *The Blood of the Lamb*, quarrels with his Dutch immigrant father. He has been dating a woman from outside the "Covenant," and his father has angrily called him to account. Don casually walks away: "I laughed softly as I hurried to my bedroom, a chuckle of affection for origins from which I would soon be gone, had already in spirit flown" (34). DeVries liked the joke well enough to have Jim Tickler repeat a variation of it in *The Glory of the Hummingbird*: "I cherished even the origins I seemed to be soaring above" (70).

Such parodic treatments of the myth of origins—presented in *The Blood of the Lamb* as a version of the melting-pot myth; in some other novels as self-conscious re-enactments of Jay Gatsby's invented identity—recur throughout DeVries fiction. These origin stories, and the stories characters tell to disguise their origins, are incised most sharply when DeVries writes about Chicago and the Midwest, particularly when he deploys a rhetoric of ethnicity. His characters' desire for another life and another social identity, their brooding sense of exclusion from that richer life, their often comic efforts to escape from what DeVries and his character Don Wanderhope call "immigrant inferiority" (*Blood* 45)—these themes and narrative forms are, as a matter of course, expressed through the filtering lenses of parody and satire. Characters like Don Wanderhope and Al Banghart of *Into Your Tent I'll Creep* naturally speak in the polyethnic accents of Chicago, but they are also given to imitating, often comically, the voices and gestures of what they believe is a higher culture and superior society. Until the end of *Forever Panting*, Stew Smackenfelt—ham actor, second-rate playwright, and the novel's comic hero—cannot seem to escape the habit of impersonating Winston Churchill reciting Longfellow's "Hiawatha." Like Wanderhope and Banghart, Smackenfelt, in trying out a half-dozen voices and personae, hopes to mask his ethnic and South Side origins, and, having entered the "worldly" world, fulfill his heart's desire.

I.

De Vries' first three novels were set in Chicago, and these, like many of his later works, recast autobiographical fragments from this past into fictive form. But none of the first three novels—*But Who Wakes the Bugler?* of 1940, *The Handsome Heart* of 1943, and *Angels Can't Do Better* of 1944—gives a prominent place to either immigrant parents or to the pains of escaping ethnic origins.[1] DeVries' treatment of his principal character's ethnicity in *Angels Can't Do Better*, for example, seems abstract, distanced, and sometimes comically muted. Peter Topp, a young faculty member in Lebanon College's political science department, is of Dutch descent. He's also a "ward heeler" and a reform politician in Chicago's eighteenth ward, first fighting "the machine," but ambitious to switch sides in the vain hope of rising to elected office (4, 21). His father, the chair of the political science department at Lebanon, is a lapsed member of the Dutch Reformed Church. At periodic intervals, Reverend De Bruin, a minister in the Dutch Reformed Church, pops up and threatens to excommunicate him. Since Mr. Topp feels that he's already quit the church, their conversations devolve into comic and hairsplitting doctrinal arguments over his precise standing in the church. None of these trappings of an ethnic past and identity seem to matter to either the elder Topp or his son.

And so, as a result of his father's indifference to the Dutch Reformed Church and his general indifference to his son's comings and goings, it does not seem to matter whether the young Topp dates and marries in or outside the Covenant. De Vries seems to have reflexively carved the character of Peter Topp's Dutch-American father out of the memories of his own painfully restricted immigrant childhood. Peter Topp, that is, exercises the worldly freedom the young Peter De Vries was forbidden. The woman Topp dates, Lucy Mayhew, the daughter of a wealthy, though crooked, contractor, bears no particular ethnic identity. While in later novels, a woman from outside the sacred circle of the Dutch community will hold a near fatal attraction because she is an "outsider." Here, it is Lucy Mayhew's claims to a higher social status and a cultural superiority that make Peter Topp fear marrying her would make him into a "prisoner of respectability" (44).

That he does not marry her, but the more sensuous and unpretentious Bessie Murdock, is fully in keeping with a narrative pattern that will dominate later DeVries novels. Drawn at first to an elegant society woman, or one who projects such an image, the DeVriesian hero will usually turn, in the final chapter or before, to an earthier woman, one like Bessie, who possesses no glittering social standing. The treatment of the well-connected Lucy Mayhew does, however, depart from this usual pattern in one other revealing respect. The clouds of luxury and culture trailing behind her, the beckoning lights of social respectability that will hold such a seductive allure for later heroes like Don Wanderhope, Joe Sandwich, Joe Tickler, and Eddie Teeters—these seem to be the very things that repel Peter Topp:

> I see myself ten years hence married to this subtly firm woman with the gentian eyes: prisoner of respectability; Schumann and chocolates and sadness in the afternoon . . . dressing for dinner, the warm boredom of the opera. . . . This spectacle gives me an exquisite pleasure, for I am in spirit already running like hell. (44)

His sarcastic response, read against the grain of narrative in later novels, carries an understandable, if idiosyncratic logic. He flees from respectability, while other De Vries heroes flee from ethnic identities and the disrespectable status attached to that ethnicity. Because Topp feels no Calvinistic restraints and rubs against none of the inhibitions about "worldly" pleasures that other DeVries heroes of Dutch descent must suffer, the lovely Lucy Mayhew and what she symbolizes holds no forbidden or fatal attraction for him.

For young Don Wanderhope's immigrant father in *The Blood of the Lamb*, whether a young woman belonged to the Covenant poses a question of great emotional and religious importance. "Any girl you go out with," Don's father tells him, "you bring here, *verstaan*, because I want to see what Jesus would say." Don's been dating Maria Italia, daughter of an Italian immigrant, an organ grinder who keeps his monkey in the basement of their apartment building. Her father sports huge handle-bar moustaches, receives Don while eating olives from an open bottle, and speaks with a cartoon character's Italian accent: "That's a good a wan." He's unmistakably, if stereotypically, Italian. But when Don faces his Dutch father's violent questioning about the girl's nationality, he feigns ignorance, even as he recites her eponymous name. His father, having spotted lipstick on Don's cheek, asks without any preliminaries:

> "Outsider?"
> "I don't know her name. Well, I think it's Italia."
> "What nationality is that?"
> "I'm not sure. They're nice people. Dark complected but nice. Awful strict." (34)

Don will be quizzed, with almost the same harshness, by Mr. Italia, an immigrant father as sternly wedded to old world ideas of family and ethnicity as Don's own father. This questioning takes place "under a pair of oval-framed photographs of parents" and a picture of Mr. Italia's wife "in her casket, gazing out at us with an eerie simulacrum of motherly love" (34).

The effect of these back-to-back interrogations is the same. After each one, Don begins to dream of an escape from the entanglements of family origins and ethnic identity. His dream, one that will possess other DeVries heroes, takes concrete shape in a mansion of a distinctly English (or Anglo-American) design. "I had a vision of polished doors opening, and myself in faultless tweeds in a party moving toward dinner across a parquet floor, under a chandelier like chiseled ice" (27). Through his older brother Louie, a pre-med student at the University of Chicago, he has already gotten a glimpse of this elegantly polished world, "the 'worldly' life denounced by the church." For him, the houses around the Midway near the University of Chicago "embodied" this dream and the vision of escape from home and family (27).

The American Dream, then, haunts and persistently eludes him. What gives his desire a particular charge, in this context, is that he comes to believe he can only enter the mansion of earthly delight by becoming "a sort of reverse Pilgrim." He must "progress *away* from the City of God" (66). He will invert his father's religious vocabulary and beliefs and come to see himself—not others—as the "outsider."

The scene that most vividly dramatizes this position as an outsider, and makes visible the dream he's pursuing, is cast in parodic religious language, as an inverted conversion. This parodied conversion occurs shortly after his father has sold his ice route, and, like some other Dutch "folk" in Chicago, has bought into the garbage hauling business. Don begins working with him in fashionable Hyde Park, near the University of Chicago. Together they collect garbage from high-toned restaurants, grocery stores, and bars. At one lunch break, he and his father pause to rest. He hears piano music and recognizes strains of Chopin's *Etudes*:

> I passed my father snoozing under an elm, a bandanna over his face to discourage flies. . . .I strolled on. I had made one right turn. . .when the sound of the piano became once more audible. It flowed from a red-brick Georgian house furred with ivy, its chaste design relieved by a burst of baroque over the doorway, where twin scrolls crowned a broken white pediment like a pair of swan's wings beating valiantly in the cause of Romance. To this visual note the music seemed an answering echo from some pining ally. . . .(43-4)

Drawn onward by the music, he "recklessly" steals up to an open window, and, "gaping at the casement ledge," watches a young man playing the piano. A young "woman . . . in a silk dressing gown" listens intently. This scene of "worldly style" thrills him, he says, to his "roots." His pleasure in this music and the glimpse of "Worldliness" in the "tastefully assembled opulence of red velour chairs" are, he tells us as he formally cites a Calvinist doctrine, a "specificable sin of a higher order." Yet the act seems to liberate him, and renew him. He feels, at this moment, that he's well on his way to escaping from his "long incarceration" in "immigrant inferiority" (44-5).

But a final escape proves to be difficult. Proceeds from his father's prospering "Mid-City Cartage: Sanitary Sanitation" business pay his way into the University of Chicago. Now, making his way among what the Dutch of Chicago called, the "American people," he gains a foothold inside a Hyde Park mansion and discovers an unexpected falseness and shabbiness. Archie Winkler, who has invited him into his parents' many-splendored mansion, borrows money from Wanderhope, and, though he regularly throws lavish parties, will not repay the loan. Don, after a quarrel with Winkler, confesses his "first assault on the strongholds of fashion" to be a failure (66). But, like Dreiser's Carrie Meeber or Balzac's Eugene Rastignac, he plans to storm these bastions again. He's not lost the dream. Still speaking like a misplaced character from an F. Scott Fitzgerald novel, he rhapsodizes about "the Babylonian hotels with names like Windermere and Chatham." Their "lights inflated the heart" (66). He dreams, with his heart lifted up by the lights of Michigan Boulevard, about a passage "northward through the Gold Coast and out to the suburbs of Evanston and Winnetka, where the last mansions waited" (66-7). He maps a campaign that will take him to these and into these everlasting mansions, where his every desire will be satisfied.

What he finds, instead, is a romance and, eventually, a marriage with Greta Wigbaldy, a lively Dutch Reformed girl. Greta's father, once a partner of the elder Wanderhope, has turned to real estate development. He has built what Don Wanderhope calls a "bourgeois paradise," a grouping of tract houses poetically named Green Knoll.

Greta decides they will use the model home, or rather the bedroom of the model home, for their first sexual adventure. They walk to Green Knoll, passing under a shingle advertising the place as 'The American Dream." Don carries sheets for the bed (70-1). They walk down a darkened Willow Lane and into the unlit model home. This journey to a darkened house—rather than the passage northward to the gloriously lighted mansions and baroque English interiors of Don's dreams—ends with a rewriting of all his expectations. He has entered the American dream, the paradise he longed for, though he does not recognize it in the tract home. No surprise, then, that Greta's parents and a pair of buyers walk into the model home at the same moment that Greta and Don are slipping under the sheets. Don's discovered the American Dream, but, ironically, he's found it somewhere within the ethnic community and Covenant he thought he was escaping.

When Don stormed the mansions of light and pleasure, he knew that he was obliged to dissemble; he knew that he had to pass himself off as an American. At the Winklers, whom he regarded as "a rich American family," he feeds the illusion that he himself descends from an "old New York Dutch" line. Asked, unexpectedly, if he's been abroad, he answers: "No, but my parents have. They've spent many years in Europe" (56). As he spins out the tale, he's thinking of his father's ghastly seasickness, a week spent in steerage "while the worst storm in recent Atlantic memory flung him about the bed and even to the floor" (3). And so he masks his own origins, parodying a story of passage that is already a parody of an immigrant narrative. His father had sailed from Rotterdam for the sole purpose of visiting relatives in America. But so seasick did he become that he cancelled his return passage, unwilling to face "open water" again. "Thus," Don Wanderhope adds in this ironic retelling of his father's story, "was added Ben Wanderhope's bit to that sturdy Old World stock from which this nation has sprung" (3).

To complete this act of dissembling, to persuade the Winklers he is of old native stock, Don must also learn to disguise his speech, a blend of Dutch, American English, and "Chicago street diction" (32). Like Stew Smackenfelt, Jim Tickler, and other of DeVries

Dutch-American characters, he first learned to speak in a macaronic mix of Dutch and English. Almost at the same time, he comes to hold a linguist's command and understanding of the polyglot speech patterns in his ward and the larger city:

> The number and variety of accents and brogues to which I was early subjected seems notable now, though they were not untypical of that part and period of Chicago. Beyond the horizons of our Dutch household—whose speech was Americanized at best into "dese" and "dem" and "de bot' of us"—lay the vast crazy quilt of other European-born elements composing the Eighteenth Ward in which we lived. Even today, after more than a quarter century . . . correct English still rings a trifle strangely on my ears . . . . (39)

Don routinely answers his mother's Dutch in a mix of English and Dutch, calling her "*moeke*" (33). The minister who visits his brother introduces himself as that "old *klets*," adding "'*Och, ja, ik ben en kletskous.*' (I am a chatterbox)" (29). Doc Berkenbosch, the quack doctor who tends to Don's father, pronounces ulcers and arthritis as "ulsters" and "arthuritis." Everyone in their community, according to Don, spoke a "loosely colloquial" and often comic blend of Dutch and American (17).

Into Your Tent I'll Creep of 1971 inflated this kind of burlesque almost to bursting. The hero of the novel, Al Banghart, while working as a door-to-door salesman in Chicago, develops a parodic ethnic language, rotating among "Italian, German, Spanish, and a kind of all-purpose Eastern-European speech you can't pin down." He makes his sales pitch by pretending, in a largely immigrant and ethnic neighborhood, to be "an immigrant struggling to get a foothold in this great land I wanted so much to be a part of" (146-7):

> "I lawv zis countree. I want to be good loyal American . . . . Make living here. Becawn citizen. I study to be doctor, when I can brink poor parents over from awld cawntree, but first must work way through school. So I paint noombers on corbs...for two dollars, plez?" (147)

His simulation of Chicago's poly-ethnic language—and the retelling of a typical immigrant's story—suggests that many of DeVries' ethnic characters have hidden roots and origins that they feel they can disguise or disclose at will.

Don Wanderhope replays samples of a fractured language not to remember his cultural roots or ethnic past, much less to define a divided heart, that familiar trope of second-generation autobiographical narratives. Recovering these fragments of his past, he illustrates "the special pains of a boy chafing under an immigrant culture," dreaming of "'wider horizons'" (27). Don imagines those "wider horizons" opening to a place free from the "pain" of the ethnic slurs and taunts that "people shouted at you on the street." He then quotes a ditty that DeVries will repeat in other novels: "Oh, the Irish and the Dutch/Don't amount to very much" (27). More, and still more intensely, he imagines himself lifted up into the high life, where he takes a "charmed" place among the urbane and sophisticated (42). Like Gatsby and a dozen other Fitzgerald heroes, he is consumed by wonder and dreams of reinventing himself nearer to the desires he has stored "in his ghostly heart" (Fitzgerald 97).

These dreams and the pattern of a *Bildungsroman* end abruptly somewhere near the middle of the novel. After Don marries Greta, he takes a job with an advertising firm and, before long, is transferred to New York. Within a few pages, the narrative shifts to a foreshortened account of Greta's depression and suicide and, with another quick move, to the progression of their young daughter Carol from sickness into death. (Here, DeVries is retelling, in fictional form, the death of his own daughter.) Though many readers find the quick step from comedy to suffering and pathos too abrupt, and the novel's structure broken because of it, we can also understand that Don, in the end, is confronting "undeluded" the randomness and the chaos of the universe and comes to believe, as he says on the last page, that "time heals nothing" (246).

II.

Little of what DeVries wrote in *The Blood of the Lamb* suggests that he drew on the tradition of Chicago and Midwestern humor that he might have found in predecessors like George Ade, Kin Hubbard, John T. McCutcheon, and James Whitcomb Riley. Throughout his career, he reworked the forms of the mock oral narration and recast the innocent comic hero that so often sat at the heart of their humor. But their nostalgia for the Midwestern farm and village—the values of plain speaking, simple folk, and cracker barrel wisdom—represented soft targets for his burlesque and satire, rather than inspirational examples. His characters, especially the young men from farm country, aspired to be urbane and modern. DeVries was certainly aware of the Chicago humorists, admired the fiction of Ring Lardner, and may well have drawn some influence from Ade's "Fables in Slang." His old friend from the 1930s and his days of radical politics, Jack Conroy, collected Ade, Hubbard, Lardner, with other "Midwest funny men," in an anthology titled *Midland Humor: A Harvest of Fun and Folklore* (1947). He placed DeVries in their company, using his early short story, "Different Cultural Levels Eat Here." Conroy no doubt had him in mind when, in his introduction, he spoke of the "present day writers" who, though they may have lost some "uniquely regional flavor," still reflect the "impress of their environment" (viii, xi).

The Glory of the Hummingbird, written about a dozen years after *The Blood of the Lamb*, toyed with the idea of regional differences and, in broad caricature, limned the type-characters and the stereotypes associated with Midlands local color.[1] Joe Tickler the protagonist, like Don Wanderhope, is Dutch American, young, ambitious, and verbally adept. Tickler comes from Wabash, Indiana, balks at its "cruel limits," and never seems to tire of singing to himself the sad lyrics of Sidney Bechet's classic "The Wabash Blues" (22). As he insinuates himself into what he calls "the cream of Chicago and North Shore Gold Coast society," he remembers his Hoosier origins and the simple rural life without a trace of nostalgia or sentimental coloring (75-6). At one point in his recollections of Indiana, he jabs at the mythos of "barefoot boys in the state of James

Whitcomb Riley." Parodying local color conventions and some once-familiar lines from Riley's poem, "A Barefoot Boy," Tickler tells of Saturday nights his mother, with a vegetable brush in hand, scrubbed and scoured "the crust of dirt" on his soles and heels. He says he is touched "to the quick by this exquisite memory" (124). When he talks of inviting his family and relatives to his wedding in Chicago, he describes them as "The Creatures from Out of Town" or, in equally sarcastic tones, as "just plain folks from the hinterlands" (100-01). His uncle drinks his coffee cold, straight from the spout of a percolator; a friend of the family seasons "his breakfast eggs with snuff" (255). His mother, for many years, has been saving up green stamps for a divorce. His father, having established himself in the local literary colony, aimed to write an epic modeled on Longfellow's "Hiawatha." A sample of his poetic effort: "Did they gigs in Escanaba/ Oshkosh and Balenciaga" (46). No wonder, Tickler so much wants to take "wing" and soar "above the vulgarity of [his] origins" (82).

The map of this flight from his origins follows a familiar route in DeVries' fictional world— north, to the rich suburbs of Chicago. There, Tickler meets the object of his desire in the beautiful and charming Amy Wintermoots, a young woman from Evanston. Marrying her, and winning a place in her father's marketing firm, intensifies his ambition to become "one of the Beautiful People" (138). His delusions about "the Cream of Gold Coast society," that they represent "'something better,'" will slowly be wiped away (99, 75). But his self-delusions fade slowly. Pitted against a Charles VanDoren look-alike in a rigged quiz show, he characterizes his opponent as an aristocrat and the "Champ of the Eastern Establishment," while casting himself as a yokel, "the rustic come to the metropolis" (158, 167). Not until the end the novel does he stop defining himself against this typology of character: he finds peace and understanding as he and his wife Amy drive through a pastoral Ohio "along still green rolling countryside, on a day balmy with white clouds and bright sunshine [where] the hills lay like fondled breasts" (275-6).

Stew Smackenfelt—one of DeVries' Chicago-born, Dutch American characters now living in suburban Connecticut —suffers from a somewhat different identity crisis. He is a television actor and a ham on stage, a second-rate playwright, and the comic hero of *Forever Panting*. He does not seem to have full command of his own voice or persona. At cocktail parties, in his house alone, and in unexpected places, he feels compelled to imitate celebrities' voices, to impersonate them reading or reciting words they would never speak. (Almost no one recognizes his impersonations.) For reasons he cannot explain, he takes to impersonating Churchill reciting Longfellow's poem "Hiawatha." Near the end of the novel, while walking the rocky shore of Long Island Sound and reciting Longfellow in the persona of Churchill, he pauses, throws away his prop cigar, and shifts into a voice that he's not used before—his own voice. As he sends his "gaze" across the Sound, he fancies himself to be "the magnetized watcher." From the sight of Connecticut's Long Island Sound, in this visionary state, Smackenfelt coaxes:

> . . . some resemblance to the burning seascapes of Petoskey and Charlevoix and Escanaba, those Lake Michigan cities where you spent the summers of your youth. . . .You fling yourself back in time, trying . . . to recapture those leaps of ecstasy common to early manhood, the raptures of illimitable hope of a vista opened . . . . Thus you experience . . . that most haunting of all human memories: the memory of expectation. In Charlevoix was a restaurant with a ceiling of patterned tin panels, stamped out by a drop-forge no less indelibly than the ceiling itself is imprinted on your memory. (265-66)

No reader of American literature can scan these lines and this scene without remembering Gatsby looking across these same waters at Daisy's "green light." That resemblance or slanted quotation, though, is much less important than what it shows us about the map of desire, "the memory of expectation," recovered here. It traces the indelible imprint of expectation, memory and desires forged in the Midwest. Stew Smackenfelt, like many other DeVries comic heroes and DeVries himself, can remember these most intensely in the dialectical opposition of Midwest and East Coast, the ironic "haunting" juxtaposition youth and age.

Notes

1. DeVries excerpted his title from a line in T.S. Eliot's poem, "Marina"; with subtle comic modulations, his frequent quotations of this figure echo Eliot's stern warnings against vanity (the glittering but transient "glory" of the hummingbird's flight).

Works Cited

Daiches, David, Malcolm Bradbury, and Eric Mottram, eds. *Avenel Companion to English & American Literature*. New York: Avenel Books, 1981.

Conroy, Jack. *Midland Humor: A Harvest of Fun and Folklore*. NY: Current Books, 1947.

DeVries, Peter. *Angels Can't do Better*. New York: Coward-McCann, 1944.

_____. *Blood of the Lamb*. 1961. New York: Penguin, 1962.

_____. *Forever Panting*. Boston: Little, Brown, 1973.

_____. *The Glory of the Hummingbird: A Novel*. Boston: Little, Brown, 1974.

_____. *Into Your Tent I'll Creep*. Boston: Little, Brown, 1971.

_____. *The Prick of Noon*. 1985. New York: Penguin, 1986.

Fitzgerald, F. Scott. *The Great Gatsby*. 1925. New York: Charles Scribner's Sons, 1953.

Frank, Jeffrey. "A Critic at Large: Riches of Embarrassment." *The New Yorker* (24 May 2004): 46-52; 54-5.

Newquist, Roy. *Counterpoint*. Chicago: Rand McNally, 1964.

Pacyga, Dominic A. and Ellen Skerrett. *Chicago: City of Neighborhoods*. Chicago: Loyola UP, 1986.

RESOURCES

Additional Works of Midwestern Literature _____

Novels
The Man with the Golden Arm (50th anniversary ed.) by Nelson Algren (1999)
Winesburg, Ohio (with variant readings and annotations) by Sherwood Anderson (1997)
The Adventures of Augie March by Saul Bellow (1953)
Dandelion Wine by Ray Bradbury (1957)
The Farm by Louis Bromfield (1933)
Once Upon a River: A Novel by Bonnie Jo Campbell (2011)
Bop by Maxine Chernoff (1987)
The House on Mango Street by Sandra Cisneros (1991)
The Adventures of Huckleberry Finn: An Authoritative Text Contexts and Sources Criticism by Samuel Clemens (Mark Twain) (1999)
The Girl Who Ate Kalamazoo by Darin Doyle (2010)
An American Tragedy by Theodore Dreiser (1925)
Love Medicine: New and Expanded Version by Louise Erdrich (1993)
So Big by Edna Ferber (1924)
The Great Gatsby by F. Scott Fitzgerald (1925)
Main-Travelled Roads by Hamlin Garland (1899)
Legends of the Fall by Jim Harrison (1979)
Lake Wobegon Days by Garrison Keillor (1985)
Main Street by Sinclair Lewis (1920)
The Field of Vision by Wright Morris (1956)
In the Lake of the Woods by Tim O'Brien (1994)
Windy City Blues by Sara Paretsky (1995)
Galatea 2.2: A Novel by Richard Powers (1995)
Driftless by David Rhodes (2008)
Impotent by Matthew Roberson (2009)
Gilead by Marilynne Robinson (2004)
The Jungle by Upton Sinclair (1906)
A Thousand Acres by Jane Smiley (1991)

Poetry
Diminished Fifth by Jeffrey Bean (2009)
Death Dance of a Butterfly by Melba Joyce Boyd (2012)

A Street in Bronzeville by Gwendolyn Brooks (1945)
Blessing the House by Jim Daniels (1997)
The Undertaker's Daughter by Toi Derricotte (2012)
Thomas and Beulah by Rita Dove (1986)
The Collected Poetry of Paul Laurence Dunbar by Paul Laurence Dunbar (1993)
American Prophet by Robert Fanning (2009)
Robert Hayden Collected Poems by Robert Hayden (1982)
Flying at Night by Ted Kooser (2005)
Octavia:Guthrie and Beyond by Naomi Long Madgett (2002)
Spoon River Anthology by Edgar Lee Masters (1915)
On the Flyleaf: Poems by Herbert Woodward Martin (2013)
Collected Poems by Theodore Roethke (1966)
The Collected Works of Sara Teasdale by Sara Teasdale (1937)
Above the River: The Complete Poems by James Wright (1990)

Short Story Collections
Coast of Chicago by Stuart Dybek (1990)
In Our Time: Stories by Ernest Hemingway (1958)

Nonfiction
Grass Roots: The Universe of Home by Paul Gruchow (1995)
The Writings of William Dean Howells by William Dean Howells (1911)
Blue Highways: A Journey into America by William Least Heat Moon (1981)
Writing from the Center by Scott Russell Sanders (1995)
Working by Studs Terkel (1974)

Bibliography

Barillas, William. *The Midwestern Pastoral.* Athens: Ohio UP, 2006.

Brown, David S. *Beyond the Frontier: The Midwestern Voice in American Historical Writing.* Chicago: U Chicago P, 2009.

Cayton, Andrew R. L. and Susan E. Gray. *The American Midwest: Essays on Regional History.* Bloomington: Indiana UP, 2001.

Davies, Richard O., Joseph Amato, and David R. Pichaske, eds. *A Place Called Home: Writings in The Midwestern Small Town.* St. Paul: Minnesota Historical Society Press, 2003.

Duffy, Bernard. *The Chicago Renaissance in American Letters.* East Lansing: Michigan State UP, 1954.

Fetterly, Judith and Marjorie Pryse. *Writing Out of Place: Regionalism, Women, and American Literary Culture.* Urbana: U of Illinois P, 2003.

Gjerde, Jon. *The Minds of the West: Ethnological Evolution in the Rural Midwest, 1830-1917.* Chapel Hill: U of North Carolina P, 1997.

Hilfer, Anthony Channel. *The Revolt from the Village: 1915-1930.* Chapel Hill: U of North Carolina P, 1969.

Johnson, Victoria E. *Heartland TV: Prime Time Television and the Struggle for U.S. Identity.* New York: New York UP, 2008.

Joseph, Philip. *American Literary Regionalism in a Global Age.* Baton Rouge: Louisiana State UP, 2007.

Longworth, Richard C. *Caught in the Middle: America's Heartland in the Age of Globalism.* Bloomsbury, New York: Macmillan, 2008.

Marx, Leo. *The Machine in the Garden: Technology and the Pastoral Ideal in America.* New York: Oxford UP, 1964.

McAvoy, Thomas T., et al, eds. *The Midwest: Myth or Reality?* Proc. Of The Midwest: Myth or Reality? A Symposium, 1961, University of Notre Dame. South Bend: U of Notre Dame P, 1961.

Pichaske, David. *Rooted: Seven Midwestern Writers of Place.* Iowa City: U of Iowa P, 2006.

Poll, Ryan. *Main Street and Empire: The Fictional Small Town in the Age of Globalization.* New Bruswick: Rutgers UP, 2012.

Quantic, Diane Dufva. *The Nature of Place: A Study of Great Plains Fiction.* Lincoln: U of Nebraska P, 1995.

Raymond, C. Elizabeth. "Middle Ground: Evolving Regional Images in the American Middle West." *'Writing' Nation and 'Writing' Region in America.* Eds. Theo D'Haen and Hans Bertens. Amsterdam: VU UP, 1996. 95-116.

Shortridge, James R. *The Middle West: Its Meaning in American Culture.* Lawrence, Kansas: UP of Kansas, 1989.

Smith, Carl S. *Chicago and the American Literary Imagination: 1880-1920.* Chicago: U of Chicago P, 1984.

Smith, Henry Nash. *Virgin Land: The American West as Symbol and Myth.* Cambridge: Harvard UP, 1950.

Spears, Timothy. *Chicago Dreaming: Midwesternness and the City 1871-1919.* Chicago: U of Chicago P, 2005.

Watts, Edward. *The American Colony: Regionalism and the Roots of Midwestern Culture.* Athens: Ohio UP, 2002.

Weber, Ronald. *The Midwestern Ascendancy in American Writing.* Bloomington, Indiana UP, 1992.

About the Editor

Ronald Primeau, professor of English at Central Michigan University, has published extensively on Midwestern literature. He is the author or editor of books on Edgar Lee Masters, Herbert Woodward Martin, Paul Laurence Dunbar, and American road literature. He has also received several teaching awards. Working with filmmaker David B. Schock, he has been associate producer for the films: *Distinct and Midwestern* (2008), an interview with David D. Anderson, founder of the Society for the Study of Midwestern Literature (SSML); *Jump Back Honey: The Poetry and Performance of Herbert Woodward Martin* (2009); and the prize-winning *Star By Star: Naomi Long Madgett, Poet and Publisher* (2011), about Detroit's poet laureate. He is a recipient of SSML's MidAmerican Award for Distinguished Scholarship on Midwestern Literature and the editor of Salem Press' Critical Insights series volume *American Road Literature* (2013).

Contributors

Marilyn Judith Atlas, a member of the Society for the Study of Midwestern Literature for decades, teaches American Literature at Ohio University, specializing in the American Renaissance, realism, naturalism, modernism, the Chicago Renaissance, Jewish American literature, African American and ethnic literature, and women's studies. She often teaches classes on Midwestern literature and memoir writing. She has published widely on authors from Leo Tolstoy and Toni Morrison to Margaret Fuller, Theodore Dreiser, and Harriet Monroe.

William Barillas teaches in the Department of English at the University of Wisconsin-La Crosse. His book, *The Midwestern Pastoral: Place and Landscape in the Literature of the American Heartland* (2006), won the Midwestern Studies Book Award. He received the MidAmerican Award for Distinguished Contributions to the Study of Midwestern Literature from the Society for the Study of Midwestern Literature in 2013.

Jurrit Daalder is currently reading for a PhD in English Literature at Oxford University, where he is conducting research on the post-postmodernist works of David Foster Wallace, Richard Powers, and Jonathan Franzen and their relation to the Midwestern literary tradition. After completing his undergraduate degree in English Literature at the University of Amsterdam, he received an MA in "Issues in Modern Culture" from University College London. He has taught Dutch as a Harting Scholar at the Department of Germanic Studies of Trinity College, Dublin.

Maureen N. Eke teaches African Diaspora literatures, postcolonial literature and theory, world literature, and women writers at Central Michigan University. She is a past president of the African Literature Association (ALA) and is the editor of the ALA Annuals series. Her publications include four co-edited volumes as well as numerous articles on African literature and cinema. She serves on the editorial boards of several international publications and is at work on a book of collected essays on Nigerian playwright Tess Onwueme.

Scott D. Emmert is professor of English at the University of Wisconsin-Fox Valley and the current vice president of the Society for the Study of Midwestern Literature. He is co-editor, with Michael Cocchiarale, of *Upon Further Review: Sports in American Literature (*2004*)* and *Critical Insights: American Sports*

Fiction (2013). He is also the author of *Loaded Fictions: Social Critique in the Twentieth-Century Western* (1996).

Phillip A. Greasley is the general editor of The Dictionary of Midwestern Literature series and former president and current board member of the Society for the Study of Midwestern Literature. He recently retired as an associate professor of English at the University of Kentucky, specializing in Midwestern literature; he served concurrently as the university's associate vice president/associate provost for university engagement.

Christian Knoeller is associate professor of English at Purdue. His research interests include teaching Native American and Midwestern literature, especially with reference to cultural and ecological memory. His first collection of poems, *Completing the Circle,* was awarded the Millennium Prize from Buttonwood Press. He has received both the Midwestern Heritage Prize for Literary Criticism (2007) and the Gwendolyn Brooks Prize for Poetry (2011) from the Society for the Study of Midwestern Literature, an organization for which he has previously served as president. He also coordinates the Native American Literature section of the Midwest Modern Language Association. His recent publications include essays on Louise Erdrich that appeared in ASLE's *ISLE: Interdisciplinary Studies in Literature and the Environment* and on John James Audubon and environmental history in the *Journal of Ecocriticism.*

Sara Kosiba is an assistant professor of English at Troy University. She has published articles on various Midwestern writers including Dawn Powell, Ernest Hemingway, Josephine Herbst, and Meridel Le Sueur. She currently serves as a member of the editorial board for the *Dictionary of Midwestern Literature: Volume Two,* and as the current president of the Society for the Study of Midwestern Literature.

Matthew Low's research interests include environmental writing, Native American literature, place studies, and the hands-on fieldwork of prairie conservation and restoration. His writing has been published in *ISLE: Interdisciplinary Studies in Literature and Environment, Mosaic, MidAmerica, and Prairie Fire,* among other places. He lives and teaches in Omaha, Nebraska.

Marcia Noe is professor of English and Director of Women's Studies at the University of Tennessee in Chattanooga. She is a senior editor of the *Dictionary of Midwestern Literature* and the editor of *MidAmerica: Publications of the Society for the Study of Midwestern Literature.*

Patricia Oman is assistant professor of English at Hastings College, where she teaches courses in American literature, children's and young adult literature, film, and writing. Her research interests include representations of region, especially the Midwest, in literature and popular culture. Forthcoming publications include scholarly articles on agricultural horror films of the 1980s and the intersection of children's literature and regional literature in Eleanor Porter's Polyanna novels. Oman is currently writing a monograph on the myths of Middle America.

David Radavich's recent poetry collections include *America Bound: An Epic for our Time* (2007), *Middle-East Mezze* (2011), and *The Countries We Live In* (2014). His plays have been performed across the U.S. and includesix off-off Broadway productions and in Europe. He has published scholarly articles on many of the dramatists in this essay. In 2012, he was honored with the MidAmerica Award (from the Society for the Study of Midwestern Literature) for his contributions to the study of Midwestern literature.

John Rohrkemper teaches literature and creative writing at Elizabethtown College. He has written extensively about the works of John Dos Passos, F. Scott Fitzgerald, Willa Cather, Toni Morrison, and Mark Twain. He is also the author of more than twenty theatrical works.

Guy Szuberla has written and published frequently on Chicago and Midwestern writers, including George Ade, Saul Bellow, Theodore Dresier, Henry Blake Fuller, and John T. McCatcheon. Professor Emeritus, he taught American literature and American studies at the University of Toledo. He was president of the Great Lakes American Studies Association, the Society for the Study of Midwestern Literature, and, for several years, served on the editorial boards of *The Old Northwest* and the *Dictionary of Midwestern Literature: Volume One.*

Sarah Warren-Riley is an adjunct faculty member at Baker College in Owosso, Michigan, where she teaches composition. As an avid reader and writer in a variety of genres, she teaches writing to inspire and empower a diverse group of emerging writers to find their voices. Her professional career has focused on social justice and housing issues, where she is a passionate advocate for causes that alleviate poverty. She has been executive director of Habitat for Humanity of Shiawassee County and currently serves as the Housing Programs Manager for the City of Owosso, helping to improve the living conditions of low-income and homeless families. Warren-Riley holds a B.A. in English from Michigan State University and an MA in English Language and Literature from Central Michigan University.

Index
